D1592071

VISIBLE WOMEN

Visible Women

Essays on Feminist Legal Theory and Political Philosophy

Edited by

SUSAN JAMES
Birkbeck College, University of London

and

STEPHANIE PALMER
Girton College, Cambridge University

OXFORD – PORTLAND OREGON
2002

Hart Publishing
Oxford and Portland, Oregon

Published in North America (US and Canada) by
Hart Publishing c/o
International Specialized Book Services
5804 NE Hassalo Street
Portland, Oregon
97213-3644
USA

Distributed in the Netherlands, Belgium and Luxembourg by
Intersentia, Churchillaan 108
B2900 Schoten
Antwerpen
Belgium

Hart Publishing is a specialist legal publisher based in Oxford, England.
To order further copies of this book or to request a list of other
publications please write to:

Hart Publishing, Salter's Boatyard, Folly Bridge,
Abingdon Road, Oxford OX1 4LB
Telephone: +44 (0)1865 245533 or Fax: +44 (0)1865 794882
e-mail: mail@hartpub.co.uk
WEBSITE: http//www.hartpub.co.uk

British Library Cataloguing in Publication Data
Data Available
ISBN 1–84113–195–4 (cloth)

Typeset by Hope Services (Abingdon) Ltd.

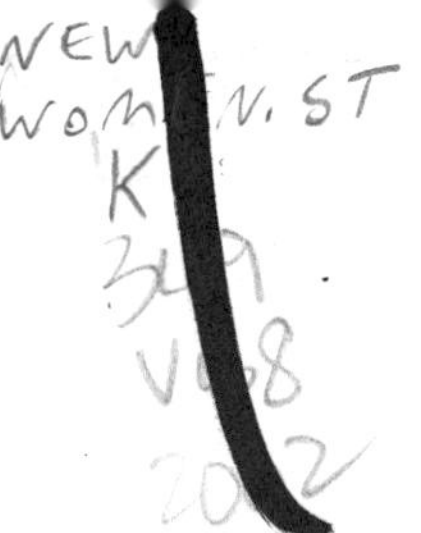

Contents

Acknowledgements

Several of the essays in this volume were originally given as papers at a seminar on current feminist work in political and legal theory. The seminar, held at the University of Cambridge, brought together people working in several academic disciplines and encouraged sustained discussion of issues that struck participants as particularly urgent and pressing. As these essays attest, there was in fact considerable convergence between lawyers, philosophers and political theorists about the central theoretical problems now facing feminism. We would like to thank the graduate students who attended and made a valuable contribution to the seminar. Two members of the Faculty of Law, Mathew Kramer and Susan Marks, were unfailingly supportive.

We gratefully acknowledge the financial support of the British Academy, and of the Faculties of Law, History and Philosophy at the University of Cambridge whose contributions made the seminar an international occasion. We are also deeply indebted to Girton College Cambridge, which offered hospitality to our speakers.

Girton College generously eased the publication of this volume by giving us a grant towards the cost of editing individual papers. We thank both the College, and Corlita Babb who did this work with great efficiency and cheerfulness. Finally, our thanks go to Richard Hart, our publisher, who has been unfailingly patient and helpful.

List of Contributors

Susan James is a Professor of Philosophy at Birkbeck College, University of London.

Stephanie Palmer is a Senior Lecturer and Fellow of Girton College, University of Cambridge.

Anne Phillips is a Professor of Gender Theory and Director of the Gender Institute at the London School of Economics, University of London.

Kristin Savell is a Lecturer in Law at the University of Sydney.

Ngaire Naffine is a Professor of Law at the University of Adelaide.

Nicola Lacey is a Professor of Criminal Law at the London School of Economics, University of London.

Seyla Benhabib is Eugene Meyer Professor of Political Science and Philosophy at Yale University.

Moira Gatens is a Professor of Philosophy at the University of Sydney.

Introduction

SUSAN JAMES AND STEPHANIE PALMER

IN JANUARY 2001 the British Equal Opportunities Commission celebrated its twenty-fifth anniversary by announcing a new vision for the twenty-first century: "sex equality is no longer just about rights for women."[1] While the Commission has, in practice, primarily dealt with cases of discrimination against women, it will now address inequalities between women and men, girls and boys, whenever they appear. The Commission's decision to campaign for equality laws which are "consistent, clear and workable" and to provide effective protection for people "of all races and creeds, at home, at school and in the workplace" is admirable in conception.[2] Nevertheless, changes of this sort, which are relatively common at the moment, trouble many women and contribute to a widespread sense that feminism is losing momentum as a political movement, both within and outside government. While feminists have always hoped for a time when there would be no special need to fight for improvements in women's circumstances because institutions would, in the ordinary course of things, devote as much attention and resources to satisfying the needs of women as of men, there is ample evidence that this era has not arrived.[3] A decline of interest in the predicament of women, whether in political life or in the academy, is therefore a cause for concern among people who fear that the advances made so far may be stalled or even reversed at a point where so much remains to be done.

This cultural shift away from feminism is a feature of intellectual as well as political life, and arises in part from developments within legal and political philosophy. During the past twenty years or so, insights into sexual difference which originated within feminism have been incorporated into broader conceptions of difference and its place in politics. As a result, feminism has sometimes come to be represented as an outmoded and unduly partisan position which has been transcended by a more wide-ranging analysis of social diversity. Rather than concentrating on the disadvantages suffered by women in particular, it is held, we should pay attention to the relative powers and condition of all sorts of groups, and work to minimise structural inequalities between them.

[1] EOC Annual Report (2000–1) at 4.

[2] Reported by Maureen Freely in *The Independent*, London 17 January 2001.

[3] To cite a single example, male earnings in Britain are still on average 18 % higher than those of women.

One version of this argument has been articulated by liberal theorists who oppose what they regard as an excessive sensitivity to difference and an insufficiently robust view of citizenship.[4] Another, as Anne Phillips points out in her contribution to this volume, has been presented by multiculturalists and communitarians whose concern is precisely to find ways of respecting and accommodating differences between communities, and who view women as one community among others.[5] For them, sexual difference has to be considered alongside other differences, such as those of race, ethnicity or religion. In addition to these challenges, the relevance and coherence of feminism has been questioned from a second direction by advocates of the view that women as such do not have interests or suffer disadvantages, and that an adequate politics must focus on their diverse needs and experiences.[6] Women are members of all races, ethnic communities or nations, and rather than presenting them as a single constituency, feminism must come to terms with their complex, overlapping identities.

These powerful lines of argument pose both a threat and an opportunity: a threat to the identity of feminism as it has been understood; and at the same time an opportunity to reconsider how the interests of women are to be kept in view. Challenges of this general type are not unusual, if only because feminism has usually been an alliance of diverse and sometimes conflicting campaigns, underpinned by a range of often incompatible theoretical positions, so that contest and disagreement within it are the norm rather than the exception. What is new, however, is the precise nature of the challenges it now faces. Because many of the arguments that tend to diminish its significance have their origins in feminism itself, feminists are likely to recognise their power, and to sympathise with the conceptions of difference that—on one level at least—now threaten them. This development helps to explain why current debates have become exceptionally fine-drawn. The play of sameness and difference around which so much feminist theorising revolves is reflected in the relations between feminist positions, and in those between feminism and other stances, with the result that any unequivocal other is hard to find. Rather than confronting clearly identified opponents, feminists have set out to explore ways of recognising a range of cultural differences while retaining a voice for women.

While trying sensitively to understand difference, feminism has of course created differences of its own between academic disciplines, and between more theoretical and more practical stances. This volume grew out of an interdisciplinary seminar held at the University of Cambridge where lawyers, political theorists and philosophers came together to listen to one another and discuss the problems they found

[4] B Barry, *Culture and Equality* (Cambridge, Polity Press, 2001).

[5] There are many variants of this view. See for example I M Young, *Justice and the Politics of Difference* (Princeton, Princeton University Press, 1990); W Kymlicka, *Multicultural Citizenship: A Liberal Theory of Minority Rights* (Oxford, Clarendon Press, 1995); C Taylor, "The Politics of Recognition" in A Gutman (ed.), *Multiculturalism: Examining the Politics of Recognition* (Princeton, Princeton University Press, 1994).

[6] See for example E Spelman, *Inessential Woman. Problems of Exclusion in Feminist Thought* (London, Women's Press, 1988).

most pressing. Despite the diverse backgrounds of the participants, their concerns turned out to converge, as the articles collected here attest. Nor was there a striking gap between philosophical interpretation of issues such as identity or embodiment and proposals about the way these might figure in the law. The following essays therefore form a whole, within which the argument moves easily back and forth between theoretical problems and issues of social policy, and focuses on a small range of themes that are tenaciously pursued. Some contributors reflect directly on the intellectual strategies currently available to lawyers and political philosophers who wish to oppose injustices to women. Others examine the materials on which such strategies depend, the categories in terms of which women and their situations are constructed or questioned within legal, philosophical and political discourses. The essays are marked by a common ambition to engage critically and constructively with contemporary theory and practice, and to develop intellectual tools which can successfully maintain and increase the visibility of women.

The decline of feminism as a political movement is most explicitly addressed by Anne Phillips, who begins by asking why feminism proceeds in cycles. This is partly because women find it difficult single-mindedly to promote their own interests, she suggests, and partly because it is not easy to sustain a politics on the margins. However, it is also due to the fact that insights originating within feminism have been taken over by other political movements. In the present cycle, the politics of difference threatens to obscure women by representing sexual difference as just one axis of variation alongside others. At the same time, multiculturalists sometimes occlude the distinctiveness of women's situation by treating them as a relatively homogeneous group with a culture in need of protection. This latter approach directs attention away from women's diversity and subordination, and can also make it more difficult to recognise conflicts and inequalities within cultures, including those between men and women. Rather than revealing women's distinctive interests, it tends to render them invisible by assimilating them to those of a culture as a whole.

As Phillips emphasises, her aim is not to reverse the beneficial movement from a politics centred on women to one organised around difference. It is rather to show that this movement "can encourage an over-individualised understanding of political agency that attaches too little weight to structural differences between women and men".[7] To reap the advantages of the politics of difference while retaining the visibility of women, we need to "theorise that complex relationship between individual and group . . . in a way that retains a meaningful politics of sexual equality".[8]

The proposal that the relationship between individual and group needs to be further explored if women are to remain visible is taken up throughout this volume. One set of contributors analyses the way in which this relationship works within the law, focusing on the connection between the individual legal person who is the

[7] A Phillips, "Feminism and the Politics of Difference. Or, Where Have All the Women Gone?", *infra* chap. 1, at p. 26.

[8] Phillips, *ibid.*, at p. 27 .

bearer of rights, and the broader field of practices in which individual and group identity are constructed. Another set examines the ways in which philosophers and social theorists have tried to articulate the interdependencies between individuals and groups with an eye to providing a conception of identity that allows for individual and social change.

In concentrating on these themes, the contributors pursue an issue that has already been widely discussed and remains of great interest. Are our conceptions of individual and collective identity gendered? If so, what are the legal and political implications of this fact? Among philosophers and political theorists who have raised these questions, some have embarked on a critical examination of standard philosophical accounts of personal identity.[9] Others have focused on a central issue within political philosophy, namely, what it is to be a citizen, the kind of person recognised as a full member of the state?[10] In both these areas, research has uncovered assumptions and patterns of argument which marginalise the culturally feminine, and in some cases exclude women from full personhood. In debates about personal identity, for example, the differences between male and female bodies, and their consequences for personal identity, have been largely ignored. In broadly liberal political philosophy, norms of citizenship developed by and for men have been uncritically adopted so that women only become citizens insofar as they are able to conform to male standards.

Significantly, the gendered character of political personhood or citizenship within the liberal tradition has been matched by the case of legal personhood. This issue is addressed by Kristin Savell and Ngaire Naffine, both of whom chart ways in which conceptions of legal personhood serve to exclude and subordinate women. Savell asks how law constructs the bodies of legal persons and, taking the case of pregnant women, shows that although the law formally recognises them as legal subjects it does not always treat them as such. In practice, some pregnant women are not recognised as persons before the law and are thus denied a status otherwise accorded to all sane adults. In English law, Savell explains, the foetus is not a legal person until it is born, and therefore possesses no rights or obligations. By contrast, the mother is a legal person. Her status is regularly undermined, however, when the law intervenes to protect the interests of the foetus and violates her rights, for example by prohibiting late abortion, enforcing caesarean sections on women who refuse them, or imposing restrictions on drug addicts by whose way of life the foetus may be damaged. In grappling with the difficulty of reconciling the mother's legal status with the interests of the foetus the law is torn, Savell argues, between two main strategies, neither of them satisfactory. It can give up the claim that the foetus is not a legal person, thus clearing the way to awarding it rights

[9] See for example S Benhabib, *Situating the Self. Gender, Community and Postmodernism in Contemporary Ethics* (Cambridge, Polity Press, 1992); M Schectman, *The Constitution of Selves* (Ithaca and London, Cornell University Press, 1996); S James, "Feminism in Philosophy of Mind. The Question of Personal Identity" in M Fricker and J Hornsby (eds.), *The Cambridge Companion to Feminism in Philosophy* (Cambridge, Cambridge University Press, 2000).

[10] See for example R Voet, *Feminism and Citizenship* (London and Thousand Oaks, Sage Publications, 1998); A Phillips, *Engendering Democracy* (Cambridge, Polity Press, 1991).

of its own. Alternatively, it can, and does, find grounds for claiming that pregnant women lack capacities that are taken to be essential to legal personhood, such as the capacity for rational judgement. This method of sustaining its own doctrines excludes and diminishes a class of women, while sweeping a central jurisprudential problem under the carpet.

In elaborating her critique, Savell refers to the essay by Naffine which argues, in somewhat broader terms, that law works with a norm of a "healthy" legal person who is implicitly male. On the face of things, women are as much legal subjects as men, and are thus included in the historical development of the doctrine of legal personality. In fact, however, they remain less than "healthy legal persons", both in the circumstances discussed by Savell, and also in relation to the law of marriage and of rape. Naffine shows that their exclusion stems from their inability to conform to an accepted conception of a legal person who is unitary, assertive and self-contained. There are several arenas where the law assumes that women do not answer to this description. When pregnant, they are not unified; in marriage they complement men; and the law of rape prescribes their sexual role. These departures from a male norm underlie and explain the persistence of laws which continue to disadvantage women by denying them legal personhood, and at the same time continue to impose a hierarchical, binary understanding of sexual difference.

In the final section of her paper, Naffine asks what approach women should take to legal personality. Should they work for legal reforms aimed at establishing a more inclusive conception of personhood that allows for sexual difference, or is this strategy suspect? Naffine offers a general criticism of the modern legal subject who has been stripped of his social nature to the point where he is incapable of negotiating or renegotiating his identity. The identity of the legal person is constituted by contractual relations which do not allow for change. As a result, legal personhood fails to capture the mutability of individual identity and is unable to recognise maturation, ageing and other kinds of transformation that are crucial to our understanding of ourselves. Without these, it is of doubtful value to women or men, and rather than rushing to make it accessible to women we should view it with cautious scepticism.

Naffine here broaches an issue, at once intellectual and strategic, which is further discussed in other essays. Is it fruitful to appeal to the normative categories of theories that were not developed with the interests of women in mind in our attempts to understand and overcome the disadvantages that women suffer? Or are there reasons for believing that this strategy will backfire, either because such categories are ineradicably tainted by masculine presuppositions or because they are in some other way ill-adapted to the aims of feminism? One area in which this question is hotly debated is that of rights—the rights of the legal person. Although feminists have in the past relied on a liberal conception of rights, and although this strategy has been in some ways extremely successful, there is currently a good deal of doubt as to whether it can achieve the ends for which women now need to strive. These reservations are part of a more general debate about the extent to which liberalism can accommodate the interests of women and, like Naffine's scepticism about legal personhood, focus on the juridical concepts at the heart of liberal political philosophy. They therefore pose a major challenge to the legal and political institutions of Western-style democracies, and to one of the theoretical frameworks within which women's disadvantages have been powerfully articulated.

In the opening section of her essay, Stephanie Palmer summarises a number of key objections to rights theory. The abstract universalism that lies at the heart of liberal rights presupposes sameness: the notion that has been at the root of women's historical difficulty in using rights to their advantage. The enormous obstacles that women have encountered in obtaining equality in the workplace and in public policy has led many feminists to reject rights as fundamentally inappropriate to feminist politics and theory.[11] On a more pragmatic note, some feminists have expressed fear that by diverting attention away from more direct political action and into legal disputes, "rights-based strategies will limit aspirations by merely reframing debates within the dominant discourse".[12] Nevertheless, she argues that rights have become a fundamental part of our legal philosophy and that women cannot afford to abandon law as a potential medium for change. She identifies an affinity between feminist ideals and human rights which have taken on a greater prominence in the United Kingdom since the enactment of the Human Rights Act 1998. As a consequence there exists an opportunity for feminist engagement with public law and new ground for theorising and strategy making.

Any excavation of the relationship between law and feminism exposes paradoxes and raises more questions than it answers. If feminism is based on a claim to speak not only "for" but "of" women, then who is this universal "woman"? If only partial knowledge is possible, then feminist theory cannot speak on behalf of the essential universal "woman". How then can any political or legal claim be made on behalf of women as a group? Is it possible for feminists to seek access to the law without being silenced by it? Can a more contextual position be adopted when formulating feminist legal claims? While cautiously adopting a rights based strategy, Palmer suggests possible ways in which the adoption of the Human Rights Act may provide a "space" for feminist voices; a chance to unsettle liberal categories. The challenge lies in giving meanings to rights that are consistent with feminist values and that are responsive to the realities of women's lives.

The question of the extent to which women's interests can be furthered by appealing to theories designed for other ends is also raised by Nicola Lacey, who integrates a discussion of legal subjectivity into a wider examination of the nature of law and the possibility of using it for ethical purposes. As Lacey points out, feminists have often taken it for granted that some of the wrongs and injustices suffered by women can be redressed by law, and have thus fought for legal reform or imagined legal utopias. The assumption that law can be assessed in ethical terms is put in doubt, however, by the view that it is intrinsically and inevitably violent. This

[11] See for example, C Smart, *Feminism and the Power of Law* (London, Routledge, 1989).

[12] S Palmer, "Feminism and the Promise of Human Rights: Possibilities and Paradoxes", *infra* chap. 4, at p. 96.

position has recently been defended by Derrida,[13] who argues that the very process of applying general rules to particular cases, thereby fixing subjects and events and imposing unchallengeable judgements on them, is a violent one. Such pervasive violence undercuts the possibility of ethically assessing particular laws or decisions, so that if an ethical sphere exists, it must lie beyond law.

The conflict between a conception of law as ethical, and the Derridean claim that law and ethics are mutually exclusive, prompts Lacey to consider how feminists committed to the value of deconstruction should resolve this clash. Taking the case of the legal subject, she argues that feminist deconstructions of legal categories work at three levels: they reveal how law violently excludes the feminine; they draw attention to the dynamic role of law in constructing sexed subjects; and they point towards the possibility of a form of law less oppressive to women. Writers who focus on the last two levels employ an approach that Lacey labels "contextualisation as strategy". By drawing attention to social relations that the law excludes, and in this way setting legal concepts and procedures in broader contexts, they aim to show how we can begin to formulate categories that are no longer culturally masculine and are less violently exclusive than the dominant ones. This project can be either reformist or utopian. Some contextualisations aim simply to modify existing categories, and therefore uphold a conception of law as ethical. Others, such as Irigaray's utopian reinterpretation of rights, envisage a society so different from our own as to be barely imaginable, and conceive the ethical as lying beyond law as we know it. As ways of furthering the interests of women, Lacey argues, both variants encounter practical and intellectual pitfalls which serve as a warning against an unqualified commitment to any philosophical analysis of the relation between ethics and law. Rather than taking an abstract stand on this matter, feminists will do better to adopt a pragmatic approach to theorising, and realising, the interests of women.

As the essays by Savell, Naffine and Lacey reveal, deconstruction of the legal subject often aspires to replace a narrowly individualist conception of the person with one whose identity is constituted by a wider range of relations with other individuals and groups. The central task of articulating such a conception of identity is taken up by Seyla Benhabib and Moira Gatens. According to Benhabib, this is an urgent project. We need to reassess the place of sexual difference in a world where traditional identities are becoming increasingly fragmented. We also need to hang on to a conception of political and moral agency in the face of post-modern views which threaten to dissipate it. (While allowing that the identities of individuals alter, we need to retain a space for the self who subverts, conforms to, or revolutionises social practices.) Finally, we need a sense of identity which will enable women to be full members of the polity, rather than strangers or nomads. Responding to these demands, Benhabib proposes a narrative view of the self. Rather than focusing on a core self-constituted by a set of relatively stable and

[13] J Derrida, "Force of Law: The 'Mystical Foundation of Authority' " in D Cornell, M Rosenfeld and D Gray Carlson (eds.), *Deconstruction and the Possibility of Justice* (New York, Routledge, 1992).

enduring characteristics, or by a horizon of deep commitments and values, we should think of selfhood in dialogical terms, as "an ability to insert oneself into webs of interlocution". The identity of an individual or group consists in its ability to go on telling a story about itself that makes sense of its own existence and answers the questions that confront it. What matters, as Benhabib elegantly expresses it, is not the document but the signature, not the content of the story but its narrative function of holding together past, present and future.

In developing her account, Benhabib acknowledges the embodiment and fluidity of the self. Here her interests overlap with those of Moira Gatens who argues in her essay that feminist theory needs to develop a politics able to accommodate difference, "whilst retaining a conception of identity as dynamic and open to transformation through encounters with others".[14] To meet this challenge, we need to avoid two unsatisfactory positions: on the one hand, a liberal outlook which recognises differences in people's ideas but fails to acknowledge the relation between who we are and what we think; on the other hand, a politics of difference which views identities as relatively fixed and fails to do justice to the ways in which they change. Gatens suggests that we can overcome the limitations of these approaches by drawing on the philosophy of Spinoza, and at the same time on a feminist understanding of the self as embodied, to arrive at what she calls an ethico-political ontology—an account of how political identities are formed and transformed, and of why, and when, we should value their transformation.

Recent feminist work has provided powerful arguments for the view that our ideas—our desires, beliefs, passions and preferences—are not independent of, and separable from, our bodies, but are formed and limited by different forms of embodiment and associated ways of life. We now face the problem of seeing how this insight bears on ethical and political theory, and here, Gatens suggests, it is helpful to turn to Spinoza, for whom individual identity is always embodied and only emerges from our relations with others. As well as being shaped by our relations with individuals, however, our capacities and ideas are shaped by our relations with institutions and associations, and with the values and ways of life they sustain. Their shared imaginaries provide individuals with a sense of identity and belonging, and confer meaning on their actions. Besides articulating this view, however, Spinoza allows for diverse forms of individuality, or difference, and for the transformation of identity as we move through the world. Gatens goes on to show how this Spinozist conception of identity is applied and developed by George Eliot (who translated Spinoza's *Ethics* into English) in her novel, *Daniel Deronda*. The great strength of these two writers is that they offer us a way to acknowledge the material presence of the past and the embodied nature of our beliefs, together with an account of our ability to transform them.

In much of her work about the construction of subjectivity and its relation to agency, Gatens makes use of the notion of the imaginary, the category that Susan

[14] M Gatens, "The Politics of 'Presence' and 'Difference': Working Through Spinoza and Eliot", *infra*, chap. 7 at p. 174 .

James goes on to examine. The imaginary has played an important part in the work of several feminist philosophers who use it, James suggests, in strikingly diverse ways. For some of them it is primarily a psychological phenomenon, a structure of the individual mind, whereas for others it is social and refers to the images and symbols embedded in a discourse or culture. James begins by analysing the differences and overlaps between these two conceptions, and traces the origin of the division between them to the work of an earlier generation of theorists. She then examines the way in which the division is perpetuated in contemporary writing, concentrating on the work of Michéle le Doeuff, Moira Gatens, and Drucilla Cornell. Cornell has recently claimed that each individual has an imaginary domain, and also a right to have it protected. James questions this latter view. The assimilation of the imaginary into a theory of rights is only achieved, she argues, at the expense of the traits that make it most valuable as a means of reflecting critically on the forces that shape our understandings of ourselves as women and men. We therefore should not allow ourselves to lose sight of the sense in which the imaginary is a social phenomenon, but should investigate it further.

This volume raises as many questions as it answers, and can be read as an invitation to further conversation about the tools that feminism has at its disposal and the problems it needs to address. As with any serious political movement, the obstacles by which feminists are confronted often appear substantial and intractable. If these essays contribute to the project of inventing ways to shift them, they will have served their purpose.

1

Feminism and the Politics of Difference. Or, Where Have All the Women Gone?

ANNE PHILLIPS

Personally, I am a feminist, and an Old Feminist, because I dislike everything that feminism implies. I desire an end of the whole business, the demands for equality, the suggestions of sex warfare, the very name of feminist. I want to be about the work in which my real interests lie, the study of inter-race relationships, the writing of novels and so forth. But while the inequality exists, while injustice is done and opportunity denied to the great majority of women, I shall have to be a feminist and an Old Feminist, with the motto Equality First.[1]

WINIFRED HOLTBY, NOVELIST, journalist, harsh critic of South Africa's racial policies, and active if reluctant feminist, wrote this in 1926 in the context of a debate then raging between old and new Feminism. The old feminism she defended pursued equality between the sexes in education and politics and employment; the "new feminism" challenging this focused on policies to improve the condition of women as mothers. A similar debate surfaced in the 1980s, when feminists found themselves embroiled in a rather unhelpful opposition between either equality or difference. When women claimed equality with men, did this mean they were accepting male conventions about what constitutes a good life, like the equal right to sacrifice one's children to one's career advancement, or the equal right to brutalise oneself in the army? If they insisted instead on what made their lives different from men's, did this confirm traditional stereotypes about the sexes—notions about women finding their fulfilment in motherhood not employment, or caring more about their nearest and dearest than any abstract justice claims? These are not the questions I focus on here, for my perception of the current state of feminist debate is that it has moved beyond that dichotomy between either equality or difference. What interests me in Holtby's comment is the reluctance it suggests about having to keep going on about the women.

There is a curious cycle within feminism that starts with exposing the once-invisible woman (attacking the many ways in which her needs, concerns, or interests have been submerged under those of men or mankind), but then gets frustrated with what comes to be experienced as an obsessive preoccupation with sex difference, and wishes it could submerge those women again. In mid-nineteenth

[1] W Holtby, "Feminism Divided" 1926, reprinted in P Berry and A Bishop (eds.), *Testament of a Generation: The Journalism of Vera Brittain and Winifred Holtby* (London, Virago, 1985) 48.

century Britain, women were literally obliterated as legal persona on entering marriage. They were subsumed under fathers or husbands for the purposes of political representation, prevented from addressing public audiences that included men, and through a combination of legal and customary practices, denied access to education and many fields of employment. Much of the campaigning activity of nineteenth-century feminism was devoted to putting these women back on the map, challenging the practices that had rendered their needs and claims invisible, and asserting their independent rights within employment, politics, and marriage. In later arguments, feminists have focused on the divisions between public and private that continued to obscure women from view even after the achievements of formal equality, and much contemporary analysis deals with the apparently inclusive categories (like humanity or citizenship) whose masculine provenance still keeps women out.

A great deal of feminism is about breaking the silence on women: disentangling the supposed unities of the family that conceal relationships of power and subordination; identifying the new issues that arise when we turn from the abstractions of humanity to put the spotlight on women themselves; drawing attention to conflicts of interest between the sexes; battling on behalf of women's rights or needs. In one particularly strong formulation of this, Carole Pateman has argued that our understanding of citizenship has to be reformulated "to open up space for two figures: one masculine, one feminine".[2] Instead, that is, of subsuming women under the false universalisms of humanity, feminists have sought to reframe views on freedom, equality, or democracy with the knowledge that there are both women and men.

This has always been a key moment in the feminist cycle, and yet the preoccupation with women never seems to last very long. It is as if we lose heart with what we come to see as an over-emphasis on women, begin stretching out towards broader implications, towards pacifism, perhaps eco-feminism, or as in the example discussed here, towards a more generalised politics of difference. This process can be extraordinarily productive, but it also threatens to return feminism to the beginning of the cycle. Women may then drop out of the picture, to become invisible again.

There are a number of reasons for this, and my own guess is that there are three particularly important contributory factors. One is that women have trouble insisting on their own special needs and interests (self-denial being part of the construction of femininity), and that feminists have proved no better at dealing with this than other groups of women. In the history of feminist campaigning, there has always been an attempt to associate women's needs with the broader needs of humanity as a whole, and it is only in rare moments that feminists have felt tough enough—or angry enough—to insist on their own "selfish" concerns. The case for women's suffrage was typically argued in terms of the way women would civilise and moralise politics, and even the most ardent of suffragists found it hard to say she wanted the vote just to make life better for herself. When Britain entered the First World War, the Women's Social and Political Union immediately suspended

[2] C Pateman, *The Sexual Contract* (Cambridge, Polity Press, 1988) 224.

its militant campaign for the vote, and in the aftermath of the War, many erstwhile feminists found it hard to continue to define themselves in these terms. This was less, in my view, because they felt their own battles were now won (British women did get the vote in 1918, but the franchise was still restricted to those over thirty), and more because the devastation of the War had been borne primarily by men. Focusing on women seemed hardly appropriate, when so many men had died.

The second reason is that sexual equality comes to seem so obvious, and it is boring to have to keep making the same old points. Writing in 1927 (and from a perspective very close to that of Winifred Holtby), Vera Brittain commented on the feelings of the typical feminist:

> "The fight for acknowledgement now bores rather than enthralls her; its postponement seems illogical, an anachronism, a waste of precious time . . . she continues to agitate, often a little wearily, only because she desires to abolish the need for agitation."[3]

In our own time, I am often struck by the disjunction between the theoretical sophistication and innovation of feminist writing and the policy recommendations most feminists support. However varied their views on psychoanalysis, post-modernism, post-colonialism, the nature of subjectivity, or whether it makes sense to talk of "women" at all, most tend to agree that there should be more nurseries, equal pay, protection against sexual harassment and domestic violence, non-sexist education, more women in positions of power. The disagreement is largely in the details, and the real difficulty is that progress is so slow. There has been no great theoretical challenge working out what needs to be done; the more intellectually exciting areas have been those where feminism stretches beyond its initial pre-occupation with women to develop new connections.

The third point is that it is hard to sustain a politics on the margins. There are exceptional periods when this becomes both possible and desirable: the typical feminist of the 1970s had little fear of marginalisation, both because she took a pride in her "outsider" status, and because she was sustained by an active community in the women's movement. Thirty years on, there is a more palpable anxiety about remaining on the margins, and this often surfaces in a dislike of feminist "ghettos" or a need to show that feminism is not "just" about women. My own work falls within what would be described as feminist political theory. When asked what I work on, however, I commonly say I deal with issues of democracy or representation or political equality: it is as if I like to think of myself as a feminist who works on democracy, rather than someone defined and delimited by a field called "feminist political theory".[4] Offering oneself up to the accusation of focusing

[3] V Brittain, from a Six Point Group Pamphlet, 1927, reprinted in Berry and Bishop, *supra* n. 1, at 99.

[4] In similar vein, Nicola Lacey has commented on her studious avoidance of the field of sexual offences, and linked this to the way that work on sexual offences in general, and the law of rape in particular, became pigeonholed as a peculiarly feminine or feminist concern. She makes this observation in the context of an essay that breaks with her previous practice to focus on the way that criminal law constructs the wrong of rape. See N Lacey, "Unspeakable Subjects, Impossible Rights: Sexuality, Integrity and Criminal Law" in N Lacey, *Unspeakable Subjects; Feminist Essays in Legal and Social Theory* (Oxford, Hart Publishing, 1998).

"only" on women suggests a narrowing of focus that most of us would prefer to avoid. One consequence is that the moments of dissidence can be distinctly short-lived.

I begin then with a warning. When looking at developments in feminist political theory, it is possible to trace a powerful movement that takes feminism beyond an exclusive preoccupation with women to link analyses of sexuality and gender to analyses of race, ethnicity, the politics of multiculturalism, and what has come to be called the politics of difference. This is an impressive achievement. It also poses a challenge. The movement testifies to the power of feminism, demonstrating that its insights can illuminate far more than the condition of women. But it also fits—rather too closely for comfort—into a cycle that begins with making women visible and ends with concealing them again. In the course of the 1980s, feminists sometimes talked confidently of a movement "from margin to mainstream"; my question in this paper is whether that consolidation might not prove to be a capitulation as well. I start with a brief indication of what I understand by the politics of difference, and identify three problems that can arise with this. My conclusion is that there are indeed risks associated with the generalisation of feminism into a politics of difference, but that these are currently more apparent in the non-feminist than feminist literature.

THE POLITICS OF DIFFERENCE

The "politics of difference" has been widely used in recent years, partly as an analytical, partly as a normative category. It seeks to capture the complexities of identity in societies where class is no longer (if it ever was) the predominant source of political identification but has given way to multiple axes of identity organised around sex, race, ethnicity, age, religion, language and culture. A politics of difference stresses the importance of recognising rather than obliterating these differences: this may be because recognising people's (differential) identities has come to be regarded as a necessary component in human well-being; more pragmatically, it may be because moves towards greater equality tend to fail when difference is not taken into account. In some versions, the key point is that identity is always forged in relations of difference, and that this uneasy mutual interdependence should encourage us to review notions of women as an identity group. In others, there is a substantive claim about the vitality and value of difference: the idea that heterogeneity is richer and more dynamic than homogeneity, and that we should welcome rather than fear our differences.

In the development of this tradition, Iris Marion Young's *Justice and the Politics of Difference* has been particularly influential.[5] Young has attacked a trend in contemporary political theory that is well exemplified in the work of John Rawls: a tendency to treat problems of social justice as a matter of what people should have

[5] I M Young, *Justice and the Politics of Difference* (Princeton, NJ, Princeton University Press, 1990).

rather than what they do. Her point is that focusing on questions of distribution (what do the principles of justice tell us about how goods should be distributed?) leads towards a politics from on-high, a politics without the politics, in which different social groups play no noticeable part in defining the principles of justice. Her related argument criticises the ideal of impartiality: the notion that it is possible to arrive at correct principles of justice by abstracting from what is particular to one's own or group position and repressing differences of gender, race, ethnicity, sexuality, culture or class. Young challenges what she sees as the assumption of a homogeneous public. She argues that this assumption renders invisible social groups whose values or practices do not fit with the dominant norms, and delivers all of us to an idealist fiction that represents the partial preoccupations of dominant groups as the last word in impartial interest. The better alternative is to recognise more rigorously the heterogeneous nature of contemporary life. This means attending to group-specific needs rather than denying them in some grand rhetoric about human equality. It also implies group-specific representation for oppressed groups so as to provide them with the empowerment and recognition that will enable them to challenge dominant norms.

In her introduction, Young describes her personal political passion as beginning with feminism, and says it was her participation in women's movement politics that first taught her to identify oppression. But it was also this participation that compelled her beyond an exclusive focus on women, for it was discussions within the women's movement on the importance and difficulty of acknowledging differences among women—differences of race, sexuality, age or culture—that ignited her reflections on the politics of difference. These discussions, as she puts it:

> "compelled me to move out of a focus specifically on women's oppression, to try to understand as well the social position of other oppressed groups".[6]

The connections Young makes have been repeated in many other works, and the politics of gender is increasingly theorised in the wider context of what have come to be called "new social movements". In recent work on political representation, I have focused on the exclusions practised against groups defined by their gender, ethnicity and race, and have argued the importance of a politics of presence in dealing with these exclusions.[7] In doing so, I have claimed that it is incoherent to promote gender parity in politics without also promoting the fairer representation of racial and ethnic minorities, and have treated these in tandem as examples of the political representation of difference. In *Justice Interruptus*, Nancy Fraser explores what she sees as a shift from a politics of redistribution, most commonly associated with class and class interest, to a politics of recognition, fuelled by "groups mobilised under the banners of nationality, ethnicity, 'race', gender and sexuality".[8] While noting important distinctions between these last groups, she argues

[6] *Ibid.*, at 13–14.

[7] A Phillips, *The Politics of Presence* (Oxford, Clarendon Press, 1995).

[8] N Fraser, *Justice Interruptus: Critical Reflections on the "Postsocialist" Condition* (London, Routledge, 1997) 11.

that the politics associated with gender and race, in particular, share crucial common features. A collection edited by Seyla Benhabib invited the contributors "to reflect upon the theory and practice of democracy after the experiences of identity politics in their 'new social movements' form",[9] and brought together essays on feminism, multiculturalism, and the rights of indigenous peoples under a general rubric of *Democracy and Difference*. There is a perception that these share important common features: most notably, that they complicate traditional views about abstract, universal rights by stressing the heterogeneity of political life.

The idea that racial and sexual inequality share common features is not new. Many of those who became active in the nineteenth-century women's movement came from a prior involvement in anti-slavery agitation, while many of those who became active in the contemporary women's movement took it for granted that racism and sexism formed a common enemy. The more unexpected alliance has been that between feminism and the defence of minority cultures, though here too one can readily identify connections. Feminists have written extensively on the relationship between equality and difference, and one of the points recurrently made is that policies of sex-blindness may not be as progressive as was traditionally assumed. Refusing to differentiate between women and men looks, on the face of it, the route to a more equal society: no more discrimination against women, no more differential treatment on the basis of sex. But in the framework of an unequal society, that refusal to recognise difference can have perverse effects. Without the sex-specific legislation that allows pregnant women to take maternity leave, for example, women are set at a disadvantage in the labour market; without the sex-specific policies that require political parties to take the sex of the candidates into account, women will continue to be grossly under-represented in politics. The refusal to recognise difference can become a covert way of elevating one group alone as the norm. Men then stand in for humanity, and humanity adopts a masculine form.

Arguments such as these have provided an important resource in addressing relationships between minority and majority cultures, for if sex-blindness is not unambiguously progressive, neither is the kind of "culture-blindness" that accommodates minority cultures only on condition that they keep their differences to a protected private zone. The pursuit of sexual equality sometimes requires differential treatment for women and men. In similar fashion, the pursuit of equal citizenship in a multicultural society may sometimes require differential rights or differential facilities for members of minority cultures. (One relatively uncontentious example is the exemption of Sikh men from the legal requirement to wear a safety helmet while riding a motorbike; another would be the provision of public funding to establish cultural centres for minority groups.) Will Kymlicka, best known for his writings on *Multicultural Citizenship*,[10] argues that the "same attitudes and habits of mind which

[9] S Benhabib, *Democracy and Difference: Contesting the Boundaries of the Political* (Princeton, NJ, Princeton University Press, 1996) 5.

[10] W Kymlicka, *Multicultural Citizenship: A Liberal Theory of Minority Rights* (Oxford, Clarendon Press, 1995).

enabled liberals to ignore the just claims of women have also enabled them to ignore the just claims of ethnocultural minorities".[11] Both feminism and multiculturalism take issue with the inadequacy of the traditional liberal conception of individual rights. Both see liberalism as blinding itself to grave injustice: in the first case by operating as if the citizen is a man; in the second, as if all citizens share the same language and national culture. Both traditions stress the institutional structures that have to be addressed in order to give meaning to an equality of rights. Both challenge the assumption that equality means identical treatment.

So when feminists defend affirmative action as necessary to deal with the deep structures of inequality that prevent women taking up their so-called equal opportunities, the argument points towards a parallel defence of affirmative action for members of racial and ethnic minorities. When feminists argue that legislation has been framed without reference to women's experience, and that giving women an equal voice would alter the prevailing norms, this points towards parallel charges that have been made by members of minority cultures. A feminism that focuses on experiences of marginalisation and exclusion has obvious points of contact with other groups that face a similar experience. This suggests a close alliance between all groups that have felt themselves defined out of the dominant norms.

The suggestions are, in my view, correct, for there **are** strong parallels between sexual and racial equality, and a close family resemblance between the issues posed by feminism and those that have to be addressed to achieve equality in multicultural societies. But the shift towards this more generalised politics of diversity and difference also carries certain risks. The first is that the preoccupation with difference can make it harder to sustain a politics focused around women or women's identity. The second is that alliances between feminism, multiculturalism, and the politics of indigenous groups can promote a conception of women's politics that pushes it too far into a paradigm derived from cultural minorities. The third is that the connections rightly made between women and other excluded groups can make it harder to articulate a critique of sexual inequality. These are substantially different points, and the fact that each can be made of something termed "the politics of difference" indicates something of the slipperiness of this term.

IDENTITY/DIFFERENCE AND THE DISAPPEARING WOMAN

The first point is that the recognition of difference can make it hard to articulate any clear sense of "women". At its most straightforward, this is because differences between women come more evidently to the fore. In the Anglo-American literature, it has become hard to sustain strong notions of "women" or "women's experience" or "women's interests": if we draw on such notions to criticise the false abstractions of "mankind" or "humanity" or "men", we may find ourselves deconstructing one

[11] W Kymlicka, "Liberal Complacencies", in S M Okin with respondents (eds.), *Is Multiculturalism Bad For Women?* (Princeton, NJ, Princeton University Press, 1999) 34.

set of fictions only to put another set in their place. Women are indeed women, and most women are probably different from most men. But sexual identities intersect with racial identities, class identities, regional or national identities, and these make it hard to articulate a strong sense of women's identity or needs.

When this critique was first developed, many feminists continued to operate with notions of group identity or group interest, but refined these to address more precise sub-groupings, like working class women or women of colour. The supposed "interests of women" then fragmented into the interests of multiple groups, and just as men could not legitimately claim to speak to or represent the interests of women, so now, it was argued, middle class women could not speak to or represent the interests of working class women, white women the interests of black women, or first world women the interests of women from the Third World. This was felt by many to be a politics of despair, for if "women" dissolves into all these sub-categories, each of which is then open to further sub-division, there seems no stopping place short of a unique description of each unique individual. This typology of differences also failed to capture the way political identities are formed, for if no-one regards herself simply as "woman", it is also the case that no-one regards herself simply as a working class woman, or simply as a black woman. It is not so much that there are many identity groups, but that each person lives in a complex of identities, some elements of which may become more important than others depending on political context.

Under the impact of such arguments, the first attack on the homogeneity of women spawned a second, this time more indebted to a post-structuralist deconstructionism that stresses the ambiguity of all identities. In the literature associated with this, the search for identity is sometimes presented as a search for false security in what is necessarily an insecure world: an attempt to close down or close off a sense of things that do not fit, instead of embracing the uncertainty and dealing with the complications that then ensue. When we define ourselves as different from others (this may be women defining themselves as different from men, or one group of women defining themselves as different from another), we are trying to fix our own identity by pushing into some other camp the unruly elements we cannot make sense of. We are trying to impose order on a turbulent existence. Think, for example, of what is happening when women define themselves as different from men because of their greater capacity for empathy or care. There may well be differences between the sexes in this respect, but when we allow ourselves to define women **through** this more caring identity, we close off our troubled perception of other elements that co-exist with this—a sense, perhaps, that women can be very aggressive, or that part of what women want is simply to insist on their own personal needs. We are trying, that is, to fix identity by expunging what is contradictory or different.

For those working in this tradition, the search for women's identity is always problematic, even when pluralised to take into account multiple differences between women. It is not just that we now have to fill in all the additional details about race or class or age or ethnicity; as Judith Butler argues, even if we were to do so, we still could not expect to end up with a meaningful category of "women".[12] For Butler, the term is a permanent site of contest; it is what we battle over rather than who we are. For Bonnie Honig, we miss the point about difference if we treat it merely as a reminder that there are different groups: that there are men and women, black people and white, Muslims and Catholics and Jews. The real point about difference is that it prevents any of us from having a secure identity, either as an individual or as a member of a group. Taking difference seriously means giving up on the dream of an identity or culture or group vision that is "unmarked or unriven by difference";[13] it means recognising conflict as built into our identities and not just as conflict between "us" and "them". From this perspective, identity can be more a source of oppression than a means to empowerment. Rather than organising around our so-called identities, we would do better to recognise that the subject is always "decentred" and identity always incomplete.

Many find this talk of the decentred subject hard to take: we might, under pressure, agree with Stuart Hall that "the fully unified, completed, secure and coherent identity is a fantasy",[14] but that seems to set an impossibly high standard for what counts as identity; to quote Hall from another context, "identity is not fixed, but it's not nothing either".[15] Yet whatever position people reach on this, few would now want to present "women" as either a pre-existing or soon-to-be-generated identity group, and much contemporary theory draws on a more troubled understanding of identity formation as organised around binary exclusions that always threaten to suppress differences on each side. The binary differences have come to seem particularly implausible, and the perhaps unexpected outcome is that what started as a pluralisation of differences (not just male **or** female, black **or** white, straight **or** gay) generates what many have felt to be an over-individualised conception of political agency.[16] This is the charge that has been levelled at Judith Butler, for example, who has been criticised for substituting individual acts of parody or transgression for the kind of political mobilisation that relies on a notion of social groups; for exaggerating the de-stabilising effects of cross-dressing as a subversion of norms of masculinity or heterosexuality, and playing down the possibilities of more traditional forms of collective action. She regards this as an unfair criticism, and I'm sure did not intend her drag example to be taken as such a paradigm for political action. It does, however, seem one consequence of the turn towards difference that any systemic differences between one group (say, women) and another group (say, men) that continue to shape and curtail our actions become less apparent. The argument builds on scepticism

[12] J Butler, *Gender Trouble: Feminism and the Subversion of Identity* (London, Routledge, 1989).

[13] B Honig, "Difference, Dilemmas, and the Politics of Home" in S Benhabib (ed.), *supra* n. 9, at 258.

[14] S Hall, "New Ethnicities" in J Donald and A Rattansi (eds.), "*Race*", *Culture and Difference* (London, Sage, 1992) 277.

[15] S Hall, "Interview on Culture and Power" (1997) 33 *Radical Philosophy* 86.

[16] See L McNay, *Gender as Agency* (Cambridge, Polity Press, 2000).

about the coherence of individual identity, but it also returns us, rather unexpectedly, to that individual. Women as a group drop out of the picture.

THE REIFICATION OF DIFFERENCE

A second problem arises in a very different part of contemporary literature, where notions of collective subjects remain almost too alive and well. Consider James Tully's *Strange Multiplicity*, which focuses on "the demands of the 250 million Aboriginal and Indigenous peoples of the world for the recognition and accommodation of their twelve thousand diverse cultures, governments and environmental practices",[17] and argues for reconciliation through dialogue and mutual respect rather than an assimilationist imposition of a uniform constitution. In this work, Tully draws on a tradition he describes as "cultural feminism", making frequent parallels between feminist critiques of the authoritative, dominant culture and the arguments put forward by Aboriginal peoples or members of linguistic and ethnic minorities.

The feminism he incorporates is one that stresses women's cultural difference, sees women as speaking "in a different voice" from men and appealing to different normative traditions. The parallels between this and the politics of Aboriginal peoples are obvious enough. In both cases, Tully suggests, the problem is how to "enter into a dialogue on equal footing with members from the authoritative tradition without being marginalised or assimilated":[18] how, that is, to claim an equal footing, but how to do this while still holding on to one's cultural distinctiveness. Many feminists will not recognise themselves in this description, will argue, on the contrary, that their feminism derives from the authoritative traditions of liberalism or democracy, and will see their task as making those traditions live up to their promises to women. But the fact that Tully draws on only one strand of a variegated tradition is not a decisive objection. The larger problem is that the assimilation of women into the category of "cultural group" has unfortunate consequences for feminist critique.

Treating women as a cultural group overstates the homogeneity of "women's culture". It also presumes that the characteristics that have come to be associated with women's way of thinking or women's way of being are ones we will want to sustain and protect, in much the same way that one might want to sustain and protect minority cultures from forced assimilation into majority values.[19] So far as women's culture is concerned, this strikes me as a dubious presumption. Women are, in my view, different from men, do tend to have different ways of talking or relating to others, do tend towards different sets of priorities and values. It would

[17] J Tully, *Strange Multiplicity: Constitutionalism in an Age of Diversity* (Cambridge, Cambridge University Press, 1995) 3.

[18] *Ibid.*, at 53.

[19] Since these, too, are tainted by the processes that produce them, there is also a question mark over the respect due to any "tradition".

be distinctly odd if this were not the case, given the markedly different treatment of boys and girls as they grow up, and the markedly different roles allocated to the sexes in carework, relationships and employment. If, with all this, men and women ended up just the same kind of people, they would have to be extraordinarily immune to the social influences acting upon them: inhuman, almost, in their detachment from social conditions. So I have no objection to the notion that women are, on average, different from men. But I cannot see that differences that derive from historical inequality or relationships of power and subordination can be treated as objects of veneration, differences one would seek to sustain.

Femininity and masculinity alike are tainted by the processes that create them, and neither, in my view, is entitled to the kind of respect that might more legitimately be accorded to traditions that have developed over centuries inside Aboriginal communities, or traditions that migrant groups have brought with them from their countries of origin. In any contest between them, I find it plausible enough that the qualities associated with femininity will win out over those associated with masculinity: that the responsibilities women carry for the care of the young, weak and old can generate a finer set of priorities than a more typically masculine experience; or that a history of subordination can generate greater sympathy for those in pain or suffering than a lifetime of being in control. But "women's culture" is formed in relations of dependency and subordination, and what is positive in it is almost inextricably intertwined with aspects that are less attractive. One of Simone de Beauvoir's complaints about women was that they were particularly prone to "bad faith", and that living in conditions of relative powerlessness, they were always inclined to blame other people or fate for the things that went wrong in their lives. Neither the master nor the slave ends up with a model culture, and while the assimilation of "women's culture" into "men's culture" is hardly a desirable objective, we cannot simply celebrate the characteristics of "women's culture" as if these were unproblematic.

The other side to this is what the analogy between women and "other" cultural groups does to the status of "men's culture". In Tully's analysis, feminism becomes "the struggles of women for the recognition and accommodation of their gender-related differences",[20] and this is taken to mean that women need something more or other than an equal say in the institutions or traditions established by men. They also need an equal say "in their own voice", which seems to imply an equal standing in a dialogue that women join from their own distinct organisations and with their own distinct traditions of interpretation. There is something rather odd in the scenario this conjures up. It suggests a dialogue between "women's culture" and "men's culture", something akin to the proposed dialogue between indigenous and settler peoples, which each party enters into in relations of mutual respect and where each comes to recognise the salience of the other's point of view. Whatever sense one might make of this in considering the relationship between minority and majority cultures, it seems peculiarly inappropriate to relations between women

[20] Tully, *supra* n. 17, at 178.

and men, who always live side by side with one another—and if feminism is right, in a relationship of subordination and inequality. When feminism is presented as claiming an equal standing for women's culture alongside men's, this not only treats women's culture as less problematic than it is; it also gives far too much credence to the claims of "men's culture".

FEMINISM AND MULTICULTURALISM

This leads to the third problem, which is that the connections made between gender and other kinds of difference can make it harder to articulate a critique of sexual inequality. The alliance between feminism and multiculturalism has been forged out of a common dissatisfaction with liberalism, contesting the excessive confidence liberalism places in a formal equality of rights, and its tendency to treat difference as something best ignored. This alliance, however, is fraught with difficulties, and this is particularly so when we consider the centrality of conventions regulating familial relationships to the definition of most cultures. What distinguishes one culture from another is very often the principles it adopts regarding the relative position of women and men: whether it regards marriage, for example, as a free contract between consenting individuals, as something that deprives women of their independent legal standing (as was the case in nineteenth century Britain), or as something best arranged by parents acting on what they conceive to be the true interests of their children. Cultures vary in their attitudes to sexuality (the most dramatic illustration being the importance some cultural groups have attached to the genital mutilation of young women), and in their willingness to recognise women as civic equals. One of the main concerns of cultural groups in their contestations with other groups or the state is to retain their authority to decide who is a group member: to decide, for example, who counts as a Jew, or who is to be recognised as a member of a particular indigenous group. As Ayelet Shachar has argued, this authority typically operates through family law, and in many cases, the criteria for membership have been self-evidently discriminatory, as when Indian tribes in North American reservations have recognised the children of men who marry outside the group as full members, but not the children of women who marry outside.[21]

The further point is that where religion is a prominent defining element in a culture, the principles regulating sexual relationships are almost always inequitable. All religions experience difficulty with sexual equality, and despite some notable exceptions (including the many early feminists who belonged to the Unitarian Church), most feminists experience difficulty with religion. That this should be so is hardly surprising, for religions tend to build into their moral prescriptions part of

[21] A Shachar, "The Paradox of Multicultural Vulnerability: Individual Rights, Identity Groups, and the State" in C Joppke and S Lukes (eds.), *Multicultural Questions* (Oxford, Oxford University Press, 1999); see also A Shachar, "Group Identity and Women's Rights in Family Law: The Perils of Multicultural Accommodation", (1998) 6 *Journal of Political Philosophy* 285 at 285–305.

what have been the customs and conventions in the societies from which they arise. They then weight these customs with all the power of religious prescription. Since no society has yet operated on the basis of full sexual equality, it is only to be expected that religions will tend towards conservatism on the position of women. To say this is not to say that religion is intrinsically misogynist, for every religion contains within itself a variety of traditions, and these have included a variety of positions on the appropriate roles and relationships of the sexes. But religion is not, on the whole, associated with a strong defence of sexual equality. What then happens to the alliance between feminism and multiculturalism when feminists find themselves defending the rights of minority cultures?

Some of the literature sidesteps this problem by overlooking religion. One of the criticisms levelled at Iris Young is that there seems to be little space in her heterogeneous public for religious groups, and that the examples she typically offers are rather too obviously drawn from what have been seen as the "progressive" end of the "new social movements" spectrum.[22] In principle, however, it is hard to see why a politics of difference should not apply equally to groups excluded or vilified because of their religious identities. The most recent survey of ethnic minorities in Britain suggests that it is people of Asian rather than African or Caribbean origin who currently bear the brunt of racial attacks and racial abuse, and the majority of Asians interviewed in the survey felt that this prejudice was primarily a prejudice against Muslims.[23] The current demonisation of Islam seems to fall well within the remit of any politics of difference—but Islam is not at its best on the question of women.

In a number of recent contributions, Susan Moller Okin sets out to prise feminism apart from its alliance with multiculturalism. "I think we—especially those of us who consider ourselves politically progressive and opposed to all forms of oppression—have been too quick to assume that feminism and multiculturalism are both good things which are easily reconciled".[24] When minority cultures lay claim to special exemptions, or argue for group rights in order to sustain their traditional practices, the cultural practices they are defending are often antagonistic to sexual equality: the examples Okin discusses include polygamy, forced marriages, female genital mutilation, and the veiling of women. The self-proclaimed leaders of these minority cultures are typically composed of their older and male members, and unless the women in these cultures speak out forcibly for the specific interests of women—and are supported in this by others committed to sexual equality—then the supposed common ground between feminism and multiculturalism will end up suppressing women's interests, making women invisible once again.

[22] The list she offers in *Justice and the Politics of Difference* does make one reference to religion—"women, Blacks, Chicanos, Puerto Ricans and other Spanish-speaking Americans, American Indians, Jews, lesbians, gay men, Arabs, Asians, old people, working class people, and the physically and mentally disabled"—but the criticism is not entirely unjust. Young, *supra* n. 5, at 40.

[23] T Modood et al., *Ethnic Minorities in Britain: Diversity and Disadvantage* (London, Policy Studies Institute, 1997).

[24] Okin and respondents, *supra* n. 11, at 10; See also "Feminism and Multiculturalism: Some Tensions" (1998) 108/4 *Ethics* 661–84.

I agree with Okin on this last point, though I also think she weights the argument unfairly by focusing on practices that are widely condemned inside minority cultures (polygamy, female genital mutilation), or ones that are already extensively contested and no longer in general use. It is easy to overstate the tensions between feminism and multiculturalism, and in so doing, to reaffirm stereotypical misrepresentations of minority cultures that contribute to their marginality. But it is also, as Okin argues, possible to exaggerate their compatibility, and one of the dangers in a radical pluralism that lists women alongside ethnic minorities, linguistic minorities, indigenous peoples, lesbians and gay men, is that the focus on heterogeneity versus homogeneity can take the edge off sexual equality.

The problem here is almost the opposite to the first one discussed, for where some have used the language of difference to dissolve the coherence of any collective identity (no more "women", no more "blacks", no more Asians or lesbians or Jews), others employ it to describe what then seem rather too solid group identities. Yet "the ethnic minority", like "the Aboriginal people" or "the lesbian and gay community", is made up of women and men, old and young, rich and poor: people often engaged in conflict and disagreeing about the interpretation of their supposedly shared culture. In some cases, these conflicts will become so acute that individuals will choose to dissociate themselves from their supposed group and redefine themselves in different ways. A more common experience, perhaps, is that dissidents position themselves for contest on two fronts: simultaneously challenging the external disparagement of "their" culture or community and the internal representations of that culture or community that reproduce inequalities and injustice. The double nature of this contest is not always fully recognised in the literature on feminism and multiculturalism, which tends to represent cultural claims as the exclusive provenance of men in the community and counterposes these to the rights and protections of women members. But it is also not well recognised in the literature on multiculturalism, some of which operates with an overly unified notion of "the community", and thinks of dialogue as taking place between rather than within and across the constituent groups.

BEYOND THE BINARY OF FEMALE AND MALE

In a variety of ways, the movement from "women's issues" to a more general analysis of difference can mean that questions once central to feminist politics become submerged under broader themes. In the first case, this is because "difference" comes to be viewed almost as a constitutive part of the human condition, associated with a lengthy (perhaps infinite) list of possible axes of differentiation, but thereby detached from any thesis about one group wielding or another group contesting power. In the second case, it is the assimilation of women into the category of "cultural group" that is the source of the problem. This encourages a perception of women as yet another culturally marginalised or threatened group, and in the process exaggerates the integrity of both "women's" and "men's" culture. In the third case, the alliance between similarly beleaguered outsiders can make it harder for feminists to articulate their critique of sexual inequality. The connections (rightly) made between gender and other kinds of difference can then end up silencing women.

At this point in the argument, many readers may feel my diagnosis is far too gloomy. After all, the assimilation of women into the category of cultural group has been more characteristic of the non-feminist than feminist literature; and if the recent voicing of concerns over the relationship between feminism and multiculturalism tells us anything, it is that feminists have retained a very healthy awareness that women in minority cultural groups can have different interests from men, and a very determined commitment to sexual equality. At this stage, indeed, one might want to stress the opposite risk. There is, of course, a danger that well-intentioned moves towards recognising the diversity and legitimacy of many cultures could encourage public authorities to turn a blind eye to practices that institutionalise women's subordination, could strengthen the power of self-styled community leaders—almost always male—who represent a very partial and often oppressive view of "their" community's most cherished traditions, and lead to a paralysed cultural relativism that puts cultural sensitivity over the rights or needs of women. But there is also a risk on the other side that the sexual equality agenda could be employed to dismiss out of hand the validity of any multicultural claims. There is a rather unsavoury strand of racism around today that uses the situation of women—"look what these people do to their women"—to characterise ethnic minority groups as backward, violent, or abusive, and then employs this stereotype to justify an arrogant assimilationism.[25] The sexual equality agenda can be adopted in a rather dishonest way—by people who otherwise show little interest in women's equality—as a means of disparaging or stereotyping the groups they regard as inferior. If this is so, we should perhaps be equally worried about the feminist challenge to the "wrong" kind of multiculturalism inadvertently encouraging a backlash against all such initiatives, or the abuse of the sexual equality agenda to promote an oppressively monocultural world. It may be that these pose a greater contemporary danger than any failure to speak out about women.

The object of my argument is not to reverse the movement from a politics centred around women to a more generalised focus on difference, for like many of those who now take difference as their central organising concept, I have found this movement enormously fruitful. It enables us to identify common patterns in processes of exclusion or marginalisation; it brings into sharper focus the connections between racial and sexual equality; it also establishes what I see as a close family relationship between feminist and multicultural concerns. But the process simultaneously makes feminism both more and less central: more central, because the analysis of gender difference becomes one of the prototypes for addressing

[25] This move is not unique to race: there has been a similar stereotyping of working class communities as peculiarly violent or abusive towards women, and one of the battles feminists have engaged in over the years is to get people to recognise that domestic violence is not an exclusively working-class phenomenon.

many axes of difference; less central, because the unravelling of group identity makes it hard to continue to speak of women as a distinct group. Once one moves from a simpler binary of female and male to a wider theorisation of difference, it does seem that generalisations about "women" and "men" miss the point: either they misread the complexities and ambiguities in the formation of identities; or they postulate an unproblematic and unified "women's culture"; or they treat women as a category outside of culture or ethnicity, and deal with culture or ethnicity as if these were exclusively male. Each of these points has a long prehistory in feminist theory and politics—there was no naïve early moment when we all thought of "women" as a simple description—but the movement that has linked analyses of gender and sexuality to the broader politics of difference helps bring them into sharper relief. In some cases it has done so by compounding the errors, as when women are listed alongside ethnic, racial, linguistic, cultural or religious minorities as the key groups challenging the presumptions of a homogeneous society: this ignores what was a central theme of feminist politics from the late 1970s, which is that women are not "just" women but make up half the membership of all the "other" minority groups.[26] In most cases, however, the very naming of the groups makes it clear that each of them intersects and shares membership with the others, for once one starts thinking about difference, it is hard to sustain for long the notion of mutually exclusive groups. What began as a heterogeneity of distinct and different groups, linked together by common experiences of marginalisation or exclusion, ends up as a more complex heterogeneity within them.

The resulting unravelling of group identity is, on the whole, a positive development—and certainly more beneficial to feminism than an uncritical reification of "women's culture" or uncritical defence of a supposedly unitary "minority culture". But the movement returns us to the problem posed earlier, which is that the logic of difference—particularly if linked to an analysis of identity formation as suppressing rather than enabling—can make it hard to talk about women. Perhaps more precisely (because we do all continue to talk about women whatever our theoretical take on the term), it can encourage an over-individualised understanding of political agency that attaches too little weight to structural differences between women and men. It is as if we either end up with a listing that places women alongside a range of minority groups as exemplars of the excluded "other" (failing therefore to recognise any specificity to gender, but also overlooking the women within each of these excluded groups); or else we dispense with these fragile group categories to fall back on the individual again. In either case, the capacity to address sexual inequality can be seriously compromised.

I have cited little so far in the way of evidence from feminist literature, and my argument has been rather short on illustrations of this supposed turn-around in feminist thought. This fits, as it happens, with my reading, for I see the dangers discussed here as more likely to mar the reception of a politics of difference outside

[26] This is particularly powerfully argued in E Spelman, *Inessential Woman: Problems of Exclusion in Feminist Thought* (Boston, Beacon Press, 1988).

feminist circles than characterise its development within. It would certainly be inappropriate to describe Iris Young's work as a case of the vanishing woman, for she has consistently argued against any tendency to submerge conflicts between women and men, and a recent collection of her essays is explicitly organised around issues of gender.[27] The problem is not so much what happens in feminism. The problem, rather, is that the politics of difference can become one of the tickets of entry into mainstream debate, but what gets taken from feminism is its critique of universalism or emphasis on diversity and difference rather than its commitment to sexual equality.

So far as feminist work is concerned, the cycle has not been completed; women have not been rendered invisible again. But in pursuing the implications of the turn towards difference, it is important to continue to theorise that complex relationship between individual and group, and to do so in a way that retains a meaningful politics of sexual equality. The stretching beyond "women" to a more generalised focus on difference has been an extraordinary achievement. In measuring that achievement, however, we have to be aware of the challenge. Like Winifred Holtby, I believe we must continue to be feminists—and keep those women still firmly in view.

[27] I M Young, *Intersecting Voices: Dilemmas of Gender, Political Philosophy, and Policy* (Princeton, NJ, Princeton University Press, 1997).

2

The Mother of the Legal Person

KRISTIN SAVELL

I INTRODUCTION

LAW'S INTEREST IN the physical body of the legal person is not uniform. In some fields, such as contract law, the legal person is primarily an economic actor whose physical body, unlike his capacity to reason, does not seem material to law.[1] In other fields, such as criminal and medical law, however, the physical body of the legal person is more central to law's concerns.[2] The genesis of the legal person is one such example. Here law prescribes the minimum physical conditions of personhood by determining that a legal person comes into being when it is "born alive" and not before. In this sense, law sees its "born alive" requirements as marking the threshold between a natural and a cultural order.

Some feminist theorists have challenged the assumption that the physical body exists prior to law.[3] This challenge goes hand in hand with the claim that (along with other discourses) law does not merely represent physical bodies but actually produces them.[4] Law does this, according to Ngaire Naffine, each time it assigns certain "qualities to the body, seeing the body in terms of some things and not others, seeing some bodies in certain ways and other bodies in others."[5] For feminists who reject law's assumptions about the naturalness of the physical body, it has become important to analyse how law does assign meanings to bodies and to document the political, social and legal consequences that follow these assignments.

[1] R Mykituik, "Fragmenting the Body" (1994) 2 *Australian Feminist Law Journal* 63, at 82–84.

[2] N Naffine, "The Body Bag" in N Naffine and R Owens (eds.), *Sexing the Subject of Law* (Sydney, LBC Information Services, 1997) 79, at 81.

[3] In philosophy, see J Butler, *Bodies That Matter: On the Discursive Limits of 'Sex'* (London, Routledge, 1993); M Shildrick, *Leaky Bodies and Boundaries: Feminism, Postmodernism and (Bio)ethics* (London: Routledge, 1997); E Grosz, *Volatile Bodies: Towards a Corporeal Feminism* (Sydney, Allen and Unwin, 1995); M Gatens, *Imaginary Bodies: Ethics, Power and Corporeality* (New York, Routledge, 1996). In bioethics, see P Rothfield, "Bodies and Subjects: Medical Ethics and Feminism" in P Komesaroff (ed.), *Troubled Bodies—Critical Perspectives on Postmodernism, Medical Ethics and the Body* (Durham, Duke University Press, 1995) 168. In law, see Naffine, *supra* n. 2; M Davies, "Taking the Inside Out—Sex and Gender in the Legal Subject" in Naffine and Owens, *supra* n. 2, at 25 XXX and I Karpin, "Legislating the Female Body: Reproductive Technology and the Reconstructed Woman" (1992) 3 *Columbia Journal of Gender and Law* 325. [hereinafter Reconstructed Woman].

[4] *Ibid.*

[5] Naffine, *supra* n. 2, at 84.

One characteristic (among a range) of the physical body that law assumes to be natural and irreducible is sex.[6] There are male and female persons. In matters concerning reproduction in particular, the sexed specificities of bodies seem most natural and most material to law. As I have already mentioned, the legal person comes into being when it is born alive, an event which is said to occur when the child emerges whole from the body of its mother and obtains an existence separate from her. At the originating moment of personhood, therefore, the female body is present in its sexed specificity. There are significant questions to ask of law's construction of the female body on both sides of this "birth" threshold. These questions concern the physical body and characteristics of the normative legal person, and the physical body and characteristics of the pregnant woman as law sees her.

In thinking about these questions in the context of the law relating to abortion and medical treatment, I have found the work of Ngaire Naffine extremely helpful.[7] Naffine argues that the body of liberal theory and of criminal law is a bounded, masculine body.[8] Moreover, she traces a relation between the bounded nature of this physical body and the integrity and dignity of the self. Dignity, she says, depends "on a respect for the physical integrity of the self".[9] Within this "logic of a bounded self"[10a], law assumes the responsibility for ensuring that "the person as flesh is treated with proper regard, the sort of regard which ensures human dignity".[10] The legal rules that govern the law of physical contact tend to bear this out. Here primacy is given to the bodily integrity of the person, whose boundaries are preserved and protected from unauthorised physical touching.[11] Authorisation for certain types of touching can be granted by the act of consent. But in the absence of consent, or in the case of touching that transgresses the bodily

[6] Davies, *supra* n. 3. It is always important to emphasise that sex is but one of a range of characteristics that is important in the construction of the body/person. It may not be the most important characteristic in producing the diminution of legal status for some or many women. Although "sex" will be foregrounded in this essay it must be kept firmly in mind that other aspects of identity, race, class and disability in particular, are critical to law's constructions of women who have medical treatment imposed on them. A US study conducted in 1986 showed that 81 % of pregnant women forced to have caesarean sections or other medical interventions were black, Asian or Hispanic, almost all were public patients: V Kolder, J Gallagher and M Parsons, "Court-Ordered Obstetrical Interventions" (1987) 36 *New England Journal of Medicine* 1192. Of the cases to be discussed in some detail later in this paper, one concerns a Canadian Aboriginal woman (*Winnipeg Child and Family Services* v. G (1997) 152 DLR (4th) 193). For the remainder, the race and class identities are not specifically recorded. On the interactions between race, class and gender in the forced medical treatment of pregnant women see D Roberts, "Punishing Drug-Addicts who have Babies: Women of Color, Equality and the Right to Privacy" (1991) 104 *Harvard Law Review* 1419. On the dangers of "sexing the subject of law" see N Lacey, "On the subject of sexing the subject . . ." in Naffine, *supra* n. 2 , at 65.

[7] Naffine, *supra*, n. 2.

[8] "What the criminal law of human contact presupposes is a standard, uniform bounded human body which is really an extrapolation from a certain liberal conception of the male body, not a woman's body. Inevitably this is very much a matter of construction, not a literal reading of the body, for, to my mind, the body does not possess a nature which can simply be read off." Naffine, *supra* n. 2, at 86.

[9] Naffine, *supra* n. 2, at 83.

[10] *Ibid.*

[10a] *Ibid* at 92.

[11] These rules are discussed below in the context of laws which govern the touching of bodies by doctors. See *infra*, Section IV at 51.

boundaries in inappropriate ways,[12] these transgressions threaten the integrity and dignity of the legal person.[13] When this occurs, the person is seen as "unbounded" and their status is diminished.[14]

As Naffine also points out, and as I will explore further in this essay, women's bodies tend not to be regarded as bounded in an equivalent manner. Women's bodies tend to be regarded as open, as "pierced" (as in the act of heterosexual penetrative intercourse) or as otherwise incomplete.[15] For this reason, female bodies are produced in law as "non-standard or aberrant (not-male) bodies"[16] and, as such, they require definition.[17] Considering some of the myriad ways that law enacts these definitions on and beneath the surfaces of (pregnant) female bodies, and their consequent impact on the legal status of pregnant women, is the task of this essay.

An important part of this investigation is to consider precisely how the physical body and characteristics of the pregnant woman are measured against the unstated norm of the legal person. There are two senses in which the legal person of criminal and medical law and the pregnant woman stand in tension with one another. First, as I have already adverted, the legal person possesses a bounded, self-contained body, a unitary model of bodily existence from which the pregnant woman departs. Extra-legal practices have amplified this conceptual exclusion. The development of advanced visualisation technologies (like ultrasound and fetoscopy) and the practices to which they have given rise, enable law to "know" and to "see" the foetus (whole) inside the body of its mother as a distinct and separable individual. But although the foetus is seen as whole, the mother is not. She is deconstructed, opaque, her physical boundaries indeterminate.

Secondly, the legal person is characterised as a self-sufficient, self-directing agent whose relations with others are antagonistic.[18] The law, however, condemns these characteristics in the mother of the legal person. Her capacity to choose and to act receive considerably less emphasis in law than her contribution as the "body" from which the child separates to achieve legal personhood. That said, the law is very concerned with the choices that pregnant women make[19] particularly when the healthcare choices she makes are thought to be detrimental to the health or life of the foetus (refusing drug rehabilitation or caesarean section being just two examples). In these situations, the transposition of a bounded, unitary model of selfhood places the mother and foetus in an antagonistic relationship. However appropriate

[12] Such as homosexual sex where, Naffine suggests, the male body is feminised by mimicking "the female mode of opening." Naffine, *supra* n. 2, at 91.

[13] These boundary transgressions have the effect of "piercing" the "body bag" so that the subject is seen as unbounded, lacking in dignity and reduced in status. As Naffine points out, and this is a critical point, the metaphor is deployed politically. Thus, "a pierced body can be regarded as either whole or invaded. A body can be enclosed by the body of another and yet still be regarded as separate and distinct . . . A body that encloses another can be regarded as pierced." Naffine, *supra* n. 2, at 84.

[14] *Ibid.*

[15] *Ibid.*, at 88.

[16] *Ibid.*

[17] *Ibid.*

[18] Mykitiuk, *supra* n. 1, at 63.

[19] See *infra*, Sections III at 45 and IV at 51.

the qualities of self-sufficiency and self-direction may be for the legal person, these qualities register as abnormal in the case of pregnant women and may signal legal incompetence.[20] From this we can infer not only that "normal" pregnant women will follow their doctor's advice and they will consent to medical interventions, but also that the normal attributes of the legal person are out of place in the pregnant woman who is expected to be compliant, nurturing and self-sacrificial.[21]

This investigation is self-evidently concerned with boundaries, both physical and conceptual.[22] It is concerned with the bounded nature of the physical body of the legal person and the open nature of the physical body of the mother in law. It is also concerned with the temporal boundaries that law observes to distinguish between foetuses of different gestational ages; and with the conceptual boundary it places between the mother and the foetus, which operates to construct the foetus as bounded while simultaneously constructing the mother as open. Finally, it is concerned with the characteristics that law assigns to the mother, and with how law interprets departures from those characteristics.

II BECOMING A LEGAL PERSON

A (human) legal person comes into being at the moment that he or she is born alive. The originating moment of personhood can be traced to Coke who claimed that in law the person "is accounted a reasonable creature in rerum natura when it is born alive".[23] But the question of when a person is "live born" is not purely a matter of fact. There is scope for interpretation as to precisely when a child is born and as to what constitutes alive.

Law has traditionally understood a person to be born when their body has been completely removed from the body of their mother. In *R* v. *Poulton,* this was expressed as the moment when "the whole body is brought into the world".[24] Glanville Williams articulates the appropriate spatial arrangement between the maternal body and the newborn child as follows:

[20] See *infra*, Section IV at 51.

[21] Ngaire Naffine argues that although the legal person is an idealised male form that tends to reflect the characteristics of middle class men, she argues that law also sustains an ideal form of woman against which actual women who come before the law are judged. The values of caring and nurturing small children are especially appropriate to the ideal woman of law. Departures from these values by actual mothers is, thus, likely to be punished. See N Naffine, *Law and the Sexes—Explorations in Feminist Jurisprudence* (Sydney, Allen & Unwin, 1990), especially Chapter 7.

[22] On the use of boundaries in legal analysis, see M Minow, *Making All The Difference: Inclusion, Exclusion and American Law* (Ithaca, Cornell University Press, 1991).

[23] Cokes Institutes, Pt. III, chap. 7 at 50. It was on this basis that Coke reasoned that the intentional killing of a foetus was not murder: "If a woman be quick with childe, and by a potion or otherwise killeth it in her wombe; or if a man beat her, whereby the child dieth in her body, and she is delivered of a dead childe; this is a great misprision, and no murder." However, "if the childe be born alive, and dieth of the potion, battery or other cause, this is murder". *Ibid.* In modern law, this is known as the "born alive" rule. See *Attorney-General's Reference (No. 3 of 1994)* [1997] 3 WLR 421 at 427.

[24] (1832) 5 C & P 329 at 330; quoted in *Rance* v. *Mid-Downs Health Authority* [1991] 1 QB 587.

"the child must have been wholly extruded from the body of the mother. No part of the child must remain within the parts of the mother if it is to be regarded born."[25]

This definition of "born", broad though it is, does not require the severing of the umbilical cord.[26] The fact that a child may, after being removed from their mother's vagina or uterus (in the case of a surgical delivery), still retain a connection to her via the umbilical cord is not material to law and does not feature in law's interpretation of when a person is born. Given law's insistence on "separation" it is interesting to reflect on why the boundary has been drawn at that moment, and not when all corporeal connections have been severed.

What does this rule tell us about the legal person? The first thing it tells us is that, generally speaking, law requires evidence of a "whole body" for its legal person.[27] This whole body comes into law's view as soon as the outer boundaries, which are to be its permanent features, are free from direct physical contact with the body of the mother. The second thing it tells us is that law is prepared to overlook extant connections between the mother's and the child's bodies and that these connections do not seem to cast doubt on the child's wholeness or its separateness. Perhaps this is so because the organs involved in sustaining this connection—the placenta and the umbilical cord—are impermanent features of bodies and, in the case of the placenta, impermanent features of women's bodies. Perhaps it is simply that a child looks substantively like a distinct individual when its entire body becomes visible to the "world". But until the umbilical cord is cut, the child is not so much separate as *separable* from the body of the mother.

While the neonate may be seen whole (even when connected) the mother's bodily boundaries remain open. This point may seem academic but it can have practical implications. In Florida, a black woman who had confided in her physician that she had taken cocaine just prior to going into labour was charged and convicted of the offence of delivering drugs to a minor. The reasoning was that she had supplied cocaine to her newborn child via the umbilical cord in the thirty to ninety or so seconds between "birth" and the cutting of the cord. This case discloses (and exploits) a contradiction that normally goes unnoticed. The child and the mother are cast as separate people (with separate bodies) and yet the means by which the "crime" was executed was the direct bodily connection between them. Only the mother's body, however, is seen to be open, its contents having leaked to the newly recognised legal person.[28]

[25] G Williams, *Textbook of Criminal Law* 2nd edn. (London, Stevens, 1983) 289–90.

[26] *Ibid.*, at 290.

[27] See *infra* n. 39–48 and accompanying text for a discussion of *Re A (Children)*. The decision appears to challenge the condition that the (natural) legal person possess a separate/whole body. In that case, the court found that conjoined twins, whose bodies were fused at the lower abdomen, were distinct legal persons. Interestingly, much attention was devoted to the fact that the bodies of each twin were "almost complete" and that it was technologically feasible to separate them. Indeed, much was made of the fact that the separation surgery would restore each twin's "natural right" to corporeal individuality.

[28] The conviction was upheld on appeal to the Court of Appeals *Johnson* v. *State of Florida* (1991) 578 So. 2d 419 (5th District Court of Appeals); but ultimately overturned by the Supreme Court of Florida (1992) 602 So. 2d 1288. For an excellent analysis of the concept of embodied maternal subjectivity in

In addition to being "born", the legal person must be "alive". The precise dimensions of this requirement have been more challenging for law. The legal meaning of "live" has been hotly contested and appears to have evolved in response to developments in medical knowledge and technology. This is a process that is likely to continue. The older authorities adopt different standards. *R* v. *Enoch* adopted the standard of "an independent circulation"[29] which was thought to occur after the child's first breath.[30] Somewhat at odds with this, *R* v. *Brain* found that a child may be alive even if it had not yet started to breathe.[31] *R* v. *Handley* adopted the standard of unassisted breathing, that is breathing through the child's own lungs "without deriving any of its living or power through any connection with the mother".[32]

More recently, the precise meaning of "live" became the subject of intense academic speculation in the context of abortion law. Some commentators contended that a beating heart or a pulsating umbilical cord was sufficient (these being signs of life).[33] Others thought that the *Handley* standard of being able to breathe without the assistance of the mother (this being a minimum condition of viability) was required for a child to be live.[34] This disagreement raises some further questions about the minimum conditions of legal personhood. Must a child be capable of independent existence to be live? What does independent existence really mean?[35] Does it mean no longer reliant on the maternal body for survival? What about reliance on machines? If a child is completely dependent on a respirator and artificial feeding and hydration for survival, are they "live"?

The meaning of independent existence is open to varying interpretations. Again, the question that interests me is where law draws the line and what this tells us about the physical requirements of legal personhood. In *C* v. *S*[36] the court indicated that

the context of this case, see I Karpin "Reimagining Maternal Selfhood: Transgressing Body Boundaries and the Law" (1994) 2 *The Australian Feminist Law Journal* 36 [hereinafter Maternal Selfhood].

29 (1833) 5 C & P 539; quoted in *Rance* v. *Mid-Downs Health Authority* [1991] 1 QB 587 at 619.

30 The independent circulation standard has been rejected by Glanville Williams as anachronistic on the grounds that it was based on the "biological misconception" that independent circulation does not exist before birth. "Some authorities lay it down that a child must have had a circulation independent of the mother, but this proposition is based on a biological misconception, since the independent circulation exists before birth. For several months the fetus has had a circulation independent of the mother in the sense that the embryonic heart maintains a fetal blood stream, which does not directly communicate with the maternal blood. The two blood-streams are separated by a thin membrane, through which oxygen and nutrients pass to the fetus, and waste products back to the mother. When the child is born, if it does not breathe, its existence is dependent on the umbilical cord, through which the blood-stream is passing in both directions, and so long as the umbilical cord is pulsating in this way the child is dependent on its mother for life." Williams, *supra* n. 25, at 290 n. 7.

31 (1834) 6 C & P 349.

32 (1874) 13 Cox CC 79.

33 I J Keown, "The Scope of the Offence of Child Destruction" (1988) 104 *Law Quarterly Review* 141; Williams, *supra* n. 25, at 290; cf. G Williams, "The Foetus and the 'Right to Life'" (1994) 53 *Cambridge Law Journal* 71 at 72.

34 See for example, J Mason and R McCall Smith, *Law and Medical Ethics* (London, Butterworths, 1999) at 130–131.

35 In obvious ways the connections persist long after birth in the case of women who nurse their babies.

36 See *infra* n. 59–71 and accompanying text for a discussion of *C* v. *S* [1988] QB 135.

to be born alive a child must breathe. It was not made clear whether mechanically assisted breathing counts as breathing for the purposes of being alive, although Lord Donaldson's comment that "it is not a case of the foetus requiring a stimulus or assistance. It cannot and will never be able to breathe"[37] suggests that initial reliance on a respirator will not affect a child's status as "live". If this is correct, then it would seem that "live" is a quality that law determines with reference to the child's state of dependency on the body of its mother only. [38]

There is support for this interpretation in the recent Court of Appeal decision *Re A (Children) (Conjoined Twins: Surgical Separation)*[39] where the Court unanimously found that conjoined twins, one of whom had a seriously deficient circulatory system and was completely dependent on her sister for oxygenated blood, were both "born alive". But even beyond this, the decision provides a particularly striking illustration of the difficulties posed by the confusion of bodily boundaries. The case involved an application to the Court for a declaration that it would be lawful for doctors to surgically separate conjoined twins, known as Jodie and Mary. There were two principal legal obstacles in the path of the proposed surgery. The first was that the parents refused to consent to the separation, though it was at least possible within the existing legal framework for this objection to be overcome by recourse to the welfare principle. The real difficulty was the second objection, which was that since the proposed surgery would result in Mary's death, it would constitute murder. It was argued, on this basis, that the surgery could not be sanctioned even if it was in the twins' best interests.

Before the Court could begin to decide what was in the twins' best interests or whether the surgery was unlawful,[40] it was necessary to decide whether, in the eyes of the law, the twins were one person or two. The reasons for this are self-evident. If the conjoined entity is one person in law, the application of the welfare principle would not, presumably, involve consideration of the best interests of the entity

[37] *Ibid.*, at 151.

[38] In *Rance* v. *Mid-Downs Health Authority*, *supra* n. 24, a case concerning the meaning of "capable of being born alive" for the purposes of the Infant Life (Preservation) Act 1929, the court adopted the criterion of "breathing through its own lungs alone, without deriving any of its living or power by or through any connection with its mother". *Ibid* at 621. However it stopped short of embracing "viable" as a pre-requisite to being "live". Counsel contended that viable meant "capable of being born alive and surviving into old age in the normal way without intensive care or surgical intervention" but this was rejected. *Ibid* at 622. The suggestion that a child must survive for a reasonable period before it can be live was also rejected.

[39] [2001] 4 All ER 961 [hereinafter *Re A (Children)*]. For a more detailed discussion of this case see K Savell, "Human Rights in the Age of Technology: Can Law Rein in the Medical Juggernaut?" (2001) 23 *Sydney Law Review* 423.

[40] The Court of Appeal adopted a two-stage analysis, considering the application of the welfare principle before turning to the question of lawfulness. On the question of best interests, the majority (Ward and Brooke LLJ) found that it was not in the best interests of Mary to have the surgery performed. On the question of lawfulness, Brooke LJ found that the surgery was excused by the doctrine of necessity. Ward LJ also found that the act would be excused, although the juridical basis of that conclusion is not altogether clear (quasi self-defence and conflict of duty were considered in the judgment). Robert-Walker LJ found that the elements of homicide would not be satisfied and, therefore, had no cause to consider defences. Despite this divergence of approaches, the Court unanimously held that the surgery would be lawful.

"Jodie" and the entity "Mary". Nor would the question of homicide arise, since law only recognises the intentional killing of a being that is a person in the eyes of the law. If, on the other hand, the twins were two people in the eyes of the law, the application of the welfare principle would require the Court to reach a determination about the best interests of Jodie and Mary as distinct from one another. It would also raise the further question of how to plot a course of action if the measures required for the best interests of one were directly against the best interests of the other and, moreover, how to decide whether the relevant acts would constitute homicide. Accordingly, the legal implications of this characterisation problem could not have been more significant.

The characterisation problem was raised in various ways. Ward LJ asked "is this a fused body of two separate persons, each having a life in being?".[41] Brooke LJ asked "is Mary a reasonable creature?"[42] and Robert-Walker LJ, "are these conjoined twins two persons or one in the eyes of the law? If they are two persons, was Mary born alive?".[43]

Each judge concluded that Mary and Jodie were distinct individuals in the eyes of law, notwithstanding the fusion of their bodies. There was also unanimous agreement that they were both "born alive", notwithstanding Mary's condition.

Robert-Walker LJ gave two reasons for deciding that Jodie and Mary are two individuals. First, they each had a brain. Second, they each had "nearly complete bodies, despite the grave defects in Mary's brain and her heart and lungs".[44] He also accepted that, as a matter of law, Mary was born alive:

> "The medical notes from the hospital show that Mary was struggling to breathe, although sadly in vain, when she and Jodie were brought from the operating theatre into the recovery ward. Mr B (who would lead the operating team) was clear in his oral evidence to this court that Mary was not still-born, but that she could not be resuscitated and was not viable. Since her umbilical cord was cut she has been dependent for life on her sister. The fact that she is alive as a distinct personality but is not viable as a separate human being is the awful paradox at the centre of this case."[45]

Like Robert-Walker LJ, Ward LJ found that Mary was a live person in her own right. This conclusion was also based, at least in part, on the evidence of the doctors. He stated that the law should not:

> "fly in the face of clinical judgment that each child is alive and that each child is separate both for the purposes of the civil and the criminal law."[46]

Two points should be made here. First, the limits and scope of the born alive rule have historically involved deference to medical understandings of "life". Although *Re A (Children)* confronts a novel legal question—whether conjoined

[41] *Re A (Children) supra* n. 39, at 994.
[42] *Ibid.*, at 1025.
[43] *Ibid.*, at 1053.
[44] *Ibid.*
[45] *Ibid.*
[46] *Ibid.*, at 996.

twins are distinct legal persons—there is a predictable homage to the medical viewpoint. Medical evidence supported the characterisation of the twins as "two" through the identification of two sets of organs (importantly, two brains) and two "almost" complete bodies.

The second point concerns the legal meaning of "reasonable creature". It was by no means clear that law has always considered conjoined twins to be two legal persons. Brooke LJ comments that seventeenth-century thinking may have been to exclude conjoined twins from the definition of murder on grounds that they did not fall to be considered as reasonable creatures. However:

> "Advances in medical treatment of deformed neonates suggest that the criminal law's protection should be as wide as possible and a conclusion that a creature in being was not reasonable would be confined only to the most extreme cases of which this is not an example. Whatever might have been thought of as monstrous by Bracton, Coke, Blackstone, Locke and Hobbes, different considerations would clearly apply today."[47]

The Court seemed very keen to draw a line between seventeenth-century conceptions of monsters as superstitious, and the modern conception of (notional) distinction as enlightened.[48] It is worth considering the role of medicine in this demarcation. Although it is not possible to claim that the difference in attitude is wholly attributable to modern medical technology, it seems at least possible that this is an influential factor. Unlike seventeenth-century thinkers, the court did not have to rely merely on what it "saw" but what it "knew" about the internal ordering of organs and, more significantly, the feasibility of applying technology to disentangle the obvious corporeal connections between the twins to reshape them as "individuals".

The manner in which law has dealt with interpretative questions about the "live born" conditions of legal personhood reveals an emphasis on separation, distinction and independence. This accords with Naffine's account of the bounded nature of the legal person. It is also consistent with the thoughts of Glanville Williams, who observes that:

> "In common sense, in everyday speech, and in religious thought, man is a discrete entity. The individual man has a body, which we recognise as in some sense continuous and identical even though its chemical constituents are always being replaced. He has a mind and a personality, which are demonstrably different from those of his parents . . ."[49]

The vocabulary of "common sense" indicates just how powerful the idea that man is discrete and individuated actually is. At this stage, however, it is important to note that despite law's theoretical commitment to "individuality" as the pre-given form of natural legal persons, there is scope for investigating the counter-claim

[47] *Ibid.*, at 1026.

[48] Robert-Walker LJ echoes Brooke LJ's remarks, stating that "it hardly needs to be said that there is no longer any place in legal textbooks for expressions (such as "monster") which are redolent of superstitious horror. Such disparagingly emotive language should never be used to describe a human being, however disabled and dysmorphic". *Ibid.*, at 1054.

[49] G Williams, *The Sanctity of Life and the Criminal Law* (London, Faber, 1958) 17.

that law plays a role in producing bodies and their boundaries. This is most vividly illustrated in *Re A (Children)* where the court constructs two individuals (each with legal personality) out of the conjoined entity. However, as I have also attempted to demonstrate, the need to specify boundaries in the context of birth has a lengthy legal history, which is similarly dependent on medical authority. The following section will attempt to demonstrate that the maternal body is neither stable nor fixed but also produced by law in concert with medical discourses. The emphasis on the foetus, as distinct, bounded and separable, is part of that production.[50]

Law's Contemplation of the Foetus

One feature of the genesis of the legal person that has generally been considered important by feminists is that foetuses are excluded from the category of legal persons. This exclusion has been significant in thwarting attempts to ascribe legal rights to foetuses and, it is thought, in protecting pregnant women from state control for the sake of the foetus. But the foetus, though not a legal person, [51] is equally, not immaterial to law. Criminal law and medical law explicitly (as in the case of abortion law, child destruction and homicide) and implicitly (in the case of forced medical treatment) recognise the foetus. One fruitful line of investigation is to examine how law constitutes the foetus in these various contexts, how it constructs the woman whose body contains the foetus and whether any diminution of the legal status of the woman is attendant on these constructions.

William Blackstone claimed that "life was a gift of God" which comes "in contemplation of law as soon as an infant is able to stir in the mother's womb".[52] To satisfy this impulse to hold the foetus "within its contemplation" without granting it personhood, law makes certain choices about how far it will go to protect the interests of the foetus, and how it will explain those choices. Blackstone substantiated his claim on the bases that law punished acts which caused the death of the foetus, and that it deemed the foetus to be born alive for certain purposes, including having a legacy or for the surrender of a copyhold estate.[53] Since the eighteenth century, the sphere in which law contemplates the existence of the foetus has

[50] R Mykitiuk, *supra* n. 1; A Bunting, "Feminism, Foucault and Law as Power/Knowledge" (1992) 30 *Alberta Law Review* 829; Karpin *Reconstructed Woman*, *supra* n. 3.

[51] In *Paton* v. *Trustees of British Pregnancy Advisory Services* [1978] 2 All ER 987 the Court stated: "The foetus cannot, in English law, in my view, have any right of its own at least until it is born and has an existence separate from the mother. That permeates the whole of the civil law of this country . . . and is, indeed, the basis of the decisions in those countries where law is founded on the common law, that is to say, America, Canada, Australia and, I have no doubt, in others." This statement was affirmed in *C* v. *S*, *supra* n. 36; *Re F (in utero)* [1988] 2 WLR 1297 (CA); *Re MB infra* n. 150 *and St Georges Healthcare NHS Trust* v. *S*, *infra* n. 150.

[52] W Blackstone, *Commentaries on the Laws of England*—A Facsimile of the First Edition of 1765–1769, Volume I (Chicago, Chicago University Press, 1979) 125–6.

[53] *Ibid.*, at 126.

expanded to the fields of child welfare,[54] tort law,[55] and medical law.[56] But it is the criminal law, in particular, that has been exercised by questions regarding the protection of foetuses.

The common law has prohibited the unlawful termination of pregnancy after quickening at least since Coke. As we have already seen, Blackstone also regarded the intentional killing of "an infant" after quickening as unlawful. The Lord Ellenborough's Act 1803 put this prohibition on a statutory footing, and also introduced the crime of abortion before quickening (although this was not punished as severely as abortion after quickening). This Act was superseded by Lord Lansdowne's Act 1828 and, thereafter, by the Offences Against the Person Act 1837. The Offences Against the Person Act 1861 replaced these earlier regimes with the current offence of "administering drugs or using instruments to procure abortion" which specifically applies to a woman trying to procure her own abortion as well as to others.[57]

The early distinction of a quickened foetus no longer exists, but the modern law nonetheless recognises distinctions based on gestational age. The Abortion Act 1967 requires two registered medical practitioners to form the opinion in good faith that the pregnancy should be terminated on one of the four grounds set out in section 1(1) in order that a termination be lawful. The first of these grounds takes account of the gestational age of the foetus and the risk of physical or mental injury to the pregnant woman or her existing children. This will be satisfied if the foetus is less than twenty-four weeks gestation and the continuance of the pregnancy would involve a risk to the woman or her existing children greater than if the pregnancy were terminated. The second and third grounds only consider the life and/or health of the pregnant woman, and the gestational age of the foetus is thus not strictly relevant. The second ground is satisfied if the

[54] Child welfare legislation, for example, has been interpreted so that a child born with a drug dependency may be taken into care immediately after birth. See *In re D (A Minor)* [1987] 1 AC 317.

[55] Tort law adopts a born alive rule whereby the child can sue to recover for damage suffered after birth as a result of negligently inflicted pre-natal injury. See *Burton* v. *Islington Health Authority; De Martell and Sutton Health Authority* [1992] 2 FLR 184. Under the Congenital Disabilities (Civil Liability) Act 1976, a mother is protected from civil liability for prenatal injury caused by her negligence, save for negligently driving a motor vehicle.

[56] There is a rich tapestry of statute and common law that contemplates the existence of the foetus and the embryo. Some of these laws have already been adverted to. The Abortion Act 1967 regulates the medical termination of pregnancies; the Offences Against the Person Act 1861 and the Infant Life (Preservation) Act 1929 contain offences regarding abortion and the intentional destruction of children capable of being born alive and may still apply if provisions of the Abortion Act are not satisfied; the Human Fertilisation and Embryology Act 1990 governs the creation of and use to which embryos created outside the body may be lawfully put. On the question of maternal treatment refusals see *infra* Section IV at 51.

[57] Section 58 provides that "Every woman, being with child, who, with intent to procure her own miscarriage, shall unlawfully administer to herself any poison or other noxious thing, or shall unlawfully use any instrument or other means whatsoever with the like intent, and whosoever, with intent to procure the miscarriage of any woman, whether or not she be with child, shall unlawfully administer to her or cause to be taken by her any poison or other noxious thing, or shall unlawfully use any instrument or other means whatsoever with the like intent, shall be guilty of felony, and being convicted thereof shall be liable to be kept in penal servitude for life." Section 59 creates a lesser offence for the supply or procuring of potions, instruments or things to be used in contravention of section 58.

termination is necessary to prevent grave permanent injury to the physical or mental health of the woman; and the third ground is satisfied if the continuance of the pregnancy would involve a risk to the life of the pregnant woman greater than if it was terminated. The final ground takes specific account of the foetus only. This ground is satisfied when there is a substantial risk that if the child were to be born it would suffer from such physical or mental abnormalities as to be seriously handicapped.

Although a relatively liberal abortion regime exists in England, it is clear that women are not entitled to terminate their pregnancies pursuant to any legal right to bodily integrity or self-determination. This provides one of many indicators of the disjunction between the rights of legal persons and pregnant women. As Naffine points out, bodily integrity is everything for the legal person and yet law does not recognise a right in women to determine for themselves, without legal oversight or interference, the question of their bodily integrity.[58] Instead, law requires justification for the termination of a pregnancy and the regime installed to police these justifications recognises a hierarchy of reasons for this purpose. The ill-health of the foetus and the serious risk to the life or health of the woman are considered to be the most important reasons for a termination, these being necessary to terminate a pregnancy greater than twenty-four weeks' gestation. In contrast to the normative legal person whose boundaries are discrete and who receives law's assistance in protecting those boundaries from transgression, the pregnant woman's physical boundaries are policed against her.

Imagining an Independent Existence

Regulating the conditions under which an abortion will be lawful merely constitutes one aspect of the law's contemplation of the foetus. Another aspect can be found in the Infant Life (Preservation) Act 1929, which confers protection on the "child capable of being born alive".[59] Section 1 of this Act creates the felonious offence of "child destruction". This occurs when a person, with the intention to destroy a child capable of being born alive, commits "any wilful act" which causes "a child to die before it has an existence separate from its mother" (unless done in good faith to save the mother's life). The Act was created to provide protection for foetuses in the process of being born on the grounds that, during the transition from the womb to independent existence, the foetus was not covered by the Offences Against the Person Act 1861 or the law of homicide. By a legal presumption enacted in section 1(2), a foetus of twenty-eight weeks' gestation is presumed to be a "child capable of being born alive" with the result that the protection conferred

[58] N Naffine, "Can Women be Legal Persons?" *infra* chap. 3, at 69.

[59] The offence of child destruction is less significant now as a result of amendments to the Abortion Act 1967 in 1990. However, the Infant Life (Preservation) Act 1929 will still apply to the intentional destruction of foetus' deemed capable of being born alive in circumstances where the requirements of the Abortion Act are not satisfied.

by the Act actually extends beyond the birthing process. The effect is an additional layer of legal protection for foetuses in utero which are capable of being born alive.

In *C* v. *S*[60] a putative father tried to injunct a pregnant woman with whom he had had a sexual liaison, from terminating her pregnancy. In support of his application for an injunction, he claimed that her foetus, which was between eighteen and twenty-one weeks' gestation, was a "child capable of being born alive". Although the court had no jurisdiction to grant on injunction at the suit of the foetus,[61] the applicant argued that the court had jurisdiction to issue an injunction to restrain doctors from committing the crime of child destruction.

The court heard detailed medical evidence about the state of development of a foetus of eighteen to twenty-one weeks' gestation and its capabilities for existing outside the womb, accepting that the meaning of "live" was at least partly a matter for medical experts. There was, however, disagreement between the experts as to the meaning of capable of being born alive.[62] The expert for the applicant contended that an eighteen-week-old foetus delivered by hysterotomy would be "live" born.[63] This claim was made on the basis that after "complete expulsion or extraction"[64] of the foetus, an eighteen-week-old foetus could be expected to show signs of life. Such signs of life would include "beating of the heart, pulsation of the umbilical cord or definite movement of voluntary muscle."[65] Although the expert accepted that an eighteen-week-old foetus could not survive independently due to an insufficiently developed respiratory system it could, nonetheless, be "live born".

The respondent contested the adoption of this definition arguing, by contrast, that "capable of being born alive" was directed to the question of foetal viability.[66] Thus, the term should be understood as the time after which, if the foetus was to be separated from its mother, it could maintain independent human existence. The respondent's expert testified that a foetus of less than twenty-four weeks' gestation is not capable of surviving "once the placental separation occurs"[67] because its lungs are "inadequately developed".[68] Furthermore, the other major organs are at an "equally primitive stage"[69] and incapable of sustaining life. The application was

[60] [1988] QB 135.

[61] Heilbron J was firm on this point. She states "in my judgment, there is no basis for the claim that the foetus can be a party, whether or not there is any foundation for the contention with regard to the alleged threatened crime." Given that the foetus has no standing, it followed that the putative father could not initiate proceedings as next friend of the foetus. In this respect, Heilbron J affirmed the decision in *Paton* v. *BPAS* that the father of a foetus has no locus standi. *Ibid.*, at 141.

[62] Per Heilbron J, "The affidavits are very important. They indicate very clearly the wide difference in thinking and interpretation between medical men, all of high reputation and great experience, in regard to the language used in the Act of 1929." *Ibid.*

[63] *Ibid.*, at 142.

[64] *Ibid.*

[65] He also relied on the fact that a foetus born at eighteen weeks would be registered as a live birth for the purposes of the Registration of Births and Deaths Act 1926. *Ibid.*

[66] *Ibid.*, at 142–143.

[67] *Ibid.*, at 144.

[68] *Ibid.*

[69] *Ibid.*

ultimately dismissed on the ground that the foetus was not a child capable of being born alive. Heilbron J did not specify that "viability" was to be the relevant legal standard, although she did indicate that she was "not greatly attracted to the very limited definition"[69a] advanced by counsel for the applicant. The Court of Appeal dealt with the issue squarely, holding that a foetus not capable *ever* of breathing (i.e. not even with the assistance of medical technology) is not a child capable of being born alive within the meaning of the Infant Life (Preservation) Act 1929.[70]

The question of when a foetus, though not born, is a "child capable of being born alive" invites law to imagine the foetus as a separate being and, having done that, to predict whether it would be alive if it was removed from its mother's womb. It is important to note that this legal calculation invokes two boundaries. First, it creates a boundary between foetuses capable of being born alive and those that are not, since its application is limited to the former.[71] Secondly, it creates a boundary between the "mother" and the "child capable of being born alive" by speculating about the prognosis of the foetus outside the womb. The overall effect is a re-orientation of law's conception of pregnancy. Whereas the offence of procuring abortion concerns the "miscarriage of any woman", the offence of child destruction concerns causing "a child to die before it has an existence separate from its mother". This shift involves an accenting of the foetus, which is positioned in an antagonistic relation to the mother. The foetus, which in law constitutes a "child capable of being born alive", is thus rhetorically cast as "other" to the woman who bears it.[72]

The Genetic Distinctiveness of the Foetus

The speculations of judges as to when a foetus could be born alive have the effect of deconstructing the maternal body to consider the foetus in isolation. This process is taken a step further when law examines the question "what is a foetus?" a question that has been asked in the context of homicide. The born-alive rule is significant to the law of homicide, which has long held the position that violence toward a foetus, which results in harm suffered after the child has been born alive,

[69a] *Ibid* at 146.

[70] [1988] 1 QB 149. See also *Rance* v. *Mid-Downs Health Authority*, *supra* n. 29, which decided that a twenty-seven week gestation foetus was a child capable of being born alive. The court reached this conclusion on the grounds that a foetus of twenty-seven weeks gestation had reached that stage of development "in the womb" that, if born, would possess the attributes of "breathing with its own lungs alone, without deriving any of its living or power of living by or through any connections with its mother", *Ibid* at 621.

[71] Subject, of course, to the operation of the Abortion Act 1967. See *supra* n. 59.

[72] Karpin explores this idea in some detail in *Maternal Selfhood* and is discussed below. See *infra* n. 181–94 and accompanying text.

can give rise to criminal responsibility. That position is unaffected by the fact that the harm would not have been criminal if it had only been suffered *in utero.*[73]

Law's attempts to grapple with the *mens rea* required to support a conviction for the homicide of a child that was not a legal person when the act of violence was committed, has recently inspired some searching legal analyses of the relationship between the foetus and legal personality. In *Attorney-General's Reference (No. 3 of 1994)* two questions of law were referred to the Court of Appeal following the acquittal of a man who stabbed his pregnant girlfriend (M), causing her to give birth to a premature child (S) who died shortly after birth. It was accepted that the wounding of M caused her to go into premature labour, and that S died in consequence of being born premature.

The questions referred[75] induced an examination of law's conception of the foetus, which was also undertaken by the House of Lords on appeal. Distinct conceptions of the relation between the foetus and the legal person grounded three different answers to the questions put to each court. The trial judge thought that since the foetus had no existence in law when the violence was committed, no person who could be a victim of murder or manslaughter existed, and urged the jury to acquit.[76] The Court of Appeal thought that the foetus was a part of its mother, so that an intention to do violence to the mother could constitute an intention to do violence to the subsequently born child pursuant to the doctrine of transferred malice.[77] The House of Lords thought that the foetus was an organism *sui generis*

[73] *Attorney-General's Reference (No. 3 of 1994) supra* n. 23, at 428. This rule was adopted in early Victorian times by the Fourth Report of the Commissioners on Criminal Law (1839) and affirmed in later Parliamentary Reports. *Ibid* per Lord Mustill.

[75] The first question referred was whether the crimes of murder or manslaughter could be committed in circumstances where unlawful injury was deliberately inflicted on a pregnant woman, or on a "child in utero", where the child was born alive but subsequently died. The second question was could the fact that the child's death was caused solely as a consequence of injury to the mother negative liability for murder or manslaughter. *Ibid* at 423.

[76] The trial judge directed the jury to acquit B of the charge of S's murder on the grounds that the *actus reus* and the *mens rea* needed to support the charge were not made out. There was no relevant *actus reus* because the foetus was not a live person and because the cause of death was the wounding of M and not S. The *mens rea* for murder was also absent because when B stabbed M he formed no intent to kill (or do serious harm) to any "live" person other than M, or to do any harm at all to the foetus. Significantly, the trial judge rejected the Crown's contention that the doctrine of transferred malice could operate to remedy the absence of intent. The doctrine could only apply in circumstances where the intent to harm one person could be added to the actual (but unintended) harm to another person. Here since S was not a person at the time of the act, the intent to harm B could not be transferred. As to the alternative verdict of manslaughter, the trial judge also directed the jury to acquit. Although the judge considered that the unlawful and dangerous act of stabbing M might be sufficient to ground a conviction for the manslaughter of S who died as a result, in the end this was rejected on the ground that at the time the unlawful act was committed, "no victim capable of dying as a direct and immediate result" existed. *Ibid* at 425.

[77] The Court of Appeal avoided the consequences of law's erasure of the foetus by revisiting the doctrine of transferred malice. To ground its analysis, the Court gave a different account of the position of the foetus in law: "In the eyes of the law the foetus is taken to be a part of the mother until it has an existence independent of the mother. Thus an intention to cause serious bodily injury to the foetus is an intention to cause serious bodily injury to a part of the mother just as an intention to harm her leg or arm would be so viewed."(*Attorney-General's Reference (No. 3 of 1994)* [1996] QB 581 at 593 (CA)). According to the Court of Appeal, law sees the foetus as a part of the mother. The Court reasoned that

distinct from its mother, rendering the application of the doctrine of transferred malice inapplicable to the circumstances, but not preventing a conviction for unlawful act homicide. The implications for the law of homicide aside, it is clear that law's conception of the foetus can be highly variable.

The House of Lords rejected a conception of the foetus as a part of the mother on the grounds that it was "wholly unfounded in fact".[78] In reasoning that the foetus was materially distinct from its mother, three factors were important. The first was a basic understanding of genetics. Lord Mustill and Lord Hope each went to some length to explain that the genotype of a foetus was constituted by the shared contribution of genetic material from its father and its mother. From this Lord Hope concluded that the embryo's inherent individuality is retained throughout the foetus' development in the womb until "it achieves an independent existence on being born".[79]

The second factor relied upon was the "science of human fertilisation"[79a] which enables the creation of embryos "outside the mother"[79b] for later placement "inside her as a live embryo".[80] For Lord Hope, this technological process "serves to remind us that an embryo is in reality a separate organism from the mother from the moment of conception",[81] thereby locating the "reality" of embryological and foetal separateness in the scientific manipulation of fertilisation.

But having enlisted genetics and IVF to emphasise the separateness of the foetus, the Court was still left with the fact that no embryo could reach the stage of independent survival without developing inside the body of a woman. The third factor relied upon by the Court, therefore, concerned the appropriate way to conceptualise the maternal body. Lord Mustill saw it in the following way:

> "There was, of course, an intimate bond between the foetus and the mother, created by the total dependence of the foetus on the protective physical environment furnished by the mother, and on the supply of the mother through the physical linkage between them of the nutrients, oxygen and other substances essential to foetal life and development. The emotional bond between the mother and her unborn child was also of a very special kind. But the relationship was one of bond not identity. The mother and the foetus were two distinct organisms living symbiotically, not a single organism with two aspects."[82]

The maternal-foetal relationship is constituted in law by physical linkage, emotional bond, and the provision of substances that are essential to life, but these features, even in combination, are subordinated to genetic identity. According to the Law Lords, it is identity that makes the foetus distinct from its mother both in fact

an intention to cause serious bodily injury to the mother (an element which was proved and not in dispute) was equivalent to the same intent directed towards the foetus, thus satisfying the requisite intent for a conviction for S's murder.

[78] *Supra* n. 23, at 428.
[79] *Ibid.*, at 440.
[79a] *Ibid.*
[79b] *Ibid.*
[80] *Ibid.*
[81] *Ibid.*
[82] *Ibid.*, at 428.

and in law. Another important point to note about Lord Mustill's characterisation of the maternal-foetal relationship is his reference to "two distinct organisms living symbiotically", connoting a relationship of mutual benefit and perhaps even equal partnership.[83]

This endorsement of a "distinct foetal identity" was not sufficiently powerful to displace the long-standing doctrine that the foetus has no legal personality. But Lord Mustill's conception of foetal distinctiveness did render implausible any contention that the foetus was an adjunct of the mother which shared legal personality with her, contrary to the view taken by the Court of Appeal. Lord Mustill thought that the foetus had no relevant type of legal personality but was, rather, "an organism *sui generis* lacking at this stage the entire range of characteristics both of the mother to which it is physically linked and of the complete human being which it will later become".[84] He goes to say that "to apply to such an organism the principles of a law evolved in relation to autonomous beings is bound to mislead".[85]

Consistent with law's conception of the foetus as distinct but physically linked to its mother, the Court found that the offence of unlawful act homicide, rather than murder, had been made out. This was principally because it is not necessary, in the case of unlawful act homicide, to show that the act causing death was committed with the specific intent of causing the victim harm. It is enough that the accused intended to do the thing that caused the death, that the victim died as a result of the act and that all sober and reasonable people would recognise the risk that some harm would result. Importantly, it is not necessary that the accused knew that the act was unlawful or dangerous. This analysis might still have been open to the objection (which was sustained at trial) that since the foetus was not a living person at the time of the unlawful act, the offence of manslaughter could not be committed. This objection was overcome, however, on public policy grounds. The foetus, the Court reasoned, was different from other "non-living" persons (i.e. dead persons), because for it "life lies in the future, not the past".[85a] Thus:

> "It is not sensible to say that it cannot ever be harmed, or that nothing can be done to it which can not ever be dangerous. Once it is born it is exposed, like all other living persons, to the risk of injury. It may also carry with it the effects of things done to it before birth which, after birth, may prove to be harmful. It would not seem to be unreasonable, therefore, on public policy grounds, to regard the child in this case, when she became a living person, as within the scope of the *mens rea* which B had when he stabbed her mother before she was born."[86]

This is a strong expression of law's contemplation of the foetus. Here law acknowledges that the mens rea for the manslaughter of a neonate may be

[83] There are two entries in the Oxford Dictionary under "symbiosis". The first is "interaction between two different organisms living in close physical association usually to the advantage of both"; and the second is "mutually advantageous association between two persons". *The Oxford Dictionary of Current English* (New York, Oxford University Press, 1992) 923.

[84] *Supra* n. 23, at 429.

[85] *Ibid.*

[85a] *Ibid.*, at 443 per Lord Hope.

[86] *Ibid.*

constituted by the intention to stab a pregnant woman. This is not because the intent to harm the woman was transferred to the foetus but because the unlawful act was likely to cause harm to *somebody* which is precisely what happened when S was born prematurely.

The *mens rea* for manslaughter having been established, the question of an *actus reus* was more straightforward. Unlike the trial judge, their Lordships took the view that the *actus reus* was the stabbing of the mother which was completed when the child died. The causative link between the stabbing and the child's death was not controverted, although Lord Mustill's reasoning on this may have broader implications. He states that:

> "the unlawful and dangerous act of B *changed the maternal environment of the foetus* in such a way that when born the child died when she would otherwise have lived" (my emphasis).[87]

It is important to pause and reflect on this analysis. It appears as though law's efforts to deliver the foetus from the consequences of its rhetorical indifference produces an erasure of a different sort. Their Lordships' emphasis on the distinctiveness of the foetus, including its genetic diversity and its potential for a future, served to temper its doctrinal invisibility to law. But as Lord Mustill's reasoning on the causative aspect of this case shows, it also has the effect of reifying the pregnant woman as a "maternal environment for the foetus". Although the consequences of this objectification may seem minimally disconcerting in a situation where "the environment" is damaged by the acts of a third party, there lies a problem that this conception may be extended to the mother's inability to maintain the "maternal environment" to a standard that satisfies law. In this scenario, Lord Mustill's view that the principles of law evolved in relation to autonomous beings could not be applied to the foetus, may resurface in a different light. With this increasing focus on the foetus as a distinct organism, what account does law give of the personhood of the pregnant woman? If, in the eyes of the law, she is a maternal environment, deconstructed and unwhole, it is important to ask how this might affect the legal personality of pregnant women.

III DECONSTRUCTING A LEGAL PERSON

Ngaire Naffine claims that law's conception of a person with discrete and unbroken bodily boundaries misrepresents the bodily realities of all human beings. But it particularly misrepresents the bodily realities of women[88] whose deviance from this norm is most irrepressible when they are pregnant. The criminal law's spatial and temporal zoning of the maternal body is consistent with the theory that the more advanced a woman's pregnancy, the less she will approximate the norm of bodily unity and the more alien she will appear when measured against the concept of the

[87] *Supra* n. 23, at 437, per Lord Mustill.
[88] See *supra* n. 5–17 and accompanying text.

legal person. It is also consistent with the obverse proposition that the more advanced a woman's pregnancy, the more she will approximate two individuals with distinct interests deserving of law's protection.

According to doctrine, the "mother of the legal person" is, unlike the foetus she carries, a legal person with the full complement of rights and obligations ascribed to that status. Among these are common law rights to bodily integrity and self-determination in medical decision-making[89] and pursuant to the Human Rights Act 1998, rights to life,[90] liberty and security,[91] respect for private and family life,[92] and freedom from torture[93] among others. But, as we have seen already, this impressive array of rights does not secure women the right to terminate their pregnancies, which raises the question of whether the status of pregnant women is diminished in law and, if so, whether this occurs as a consequence of her bodily deviation from the normative legal person. This question is significant in the context of pregnant woman who do not comply with medical or "common sense" standards of maternal conduct, especially when this non-compliance threatens the health or life of the foetus. This is the case when women refuse to consent to a caesarean section or when they use drugs when pregnant. In these cases, the mother is often said to be "acting against" the foetus by causing injury to it even though the act or omission complained of concerns her own body.[94]

Extra-legal Practices and Legal Personality

As a preliminary point it is worth noting that that law does not act alone in delimiting the boundaries of the legal person and in excluding certain people from its scope. In her work on theorising law's relationship to women's bodies, Carol Smart takes up the question of law's permeability to extra-legal knowledge and practices. She argues that a merger has occurred between law and the modern discourses of regulation, such as medicine and psychiatry, in the context of law's relationship to the female body. She argues further that these collaborations affect how law constitutes the field of persons and things over which it has power (the jurisdiction question) as well as what methods law can apply within this field.[95]

The criminal law's engagement with the foetus in the context of abortion, child destruction and homicide provides some evidence to support Smart's theory. Although law makes no claim to have jurisdiction over the foetus as a legal person, it does recognise it as "an object for scrutiny"[95a] and the myriad ways it achieves this has undoubtedly been influenced by prevailing theories about women's

[89] See *Sidaway* v. *Bethlem Royal Hospital Governors and Others* [1985] AC 871; *Re T (Adult: Refusal of Medical Treatment)* [1992] 2 WLR 782 (CA); *Airedale NHS Trust* v. *Bland* [1993] AC 789.

[90] Schedule 1, Art. 2.

[91] Schedule 1, Art. 5.

[92] Schedule 1, Art. 8.

[93] Schedule 1, Art. 3.

[94] Karpin, *Maternal Selfhood, supra* n. 28, at 47.

[95] C Smart, *Feminism and the Power of Law* (London, Routledge, 1989) 96.

[95a] *Ibid.*

bodies. We have already seen that law has adopted the foetal categories of "pre-quickened", "quickened", "capable of being born alive" and "more than twenty-four weeks gestation" at different times. The modern categories, which replaced the earlier ecclesiastical ones,[96] reflect medical opinion about the separability of a foetus of a particular gestational age from the body of its mother, so that intentionally destroying foetuses in these categories requires greater justification.

It is also important to realise that collaborations between law and medicine create new ways for law to operate. Smart finds evidence of the merger between law as a traditional discourse of control, and medicine as a modern discourse of regulation, where law appropriates medical categorisations and welfare-oriented practices.[96a] But, as Smart also points out, law retains its traditional methods of control via the distribution of rights and penalties as between the individual and the state.[97] Returning again to the context of abortion, we can see that law has "recourse to both methods".[98] The Offences Against the Person Act 1861 and the Infant Life (Preservation) Act 1929 each proscribe the killing of foetuses and penalise those who do so with criminal sanctions, thus typifying law in the traditional mode of control. Although these laws continue in force they are now subject to the operation of the Abortion Act 1967. This Act makes the "medical termination of pregnancy" lawful as long as certain requirements are met. These requirements concern questions of "health", "well-being" and foetal gestational age as determined by doctors and, thus, form part of a regime of surveillance and regulation.[99]

Visualisation Practices and Foetal Rights

There is a body of literature that connects the emergence of the foetus as a separate patient to advancements in scientific technology and, beyond this, to personhood. One example of this type of reasoning is contained in the following passage:

> "For centuries the human fetus has been a 'medical recluse'. Until recently, the advancement of medical knowledge about the fetus was restrained by a limited ability to observe and study fetal growth and development *in utero*. Beginning in the 1960s, however, the fetus slowly emerged from its gestational hiding place with the advent of new technological developments that provided practical methods to examine and analyze fetal characteristics . . . [T]he development of ultrasound (sonography) for obstetrical use . . . provided the major technological means to transform the fetus into a full fledged patient by facilitating direct *in utero* visualization of fetal anatomy."[100]

[96] Bernard Dickens provides an excellent analysis of the ancient ecclesiastical authorities and the development of English law with respect to abortion. B Dickens, *Abortion and the Law* (London, MacGibbon & Kee, 1966).

[96a] Smart, *supra* n. 95 at 96.

[97] *Ibid.*

[98] *Ibid.*

[99] Smart provides a compelling analysis of the incorporation of health and welfare-oriented practices into law. *Ibid.*, at 96–104.

[100] Note, "The Fetal Patient and the Unwilling Mother: A Standard for Judicial Intervention" (1983) 14 *Pacific Law Journal* 1065 at 1065–6.

In one sense, this is incontrovertible. Formerly, the foetus was beyond the diagnostic reach of physicians and, accordingly, physicians' saw their role as maintaining and promoting maternal health, which would, presumably, also enhance the health of the foetus.[101] Advances in technology have, however, permitted researchers and doctors to see, access and treat the foetus in ways previously not possible.[102] The notion that the foetus, a former recluse, has emerged from its "gestational hiding place" to a "full-fledged patient" invites us to see the foetus as a distinct being with a new status. Nelson and Milliken suggest that the new technology has at least affected, and may even have created, "physicians' perception of the fetus as a separate patient".[103]

This conceptualisation of the "foetus as patient" carries with it a correlative potential to transform the way the body of the pregnant woman is perceived. The idea that the foetus has emerged from its "gestational hiding place" also conveys a particular understanding of the function and significance of the body of the pregnant woman. In this account, the pregnant woman is a now-transparent "gestational place" for the foetus, a perception that carries with it the danger of diminishing the importance of the connections between the foetus and the pregnant woman. The reasoning adopted by Lord Mustill in *Attorney-General's Reference (No. 3 of 1994)* suggests a cross-fertilisation between law and medicine on this point.

The proposition that an excessive focus on the "foetal patient" has contributed to a correlative diminution of the corporeal and social significance of the pregnant woman has been the subject of feminist critique.[104] Rosalyn Petchetsky argues that the technologies which penetrate the pregnant body to produce images of the foetus, have had the effect of fetishising the foetus and of "effacing the pregnant woman".[105] This effect has been facilitated in part by the easy assimilation of these images into humanist discourses. The image of the foetus, "free-floating" in the inner space of the womb, she claims, "merely extends to gestation the Hobbesian view of born human beings as disconnected solitary individuals".[106] To place this within Naffine's analysis, the foetus in this account is bounded and complete (despite its connections with the body of the mother) while the pregnant woman

[101] L J Nelson and J D Milliken, "Compelled Medical Treatment of Pregnant Women: Life, Liberty and Law in Conflict" (1988) 259 *Journal of the American Medical Association* 1060 at 1060.

[102] According to Nelson and Milliken: "Advances in knowledge of fetal physiology and the development of new technology have enabled physicians to see the fetal in detail with ultrasound, to assess its condition with fetal heart monitoring, and to operate on it in utero." *Ibid.*

[103] *Ibid.*

[104] See for example, Karpin, *Reconstructed Woman supra* n. 3.; B Bennett, "Pregnant Women and the Duty to Rescue" (1991) 9 *Law in Context* 70; K De Gama "A Brave New World? Rights Discourse and the Politics of Reproductive Autonomy" (1993) 20 *Journal of Law and Society* 114.

[105] R Petchesky, "Foetal Images: The Power of Visual Culture in the Politics of Reproduction" in M Stanford (ed.), *Reproductive Technologies—Gender, Motherhood and Medicine* (Cambridge, Polity Press, 1987) 57 at 59.

[106] *Ibid.*

is unbounded. Thus, while the conceptual boundary marked by the placenta is seen to enclose the foetus, it is paradoxically seen to expose the pregnant woman.

The significance attached to this boundary, and the different meanings that are ascribed to it vis-à-vis foetus and woman, becomes extremely fraught when the purpose is to construct the pregnant woman as "two patients". It is a battery to administer medical treatment to non-consenting competent adults, even if they will die without it.[107] But where a pregnant woman is not amenable to treatment regarded by physicians as necessary for the foetus, and a foetus is seen as notionally distinct, conflict looms large. [108] Christian Witting translates this to a legal context when he claims that the emerging powers of obstetrics to see and treat the foetus "have called for a judicial re-examination of the status of the unborn".[109] He reasons that the courts are faced with a dilemma,

> "because the foetus is potentially a patient in its own right. If a foetus can be seen as a patient, the question arises as to what legal and ethical duties are owed to it."[110]

This recourse to rights language in the face of disagreements about medical treatment during pregnancy reinforces the construction of separateness highlighted by Petchetsky.[111] It is also indicative of the relationship between selfhood and bounded physical bodies where claims to enact foetal rights rely on the visualisation of anatomical foetal bodies for support.

The way that law responds to maternal treatment refusals suggests that whatever law says about the bodily integrity and self-determination of legal persons, these principles do not apply consistently to pregnant women. There are two strategies that have been used to assist law to account for its denial of full legal rights to pregnant women in circumstances where her conduct might be harmful to the foetus. Both strategies construct boundaries for the purpose of differentiating the pregnant woman in question from the legal person who has rights to bodily integrity and self-determination; and also of differentiating the foetus from the mother. The first strategy re-negotiates the self/other boundary directly by jettisoning the "born alive" rule. This has been attempted in the context of women whose lifestyles

[107] At common law, it is a tortious and criminal battery to touch the body of another without their consent. This includes medical treatment. This principle has been clearly articulated by the House of Lords: ". . . it is unlawful, so as to constitute both a tort and the crime of battery, to administer medical treatment to an adult, who is conscious and of sound mind, without his consent". *Airedale NHS Trust* v. *Bland, supra* n. 89, at 857 per Lord Keith.

[108] See generally, Nelson and Milliken, *supra* n. 101, at 1067–9; J Lenow, "The Fetus as a Patient: Emerging Rights as a Person?" (1983) 9 *American Journal of Law and Medicine* 1 at 2; W A Bowes and B Selgestad, "Fetal Versus Maternal Rights: Medical & Legal Perspectives" (1981) 58 *Obstetrics and Gynecology* 209 at 209; F A Chervenak and L B McCullough, "Perinatal Ethics: A Practical Method of Analysis of Obligations to Mother and Fetus" (1985) 66 *Obstetrics and Gynecology* 442.

[109] C Witting, "Forced Operations on Pregnant Women: *In re S* Examined" (1994) 2 *Tort Law Journal* 193 at 203.

[110] *Ibid.*

[111] "If the fetus is a separate entity, questions will arise as to whether it possesses rights . . . To acknowledge the rights of the fetus is to emphasise its separate existence: there must be a distinct entity by or on behalf of which the rights may be asserted." J Seymour, *Fetal Welfare and the Law* (Canberra, Australian Medical Association, 1993) 50.

(especially drug-taking) are thought to pose a threat to the health of the foetus. Conceptually, it is a dramatic move because it represents an explicit break with the unitary conception of selfhood by ascribing legal personality to the foetus and, possibly for this reason, has not commanded wide judicial acceptance. It is however a strategy open to legislatures, and in both England and Canada courts have been more than willing to draw attention to this.[112] The second strategy, so far the preferred option in England, is to manipulate the competent/incompetent boundary by treating pregnant women as lacking legal capacity. This has been used in the context of women who refuse to consent to caesarean sections. It offers the advantage of subverting the personhood of the woman to benefit the foetus, while maintaining the committment to unitary personhood.

Both of these strategies owe a debt to medical power,[113] albeit in distinct ways. The proposal to jettison the born-alive rule relies heavily on medical technologies which, the proposal argues, dispense with the need for a child to be born alive for law to recognise it as a living person. The denial of legal capacity to pregnant women who refuse to consent to recommended caesarean sections also relies on these technologies but it does so by normalising medical practices, thereby raising questions about the competence of women who reject them.

IV RE-NEGOTIATING THE SELF/OTHER BOUNDARY

As we have already seen, the born-alive rule is critical to the concept of legal personhood. Unless and until a child is born alive it is not a person in law with legal rights or legal standing. One interpretation of this rule is that a differentiated and bounded body (in relation to the maternal body) and a capacity for autonomous existence are necessary attributes of the (natural) legal person. In *Winnipeg Child & Family Services* v. *G*, however, a strong dissenting opinion of the Supreme Court of Canada [114] challenged this interpretation. [115]

[112] See *Winnipeg Child & Family Services* v. *G* (1997) 152 D.L.R. (4th) 193 (SCC) and *Re F (in Utero)*, *supra* n. 51.

[113] On the concept of medical power and its relationship to law, see S Sheldon, *Beyond Control: Medical Power and Abortion Law* (London, Pluto Press, 1997).

[114] *Winnipeg Child & Family Services* v. *G*, *supra* n. 112 per Major J, (Sopinka J concurring); see also the first instance decision of the Manitoba Queen's Bench (1996) 138 DLR (4th) 238.

[115] It could be argued that some statutory regimes in Canada already achieve this, a matter that calls into question the wisdom of relying simply on the non-personhood of the foetus at common law to protect pregnant women from intervention. For example, express statutory provisions regarding foetuses do exist in the Family Services legislation of New Brunswick and Yukon Territory. New Brunswick's *Child and Family Services and Family Relations Act* SNB. 1980 c. C–2.1, defines child to include unborn child. Accordingly, an unborn child can be the subject of a supervisory order in circumstances where neglect is shown, and this power has been exercised. See *Nouveau-Brunswick (Ministre de la Santé et des Services communautaires)* v. *A D* (1990) 109 NBR (2d) 192, 273 APR 192 (QB). Section 134(1) of the Yukon Territory's Children's Act R.S.Y.T 1986, c.22 enables the Director of Children to apply to the court for an order to require a pregnant woman to receive counselling or supervision in respect of alcohol use if the foetus is at serious risk of suffering foetal alcohol syndrome. See *Joe* v. *Yukon Territories Director of Family and Children's Services* (1986) 5 B C L R (2d) 267 (Y T S C). This was an appeal from an earlier order granted pursuant to section 134. Although the point was moot, since the

The case concerned G, a twenty-two year old Aboriginal woman who was pregnant and addicted to sniffing solvents. In June 1996, the social services were informed that G was pregnant and they attempted to locate her "to determine if she would co-operate in taking treatment for substance abuse".[116] She refused.[117] Social services applied for orders to detain and compulsorily treat G for substance abuse. The Queen's Bench of Manitoba found that it had jurisdiction under the Mental Health Act 1987 to grant the orders sought.[118] In an addendum to the judgment, however, the Court indicated that it would be prepared to extend its *parens patriae* jurisdiction to G's foetus. The logic underwriting the proposal was that, provided that the child would be born, law should protect it from being harmed in ways that will affect it irreparably after birth. To put it simply, as the Court did, "the focus should be on the child to be born".[119]

A similar legal strategy was attempted in England in *Re F (in utero)*[120] which was a case concerning a pregnant woman who led a chaotic lifestyle, and who social services feared would not take responsibility for the imminent birth of her child.[121] The authorities petitioned the court to ward the foetus so that they could take custody of the woman and ensure that she received proper medical care during and after the birth.[122] The question of whether the wardship jurisdiction could apply to unborn children had not previously arisen in English law.[123] The Court of Appeal concluded that it could not apply to a foetus.[124] In Balcombe LJ's judgment this was not specifically because the foetus was not a legal person, because there was no requirement that a child be party to wardship proceedings.[125] Like Hollings J at first instance,[126] Balcombe LJ thought that the authorities which denied legal personality to the foetus,[127] though evidence of the "trend of authority" on the

woman had complied with the order and given birth to her child, the court questioned the constitutionality of the section. It held that the section clearly infringed the woman's right to life, liberty and security of the person guaranteed by section 7 of the *Canadian Charter of Rights and Freedoms*, but declined to decide whether it could be saved by section 1 of the Charter since the point was not raised at trial.

116 *Winnipeg Child & Family Services* v. G *(D.F.)* (1996) 138 DLR (4th) 238 at 244.

117 *Ibid.*

118 The court also found that G's mental state provided a strong foundation for the exercise of the *parens patriae* jurisdiction over adults of unsound mind. *Ibid.*, at 253.

119 *Ibid.*

120 *Supra* n. 51.

121 The psychiatrist that had seen her most recently expressed concern about her condition following the birth of the baby she now carried, and formed the view that "he did not think her competent at the time to make sensible plans for her own welfare or that of the new baby". *Ibid.*, at 1291.

122 *Ibid.*

123 Hollings J *ibid.*, at 1293, May LJ *ibid.*, at 1300, Balcombe LJ *ibid.*, at 1302.

124 *Ibid.*, at 1295–6.

125 *Ibid.*, at 1302, per Balcombe LJ.

126 "In wardship proceedings it is not, of course, necessary for the child to be made a party, so that in itself is not a reason why wardship proceedings could not apply to an unborn child . . . The fact that a child does not need to be made a party underlines again the difference between the wardship proceedings and proceedings in the other jurisdictions, such as in the *Paton* case." *Ibid.*, at 1295.

127 *Paton* v. *British Pregnancy Advisory Service Trustees*, *ibid.*and *C* v. *S*, *supra* n. 36.

question of the foetus' position in law,[128] were not decisive of the question of wardship.[129] May LJ was less clear on this point. He thought that the "only permissible inference" to draw from section 41 of the Supreme Court Act 1981 was that wardship could only apply to "minors" who, by operation of the Family Law Reform Act 1969 were born children.[130]

Nonetheless, all the judges did agree that the foetus could not be the subject of the wardship jurisdiction. First, because it had no existence independent of its mother and therefore could not be "protected" without infringing the liberty of the mother;[131] and second, because application of the paramountcy of the ward principle would entail elevating the foetus' interests over the woman's in the event of a conflict.[132] In the final analysis, the Court could not reconcile itself to the incongruity of granting paramount consideration to the welfare of an entity contained within the body of another person, without explicit authority and without guidelines as to how the legal rights of the mother were to be taken into account.

The Manitoba Queen's Bench in *Winnipeg Child & Family Services* v. G was not persuaded of the "insuperable difficulties"[133] of enforcing a wardship order in respect of a foetus against its mother. It recognised that "some interference with the freedom of the mother" was likely, but it also thought that "in appropriate circumstances that interference would be justified".[134] Although the Court of Appeal in *Re F (in utero)*, and a majority of the Supreme Court of Canada in the same case disagreed, this view found favour in the dissenting opinion of Major J (with whom Sopinka J concurred).

[128] "Of particular significance in the present case is that there is no recorded instance of the courts having assumed jurisdiction in wardship over an unborn child. Indeed the whole trend of recent authority is to the contrary effect." *Supra* n. 51, at 1302.

[129] In reference to the decisions denying legal personality to the foetus, Balcombe LJ said: "these decisions only relate directly to the legal rights of the foetus: they are not decisive of the question before us, namely, has the court power to protect a foetus by making it a ward of the court?", *ibid.*, at 1303. Balcombe LJ did not think that section 41 of the Supreme Court Act or section 1(1) of the Family Law Reform Act 1969 provided the answer to this question, "neither Act contains anything to indicate whether it is possible for a person to be a minor before birth". *Ibid.*, at 1304.

[130] "Finally, when one turns to section 41 of the Supreme Court Act 1981, although it is not so provided directly, I think that the only permissible inference to draw from the wording is that it is only 'minors' who can be made wards of court. Then in the light of section 1 of the Family Law Reform Act 1969 I think that minor can only be a person, in the sense that he or she has been born." *Ibid.*, at 1301.

[131] *Ibid.* Per May LJ; Balcombe LJ *ibid* at 1305.

[132] In reference to the inherent practical difficulties, Hollings J stated: "It is this principle which I think underlines and illustrates why it must be right that, as the law and practice at present stands, wardship can only apply to a living child. For it to apply to a child still within the body of the child's mother, very serious considerations must arise with regard to the welfare of the mother. I do not intend to spell out by examples in this judgment the difficulties that one could anticipate, but one can well imagine that there would be a repugnance on the part of a right thinking person in certain circumstances to think of applying the principle of paramountcy in favour of the child's welfare at the expense of the welfare and interests of the mother." *Ibid.*, at 1296. See also May LJ at 1301; Balcombe LJ at 1305 and Staughton LJ at 1306.

[133] *Ibid.*, at 1301, per May LJ.

[134] *Winnipeg Child & Family Services* v. *G*, *supra* n. 116 at 253.

Jettisoning the Born-Alive Rule

The minority opinion has three features that bear special mention. The first relates to the born-alive rule. The minority judges thought that the born-alive rule should be jettisoned, at least for the purposes of protecting a foetus from the ill-effects of substance abuse. They reasoned that the born-alive rule was an evidentiary, rather than substantive, rule that was originally conceived because the "rudimentary" state of medical knowledge made it impossible to know whether a foetus was alive until it was born.[135] It is important to notice, in the context of Carol Smart's thesis, the importance of medical knowledge and practices in the reasoning of the minority judges on this point. They reasoned that,

> "present medical technology renders the 'born-alive rule' outdated and indefensible. We no longer need to cling to an evidentiary presumption to the contrary when technologies like real-time ultrasound, fetal heart monitors and fetoscopy can clearly show us that a foetus is alive and has been or will be injured by the conduct of another."[136]

The second point that deserves mention concerns the relationship between the born-alive rule and the *parens patriae* jurisdiction. The minority (and indeed the majority) judges read *Re F (in utero)* as standing for the proposition that the foetus could not be the subject of the wardship jurisdiction because it is not a legal person. Balcombe LJ certainly did not reach his decision on this basis. May LJ was more equivocal[137] and Staughton LJ did not comment on this point. Nonetheless, Major and Sopinka JJ took the view that the *parens patriae* jurisdiction had not traditionally extended to foetuses because they had no legal personality. They went on to hold that the born-alive rule, though still important to the criminal law, should not bar the operation of *parens patriae* over foetuses.[138] The purpose of the *parens patriae* jurisdiction was to protect "those who are unable to protect themselves"[139] and this foetus having "no means of escape from the toxins ingested by its mother"[140] was in a vulnerable position.

The minority judges regarded the extension of the *parens patriae* jurisdiction to the foetus as analogous to existing forms of recognition of the foetus, in particular, the application of negligence principles to compensate for harm occasioned by third parties and inheritance rights prior to birth. These examples of legal recognition of

[135] The dissenting judges quoted liberally from Clarke Forsythe's article "Homicide of the Unborn Child: The Born Alive Rule and Other Legal Anachronisms" (1987) 21 *Val. U L* Rev 563. The essence of Forsythe's argument is that if the born alive rule was in truth a substantive rule about when a human being comes into being then the law of homicide would not find criminal liability in circumstances where the death of a child occurs from injuries inflicted in utero. *Ibid*, at 589.

[136] *Winnipeg Child & Family Services* v. G *(D.F.)*, *supra* n. 112, at para. 109.

[137] Finding that the operation of the Supreme Court Act and the Family Law Reform Act did support the inference that the *parens patriae* could only be exercised in relation to minors, which a foetus is not.

[138] *Supra* n. 112, at para. 113.

[139] *Ibid.*, at para. 103.

[140] *Ibid.*

the foetus could be explained, they argued, on the basis that law seeks to protect "the interests of the child upon its birth".[141] This rationale, they thought, applied equally to the case of prenatal neglect, a chain of reasoning which culminated in the plea:

> "society does not simply sit by and allow a mother to abuse her child after birth. How then should serious abuse be allowed to occur before the child is born?"[142]

The final point that deserves a mention concerns the impact of the operation of the *parens patriae* jurisdiction on the pregnant woman. The minority judges argued that the born-alive rule was anachronistic in the context of modern medicine, but they did not engage in any detail with objections which were (arguably) more important to the decision in *Re F (in utero)*; in particular, the imposition on the liberty of the pregnant woman and the difficulties that could arise in the application of the paramountcy principle. Their focus was on the foetus and the infringement of the mother's legal rights only received perfunctory attention. It was acknowledged that some of the rights possessed by the mother would need to be overridden and that these were potentially serious impositions.[143] However, they were "fairly modest when balanced against the devastating harm substance abuse will potentially inflict on her child".[144] And, "in any event, this interference is always subject to the mother's right to end it by deciding to have an abortion".[145]

This minority opinion seeks to create new legally relevant categories of foetuses—foetuses that will be born and foetuses that will be aborted—where the former could attract the *parens patriae* jurisdiction.[146] This echoes the zoning effects of abortion law, but there are two important differences. The first is that the abortion law proscribes the unlawful killing of foetuses (and this proscription is always subject to overriding justifications) whereas this proposal to extend the *parens patriae* jurisdiction is to "protect the health of the child". This goal is considerably more vague than law's proscription of intentional killing. The second important difference is that the *parens patriae* jurisdiction requires a court to consider the interests of the ward above all others. This would mean subordinating the interests of the pregnant woman to those of the foetus. This goes much further than abortion law, which will not place the life of the foetus above that of the pregnant woman in the case of a direct conflict.

Unstable Boundaries

The minority judges reliance on the rights of children and the visually accessible anatomically human foetus echo with Petchetsky's insight about representing the

141 *Ibid.*, at para. 117.
142 *Ibid.*, at para. 103.
143 *Ibid.*, at para. 124.
144 *Ibid.*, at para. 132.
145 *Ibid.*, at para. 93.
146 "A fundamental issue always will be to determine, on a reasonable basis, that the child will indeed be born. This will depend on the evidence which will include evaluating the intention of the mother." *Ibid.*

foetus as autonomous man. An important effect of this representation is the ascription of "self" and "other" to the relationship between mother and foetus.

The interplay between the notions of self, other, responsible action and control can be explored from this perspective. In the case of a pregnant woman who refuses to cease using drugs, as we have seen, the relationship is constructed as adversarial. The foetus is the victim of the mother's ingestion of toxins, from which it cannot (without the law's help) escape. But this representation of the foetus as "prisoner" highlights the further point that the boundary constructed for the purpose of differentiating the foetus from the mother is not fixed, but rather, permeable and unstable. It is precisely the instability of the boundary that gives rise to the fear that the foetus may be harmed by the mother's body if she behaves inappropriately. Discourses about the risk posed to the foetus by maternal conduct then provides the inspiration for a regulatory project to restore stability and to control the maternal body.[147] Karpin describes the rationale for such a project:

> "As the woman is no longer seen as a protector of the fetus, the modern project has been one of wresting control of the 'endangered' fetus from the woman and removing it to a place of masculine security and control—the clinic, the laboratory, and, if need be, the courtroom."[148]

From this perspective, the attempt to jettison the born alive rule to constrain the actions of the pregnant woman can be read as an attempt to police the boundary between mother and foetus.[149]

V MANIPULATING THE COMPETENT/INCOMPETENT BOUNDARY

As we have seen, law's negation of the foetus is incomplete and it becomes particularly strained as the moment of birth approaches. Although law may rhetorically adhere to a unitary conception of personhood (which excludes the foetus), it can nonetheless use other means to deny full personhood to pregnant women. The denial of legal capacity to women in or close to labour provides a good illustration of how law can countenance non-consensual intervention without explicit reliance on foetal rights or interests and without explicit reference to her sexual difference.[150] By failing to acknowledge these as a basis for the intervention, law is able to appear to maintain its commitment to sex neutrality.[151]

[147] Karpin, *Reconstructed Woman*, *supra* n. 3, at 333.

[148] *Ibid.*, at 333–4.

[149] For a general discussion of "policing boundaries" see Karpin, *Maternal Selfhood*, *supra* n. 28, at 53.

[150] *Re MB* [1997] 2 FLR 426; and *St Georges Healthcare (NHS) Trust* v. *S; R* v. *Collins Ex parte S* [hereinafter *St Georges Healthcare Trust* v. *S*] [1998] 2 FLR 729.

[151] Cf. *Re S* [1992] 4 All ER 671 where Sir Stephen Brown made orders for the non-consensuai caesarean section of a Nigerian woman notwithstanding her competent refusal; and the comments (obiter) of Lord Donaldson concerning a possible exception to the general rule in the case of pregnant women carrying viable foetuses; *Re T, supra* n. 89. Both these departures from the official line of sex neutrality were criticised by the Court of Appeal in *St Georges Healthcare Trust* v. *S supra* n. 150.

This has been a more successful strategy for circumventing the pregnant woman's legal rights.[152] It has the effect of relegating her to the category of "incompetent persons", whose legal rights to bodily integrity and self-determination in medical decision-making are limited. In England, a number of applications have been made by doctors to courts seeking declarations to permit the use of force (if necessary) against women who refuse to have caesarean sections.[153] All have been successful, although one case was overturned on appeal after the operation was performed,[154] yet none of these women were mentally "disordered" or "disabled" within the meaning of the Mental Health Act 1983.

This denial of legal capacity to women who are close to, or in, labour does not rest (explicitly) on law's recognition of any foetal rights. The Court of Appeal has been resolute in its determination that pregnant women do not comprise a special category of patients for whom the common law principles regarding the right to refuse medical treatment ought not apply.[155] Any competent refusal must be respected whether or not the pregnant woman may suffer harm or die, and whether or not the foetus may suffer harm or die, as a result. An incompetent woman, on the other hand, does not have the legal capacity to exercise her rights to self-determination. In her case, doctors may provide her with any treatment that they consider to be in her best interests, and treatment will be in her best interests if it is necessary to preserve her life or health or prevent a deterioration in her health.

[152] Even in *Re F (in utero)* [1988] 2 WLR 1289 (HC) where the High Court felt unable to extend the wardship jurisdiction to the foetus, it nonetheless suggested that the applicants use the Mental Health Act to effect the same result. Hollings J said: "The history of mental instability in this mother raises at once the question whether the provisions of the Mental Health Act are not appropriate to deal with this situation. I was told yesterday that her mental condition was not believed to be such as to justify a recommendation to be made in accordance with . . . the Act. . . . I only mention that to indicate that in a case of this kind there may well be a way of safeguarding mother and unborn child other than by seeking to bring that child within the provisions of the wardship jurisdiction." *Ibid.*, at 1292.

[153] *Tameside and Glossop Acute Services Trust* v. *CH* [1996] 1 FLR 763; *Norfolk and Norwich (NHS) Trust* v. *W* [1996] 2 FLR 613; *Rochdale Healthcare (NHS) Trust* v. *C* [1997] 1 FCR 274; *Re L (An Adult: Non-consensual Treatment)* [1997] 1 FCR 609; *Re MB, supra* n. 150; and *St Georges Healthcare Trust* v. *S, supra* n. 150.

[154] *St Georges Healthcare Trust* v. *S, supra* n. 150.

[155] Although it was not strictly necessary to decide the matter in *Re MB*, the Court nevertheless stated that "On the present state of the English law, the submissions made by Mr Grace that we should consider and weigh in the balance the rights of the unborn child, are untenable. The only support in Lord Donaldson's observation in *Re T* cannot stand, in our view, against the weight of earlier decisions, which are far more persuasive as to the present state of the law and which are applicable by analogy to the present appeal. The law is, in our judgment, clear that a competent woman who has the capacity to decide may, for religious reasons, other reasons or for no reason at all, choose not to have medical intervention . . .", *supra* n. 150, at 444. This position was reaffirmed in *R* v. *Collins et al; Ex parte S* where the Court set aside the declaration set aside by Justice Hogg concerning the lawfulness of a non-consensual caesarean section on Ms S, on the basis that because she was competent her right to refuse should have been respected. After reviewing the authorities in England, Canada and the United States, the Court stated that: "In our judgment, while pregnancy increases the personal responsibilities of a woman it does not diminish her entitlement to decide whether or not to undergo medical treatment. Although human, and protected by the law in a number of ways set out in the judgment of *Re MB*, an unborn child is not a separate person from its mother. Its need for medical assistance does not prevail over her rights. She is entitled not to be forced to submit to an invasion of her body against her will, whether her own life or that of her unborn child depends on it." *Supra* n. 150, at 746.

As a matter of law, then, the decision whether or not to accept doctors' advice to have a surgical delivery can be taken out of the hands of a woman if she is incompetent. A woman would certainly lack legal capacity if she was unconscious and unable to communicate her decision about treatment.[156] She may also lack legal capacity if she is sufficiently mentally disordered[157] or disabled[158] to be unable to make a decision about having a caesarean section. The legal test for determining whether or not a woman has the requisite capacity to make treatment decisions involves three steps.[159] The first is that she can understand the nature of, and reasons for, the proposed caesarean section. The second is that she believes the caesarean section to be necessary, and the third is that she can weigh the factors for and against having a caesarean section in the balance to reach her decision. If, in the opinion of doctors and the court, the woman does not meet these three requirements, she is deemed in law to be incapable of giving or refusing consent to the operation.

Competence

The Court of Appeal has twice considered the refusals of pregnant women to consent to caesarean sections. In the first case, *Re MB (Medical Treatment)* the Court heard an immediate appeal from the declaratory judgment of the High Court and before the caesarean section was carried out. The second case, *St Georges Healthcare NHS Trust* v. *S; R* v. *Collins & Ors Ex Parte S*, was heard as an appeal after the caesarean section had already been performed on Ms S. The Court decided that MB was incompetent and made a declaration permitting doctors to perform a caesarean section using force if necessary. In contrast and reviewing all the evidence after the surgery had been performed, the Court of Appeal found that Ms S was competent at the relevant time and, accordingly, that the caesarean section performed on her was unlawful. It is difficult to say whether the timing of the hearing was significant

156 This was the case in *Re T* where, although when conscious Miss T had made it clear that she did not wish to have a blood transfusion, the court held that since her refusal was made at a time when she was not aware that a transfusion might be required to save her life, and taking into account her loose connections with the Jehovah Witness faith and the possible influence of her mother who was a devout follower, the refusal did not apply to her present situation. *Supra* n. 89.

157 Section 63 of the Mental Health Act 1983 provides that the consent of a patient detained under the Act is not required for medical treatment given for the mental disorder from which they are suffering. The section specifically excludes some treatments, such as ECT for which specific procedures apply. Precisely what constitutes a treatment for a mental disorder, however, seems open to wide interpretation. In *Tameside and Glossop Acute Services Trust* v. *CH, supra* n. 153, the court held that a caesarean section was medical treatment for CH's schizophrenia. The courts have also held that the forcible provision of food to a patient suffering borderline personality disorder with a compulsion to self-harm constituted medical treatment for the purposes of section 63; *B* v. *Croydon Health Authority* [1995] 1 FLR 470.

158 See in particular, *T* v. *T and Another* [1988] 2 WLR 189 respecting the termination of pregnancy and sterilisation of a mentally handicapped woman, *F* v. *West Berkshire Health Authority and Another (Mental Health Act Commission intervening)* [1989] 2 All ER 545, and *Re GF (Medical Treatment)* [1992] 1 FLR 293 respecting the sterilisation of a mentally handicapped women.

159 *Re C (Adult Refusal of Medical Treatment)* [hereinafter *Re C*] [1994] 1 WLR 290 at 295.

to the outcome of each case. It is at least possible to say, that the Court of Appeal had more time to consider their judgment in the case of Ms S.

MB was a near-term pregnant woman whose foetus was in the breech position. Doctors advised her to have a caesarean section because this procedure would be safer for the foetus. MB was extremely concerned about the well-being of the foetus and, in principle, understood the reasons for recommending a caesarean section but she nonetheless refused to consent because she was frightened of needles and did not want an anaesthetic. The doctors made repeated attempts to persuade MB to be anaesthetised, all of which were unsuccessful. A declaration to perform the surgery, using force if necessary, was obtained by the health authority and MB, who was by that time in labour, appealed to the Court of Appeal.

The focus of the Court of Appeal's attention was MB's competence. Like the cases of *Norfolk and Norwich (NHS) Trust* v. *W*, *Rochdale NHS Trust* v. *C* and *Re (Non-consensual medical treatment)* before it, the Court found that MB was not competent to make a decision about the surgical delivery. This was because MB failed the final prong of the competency test. In particular, she was not able to weigh the considerations in the balance because her fear of needles dominated her thinking at the moment that the anaesthetic was to be administered. This is why she changed her "yes" to a "no" at the last minute.

The last minute withdrawal of consent is a matter that has arisen in the context of sexual assault and this provides an interesting point of comparison. In the context of sexual intercourse, it is hardly likely that a court would entertain the suggestion that a woman who initially agreed to sexual intercourse and then changed her mind was legally incapacitated (thus vitiating her refusal). As far as the law is concerned, if sexual intercourse occurs without consent it is rape. This point of comparison can clarify the critical difference between MB's non-consensual caesarean section and non-consensual sexual intercourse. This, I suggest, is that while rape can never be in a woman's best interests, performing a caesarean section to save her foetus' life might be. But to assess competency by reference to what is thought to be a person's best interests, undermines the very value that law vows to uphold, that is, the legal person's right to make their own choice. MB's best interests provided a compelling motive for deeming MB incapable, and it may explain why the Court of Appeal seized upon the "needle phobia" as an indicia of incapacity rather than an "irrational" reason for refusing treatment. If MB's refusal was a competent (though irrational) one, no question of her best interests would have arisen and her refusal would have been respected. As it was, the Court found that:

> "on the evidence she was incapable of making a decision at all. She was at that moment [immediately prior to the administration of the anaesthetic] suffering an impairment of her mental functioning which disabled her. She was temporarily incompetent. In the emergency the doctors would be free to administer the anaesthetic if that were in her best interests."[160]

[160] *Re MB (Medical Treatment)*, *supra* n. 150, at 438.

It is worth comparing the Court of Appeal's reasoning on competence in *Re MB* with the High Court's reasoning in *Norfolk and Norwich (NHS) Trust* v. *W* and *Rochdale NHS Trust* v. *C*. Ms W had been brought into accident and emergency after a car accident in a state of arrested labour. Doctors wanted to perform a forceps delivery or a caesarean section if necessary but W would not consent. A psychiatrist gave evidence that she had denied to him that she was pregnant, but found it difficult to say whether "this was said artfully or because of a genuine lack of comprehension".[161] He could not say whether W was capable of comprehending, retaining and believing the information she received about the need for medical intervention in her labour, but he took the view that she did not seem to be able to balance the information given to her. There was evidence that Ms W had received psychiatric treatment in the past but the psychiatrist did not find any evidence of mental disorder within the meaning of the *Mental Health Act* 1983. The Court concluded that W "was incapable of weighing up the considerations that were involved" and was, therefore, legally incapable of refusing medical treatment. Although there was no evidence about W's physical condition, the judge went a step further to note that:

> "she was called upon to make that decision at a time of acute emotional stress and physical pain in the ordinary course of labour made even more difficult for her because of her own particular mental health history."[162]

The "pain and stress of labour" as a basis for negating a woman's competence approximates a status approach to legal capacity which raises the question, why assess the capacity of labouring women at all?[163] The "irrationality" of labouring women was an even stronger feature of *Rochdale Healthcare (NHS) Trust* v. *C*.[164] This case concerned a woman who did not want to have a surgical delivery because she had suffered deleterious effects from a previous caesarean section. C was considered by her obstetrician to be fully competent but the court found otherwise. Its assessment of incompetency was based on two grounds. The first was that she "was in the throes of labour with all that is involved in terms of pain and emotional stress".[165] The second ground was that:

> "a patient who could, in those circumstances, speak in terms of the inevitability of her own death, was not a patient who was able properly to weigh up the considerations that arose so as to make any valid decision, about anything of the most trivial kind, surely still less one which involved her own life."[166]

It is worth repeating that, according to doctrine, every legal person has the right to refuse treatment for any reason at all even if they might die as a result. The Court's

161 *Norfolk and Norwich (NHS) Trust* v. *W*, *supra* n. 153, at 614.

162 *Ibid.*, at 616.

163 Quite apart from this, it might be objected that a woman who experiences intolerable levels of pain and stress may be more likely to accede to doctor's advice to bring an end to their labour.

164 *Rochdale Healthcare (NHS) Trust* v. *C*, *supra* n. 153.

165 *Ibid.*, at 275.

166 *Ibid.*

denial that C was competent *because* she refused potentially life-saving treatment is difficult to square with this. It suggests that factors other than her own (potential) death were exercising the judge when he admonished her for being unable to "weigh up the considerations that arose". The same judge was more forthcoming on the "considerations" in W's case where he concluded that:

> "throughout this judgment, I have referred to 'the foetus' because I wish to emphasise that the focus of my judicial attention was upon the interests of the patient herself and not upon the interests of the foetus which she bore. However, the reality was that the foetus was a fully formed child, capable of normal life if only it could be delivered from the mother."[167]

C was denied legal capacity because she was, according to the Court, incompetent. An addendum to the judgment casts further doubt on this assessment. Justice Johnson noted that, during the time that it had taken to obtain a court order, "the patient had changed her mind and given her consent to the procedure. Accordingly, the operation was in fact performed with her consent".[167a] The inference here is clear. Mrs C is competent when her decision accords with the advice of her doctors and the court, and she is incompetent when it does not.

Although legal capacity is not to be determined by reference to the quality of the decision, or the status of the person, there is evidence of both in C's case. This raises an issue of considerable significance. It seems clear that in practice the law makes assumptions about what normal expectant mothers will do for their foetuses, a departure from which may signal incompetence or mental illness. This was a central issue in the case of *St Georges Healthcare Trust* v. *S* where Ms S, who showed signs of pre-eclampsia but refused a recommended caesarean section, was sectioned under the Mental Health Act 1983. She was detained under the powers of the Act until a declaration was obtained from Justice Hogg to permit a caesarean section to be performed on her without her consent. There is no reported judgment available of the hearing at first instance but three points seem clear. First, Ms S was sectioned under the Act because she refused the caesarean section. Secondly, she was detained under the Act because she persisted in that refusal and not because she exhibited signs of a mental disorder within the meaning of the Act. Finally, although Ms S was competent and there was no juridical basis for the declaration made, the legal process did not initially uncover this.

The Court of Appeal had an opportunity to reflect on these aspects of the case after the caesarean section had been performed on S. Not surprisingly, it did not condone the conduct of the earlier proceedings. On the question of maternal conduct and mental illness it had the following to say:

> "The Act cannot be deployed to achieve the detention of an individual against her will merely because her thinking process is unusual, even apparently bizarre and irrational, and contrary to the views of the community at large."[168]

[167] *Norfolk and Norwich (NHS) Trust* v. *W*, *supra* n. 153, at 616.
[167a] *Rochdale Healthcare (NHS) Trust* v. *C*, *supra* n. 153 at 276.
[168] *St Georges Healthcare Trust* v. *S*, *supra* n. 150, at 746.

The Court of Appeal was aware of material facts that, though available, were apparently withheld from the High Court at first instance. This included the evidence that in the view of the doctors Ms S was competent to refuse treatment, that she had articulated her refusal verbally and in writing, and that she had instructed solicitors to oppose the application (they were not told). It must be remembered that the High Court did not know these things and, for whatever reason, was not able to ascertain them before making the declaration. In these circumstances, assumption rather than fact dictated the proceedings. The Court of Appeal identified what it considered (after the fact) to be the assumptions which feed what it called the "prohibited reasoning":

> "Here is an intelligent woman. She knows perfectly well that if she persists with this course against medical advice she is likely to cause serious harm, and possibly death, to her baby and to herself. No normal mother-to-be could possibly think like that . . . . Her bizarre thinking represents a danger to their safety and health. It therefore follows that she must be mentally disordered and detained in hospital in her own interests and those of her baby."[169]

It seems possible that this prohibited reasoning not only precipitated S's caesarean section but also C's and W's, with the exception that incapacity rather than mental disorder was relied on to explain their deviance from normal maternal behaviour.

Best Interests

It is important to remember that each of these assessments of capacity took place in less than optimum conditions. In C's case, the court was told that her decision to refuse a caesarean section could lead to her death, and would probably lead to the death of her foetus within fifteen minutes. The vocabulary of separation is evident in the presentation of the facts. In each case, the court documents the risks to the foetus, followed by the risks to the pregnant woman although the risks to her health are not usually elaborated beyond vague statements like a "likelihood of damage to her physical health which might have potentially life-threatening consequences"[170] or "injurious to her health and well-being".[171] The willingness to accept vague statements as to risk, if nothing else, indicates a judicial deference to medical assessment and knowledge.[172] But it also points to the fact that the presence of

[169] *St Georges Healthcare Trust* v. *S*, *supra* n. 150, at 746.

[170] *Norfolk and Norwich (NHS) Trust* v. *W*, *supra* n. 153, at 616.

[171] *Re L*, *supra* n. 153, at 610. There was no risk to MB's life, although the obstetrician felt that C's life was in grave danger.

[172] This deference was alluded to by Lord Goff in *Bland* where he says: "It is . . . the function of judges to state the legal principles upon which the lawfulness of the actions of doctors depend; but in the end the decisions to be made in individual cases must rest with the doctors themselves. In these circumstances, what is required is a sensitive understanding of each others respective functions, and in particular a determination by the judges not merely to understand the problems facing the medical profession in cases of this kind, but also to regard their professional standards with respect". *Supra* n. 89, at 871.

the foetus, although strictly speaking not legally relevant, is a significant concern in the minds of both doctors and judges.

This becomes clearest in the judicial assessment of "best interests" which the court must undertake if it reaches the conclusion that the woman is incompetent. This exercise is paternalistic by definition and I do not seek to criticise the courts' approaches on that basis. An examination of the reasons given for the court's findings on "best interests" is still worth engaging because it is in this part of the court's reasoning that its unstated assumptions about the foetus become more obvious. Here the tension between the legal principle that a foetus is not a person, and the intuitive or "common sense" sentiment that a late term foetus is all but a person, is most apparent. The proximity of the legal boundary marked by birth, coupled with medical assertions about the levels of risk associated with a natural birthing, intensify this tension, as the Court of Appeal acknowledges:

> "Although it might seem illogical that a child capable of being born alive is protected by the criminal law from intentional destruction, and by the Abortion Act from termination otherwise than as permitted by the Act, but is not protected from the (irrational) decision of a competent mother not to allow medical intervention to avert the risk of death, this appears to be the current state of the law."[173]

Notwithstanding the clarity of the common law on the question of whether foetal interests can be taken into account in deciding whether a caesarean section can be performed without consent, there are ample indications to the contrary. In *Norfolk and Norwich (NHS) Trust* v. *W*, the Court held that the intervention proposed was in W's "best interests" on three grounds. First, it would end the stress and pain of her labour. Second, it was necessary to prevent a risk to her physical health. His Honour refers to the death of the foetus causing serious physical damage and possibly death for W as a near certainty at one point, and as a "likelihood" at another.[174] Third, and especially revealing, His Honour exhorted that:

> "despite her present view about the foetus, [the intervention] would avoid her feeling any feeling of guilt in the future were she, by her refusal of consent, to cause the death of the foetus."[175]

This third reason was repeated in varying shades in the other decisions. Its circularity is obvious. The best interests of the pregnant woman are determined by reference to what is best for the foetus, and are furthered by protecting her from suffering the guilt of her misjudgment. A similar logic was used in *Tameside and Glossop Acute Services Trust* v. *CH*, where the judge held that "the best interests of the patient lie in her producing a healthy child".[176] In *Re L*, the court held that the forced intervention would "spare her the inevitably profound stress of losing her

[173] *Re MB*, *supra* n. 150, at 441.

[174] "The death of the foetus would have immediate and increasing deleterious effects upon the patient herself leading to serious physical damage and possible death". *Norfolk and Norwich (NHS) Trust* v. *W*, *supra* n. 153, at 616.

[175] *Ibid.*

[176] *Tameside and Glossop Acute Services Trust* v. *CH*, *supra* n. 153, at 767.

child",[177] and in *Re MB* "it must be in the best interests of a woman carrying a full-term child whom she wants to be born alive and healthy that such a result should if possible be achieved".[178] As if to strengthen the force of this reason, the court in *Re L* concluded its judgment with a brief note to record L's contrition "that she had caused many people so much trouble".[179] Curiously, the deleterious effects of being forcibly sedated for the purpose of enacting major abdominal surgery were not considered at all in the cases of C, W and S; and were considered as not significant to the assessment of "best interests" in the cases of L and MB.

Finally, it is important to emphasise that non-consensual caesarean sections were performed on all the aforementioned women without disrupting the established principles concerning the foetus' lack of legal personality or the rights of legal persons to bodily integrity and self-determination in medical decision-making. In the Court of Appeal judgments, both principles are repeated and affirmed. In this way, the sex neutrality of the relevant legal principles are not challenged, nor are the sexed differences of the defendants bodies (when compared against the body of the legal person) deemed material to the legal resolution. But these factors are critical in understanding how law imposes a physical invasion onto these subjects, in direct contravention of its own understanding of the paramountcy of bodily integrity. Perhaps most ironically, law adopts the vocabulary of dignity and respect in its framing of the orders in these cases. It permits doctors to perform the invasive surgery or other necessary tests on the woman in any manner which "preserves the greatest dignity" possible in the circumstances.[180]

VI SOME CONCLUDING THOUGHTS ON INDIVIDUATION AND LAW

I have been arguing that law that the pregnant woman who carries a viable foetus does not fit law's conception of the legal person as a bounded unitary self. Her deviation from the embodied state of the legal person is located in the various strategies which law adopts to create a boundary between her and her foetus. When this occurs, control of her body/self may be ceded to other authorities who police this boundary by, for example, determining the conditions under which she might

177 *Re L, supra* n. 153, at 612.

178 *Re MB,supra* n. 153, at 439.

179 *Re L supra* n. 153, at 612.

180 The connection between bodily wholeness and dignity in judicial reasoning was also significant in the context of *Re A (Children), supra* n. 39. All three Court of Appeal judges remarked on the relationship between dignity and bodily integrity. Robert-Walker LJ observed that:

> "Every human being's right to life carries with it, as an intrinsic part of it, rights of bodily integrity and autonomy—the right to have one's body whole and intact and (on reaching an age of understanding) to take decisions about one's body." (*Ibid.*, at 83).

Against this analysis, Robert-Walker LJ reasoned that there was a strong presumption in favour of the operation *because* it would restore the bodily integrity of each twin. Thus, although the separation operation would surely violate Mary's right to life, it could be nonetheless as an attempt to restore to her "natural rights" which had been denied her. "For the twins to remain alive and conjoined in the way they are would be to deprive them of the bodily integrity which is the right of each of them." *Ibid.*

lawfully terminate her pregnancy, or make decisions concerning the delivery of her child or, perhaps in the future, whether she should be incarcerated to ensure that she does not pollute the maternal environment. In these circumstances, the boundary is made to appear more stable by restraining the mother from harming someone who is not her self although she achieved this by doing, or not doing something, to her own body.[181]

This "self/other boundary" is not always policed in an oppressive manner and I am not suggesting that law is consistent in this approach. The strategy to dispense with the born-alive rule was rejected by a majority of the Supreme Court of Canada and by the Court of Appeal in *St Georges Healthcare Trust* v. *S.* In the latter case, the idea that pregnant women who refuse caesarean sections must be incompetent was roundly condemned. But what I am suggesting is that law observes this "self/other boundary" even if it chooses not to police it for the sake of the "other". The foetus may not be a legal person but, as the Court of Appeal has said, "whatever else it may be a thirty-six week old foetus is not nothing: if viable it is not lifeless and it is certainly human".[182] This distinction is capable of transforming a pregnant woman into a "mother" and "child" in an oppositional struggle.

Isabel Karpin argues that this disembodies pregnant women and, in so doing, erodes the possibilities for maternal autonomy and selfhood.[183] She argues that the autonomy of pregnant women should be respected, not because the foetus is insignificant, but because pregnant women *are* significant.[184] When law conceptualises pregnant women as acting "outside or against our bodies"[185] she claims, it denies them this significance. Her answer is to insist on an embodied account of pregnancy which entails a resistance to the rhetorical separation of the "foetus" and the "mother".[186] This strategy, she claims:

> "would seek to place the woman in control of her body/self and the fetus, and not, as she was constructed in the pre-technological era, as subject to her body nor, as she might otherwise be constructed in the age of technology, as subject to the fetus".[187]

Marie Ashe provides a positive account of the embodied subjectivity of pregnant women in the following passage:

> "Pregnancy is experienced not so much as presence of a separate entity in the womb but as an alteration of the entire body . . . The experience of the pregnant woman who desires her pregnancy is not one of occupation but one of bodily alteration. And the alterations of bodily reality become mirrored by alterations of personhood, to maintain the balance of body and mind, of culture and nature. Many women give accounts of pregnancies as experiences of knowledge. . . So profound are the alterations that occur in the process of pregnancy that a woman may find herself to be, in some senses, a 'different person' at the

[181] Karpin, *Maternal Selfhood*, *supra* n. 28, at 41.
[182] *St Georges Healthcare Trust* v. *S* , *supra* n. 150, at 741.
[183] Karpin, *Maternal Selfhood*, *supra* n. 28, at 46–7.
[184] *Ibid.*
[185] *Ibid.*, at 47.
[186] *Ibid.*
[187] *Ibid.*

end of the pregnancy from the one she was at its start. Against her altering body, the pregnant woman defines an altering self, defining a new distance from her bodily experience at which the site of personhood will be located."[188]

The need to re-examine the location of personhood in legal accounts of pregnancy prompts Karpin to suggest a conceptualisation of maternal body as a "nexus of relations".[189] This urges law to see the mother and the foetus (and later, the child) as intimately connected selves in a physical or material sense as well in a social and political sense.[190] In contrast to the legal approaches discussed above, such an account would resist conceiving the foetus and woman as separable and perhaps oppositional and would instead explore the connective aspects of the relationship. Karpin makes it clear that she is not suggesting,

> "a relationship in which mother and fetus (or. . child) are equal partners because that would rely on a basic premise of distinction. The value of a nexus-of-relations perspective is that it makes obsolete a notion of subjectivity that is dependent for its subject status on distinction, separation and defensive opposition to others."[191]

In a framework such as this, she argues, it makes no sense to regard the actions of a pregnant woman as separable from her body, her foetus or her material circumstances.[192] Neither would it be impossible to think in terms that prescribe the failure to keep her material and social self separate from her foetus as a failure to act responsibly. In this way, "mother, child and context are all part of one extremely vulnerable selfhood".[193] This nexus-of-relations theory therefore rejects the conceptualisation of the self as separate and bounded in favour of a more flexible and open-ended subject.[194] Karpin's general point, I take it, is that the artificiality of the separateness thesis is illustrated by the interconnectedness of mother and foetus. The answer to this ambiguity, she argues, is not to draw boundaries within the maternal body in order to make it fit into a conceptual framework that relies on individuation as a pre-requisite to selfhood, but rather, to accept the connections and differentiations of mother and foetus in their complexity, without undermining the selfhood and subject status of the pregnant woman.

As I hope the foregoing analysis of law's approaches to pregnant women demonstrates, the question of whether a fuller understanding of the relational aspects of bodily experience and autonomy may be deployed to re-negotiate law's conception of its subject is important.[195] But is it an especially difficult question to analyse

[188] M Ashe, "Law-Language of Maternity: Discourse Holding Nature in Contempt" (1988) 22 *New England Law Review* 521 at 549–51.

[189] Karpin, *Maternal Selfhood, supra* n. 28, at 46.

[190] *Ibid.*

[191] *Ibid.*

[192] *Ibid.*, at 48.

[193] *Ibid.*

[194] *Ibid.*, at 46

[195] See C Stychin, "Body Talk: Rethinking Autonomy, Commodification and the Embodies Legal Self" in S Sheldon and M Thomson (eds.), *Feminist Perspectives on Health Care Law* (London, Cavendish, 1998) 211. Stychin attempts to develop a concept of self-ownership that does not rely on "property rights" in the body. He argues that a property-based conception will not secure self-ownership for all

in the context of pregnancy. Feminists will rightly be sensitive to the potential ramifications of giving recognition to the foetus in law. The danger is that an investigation of the legal significance of the foetus and pregnant woman within a relational framework might be misread as an invitation to "relate" directly to the foetus as a person, a contingency that could amplify the oppressive aspects of legal personhood as currently constituted.[196] The same objection could be made to the feminist project of re-conceiving autonomy in terms of a relational ethic of care.[197] The danger is that advancing "care" as a principle for explaining intervention could merely disguise an oppressive paternalistic interference with pregnant women. Sound though these objections are, the fact remains that the legal personality of pregnant women is routinely undermined by law, even in the absence of foetal personhood, and what is desperately needed is a more coherent vision for the self-determination of all legal subjects (male and female).

subjects because this strategy assimilates, rather than challenges, the mind/body dualism that discursively constructs the body as an object of knowledge, as "other" to reason and as irretrievably feminine.

[196] See for example K de Gama, "Posthumous pregnancies: Some thoughts on Life and Death" in Sheldon and Thomson (eds.), *supra* n. 195, at 259. De Gama considers the practice of artificially ventilating brain dead women for the express purpose of incubating foetuses, and draws attention to the fact that this practice has been in part justified on the grounds of "relationship", typically between the doctor, or the putative father, and the foetus.

[197] See for example C Wells, "On the Outside Looking In: Perspectives on Enforced Caesareans", and J Bridgeman, "Because We Care? The Medical Treatment of Children" in Sheldon and Thomson (eds.), *supra* n. 195.

3

Can Women be Legal Persons?

NGAIRE NAFFINE*

I INTRODUCTION

TO BE VISIBLE IN law and thus to have legal standing, to attract legal rights and to assume legal obligations, one must be a legal person. If a human being is not a person in law,[1] she can be treated as a species of property: she can be bought and sold. It is because animals are not legal persons that they can be destroyed by their owners, almost with legal impunity. The offences against the person are not designed to afford legal protection or dignity to the family pet. Closely allied with the legal concept of the person is the moral concept of person. For, to be a legal person is also to have moral standing, which is why animal liberationists have argued for the legal personhood of the non-human primates—it is thought that with legal standing comes moral standing.[2] To be a legal person is also to be recognised as an active participant in the polis. As one legal analyst has remarked about the former denial of personhood to Afro-Americans, it was more than just a matter of legal standing. Rather

> "it involve[d] considerations both of the fundamental legal and political concept of membership within a liberal society and the fundamental scope of understanding of civil . . . rights and liberties".[3]

Feminist legal theorists have made considerable advances in our understanding of the concept of the legal person and its pernicious consequences for women, which is itself a highly problematic legal term of art.[4] My essay draws together feminist

* I am grateful for the many thoughtful comments of Margaret Davies and Kate Leeson.

[1] One does not have to be a human being to be a legal person. The most prominent example of a non-human legal person is the corporation. However my concern here is with rights as they are awarded or denied to human beings, not artificial entities.

[2] See for example P Singer, *Animal Liberation: A New Ethics for Our Treatment of Animals* (London, Jonathan Cape, 1976).

[3] J McHugh, "What is the Difference Between a "Person" and a "Human Being" within the Law?" (1992) 54 *Review of Politics* 445 at 446.

[4] The compulsions of language, legal and otherwise, are a central interest of this paper and also cause constant problems for it. My purpose is to show how law creates and enforces a concept of a legal person in conjunction with a related concept of a legal woman (Carol Smart has called her "the woman of legal discourse": C Smart, "The Woman of Legal Discourse" (1992) 1 *Social and Legal Studies* 29). However I need also to be able to refer to women in another sense, as other than the legal construct, though never entirely other given the immense power of law to define our lives. There is no other term than "woman" that I can use for my constituency: this is the current limits of intelligibility of the language. As the later Wittgenstein put it: "whereof one cannot speak, thereof one must be silent" (L Wittgenstein, *Tractatus*

insights into law's subject, its person, in order to assess the continuing theoretical and practical significance for women of this basic legal concept. It reflects also on the sorts of conditions which could produce a non-oppressive personhood in law.

The essay first considers why legal personality, as it participates in Anglo-American and Australian jurisprudence, remains of interest to contemporary feminist theorists, especially in light of the conventional legal wisdom that the concept has ceased to function in an exclusive, discriminatory manner and now embraces all live human beings. It notes the disavowal of the continuing politics of personality by orthodox legal theorists, and replies that, despite its ostensible universality, personality remains a principal means by which law both implicitly and explicitly continues to classify and order human beings, often in an unethical manner, by giving an effective vigorous persona to some, while dulling the influence of others.

The second part documents briefly the emergence of modern legal personality, drawing on two prominent schematic histories of the concept. One is Sir Henry Maine's celebrated story of the transition from status to contract; the other is Marcel Mauss's anthropological account of the etymology of the word "person". In both histories, we witness the rise of a sovereign, self-legislating and notionally universal legal individual. We then consider the feminist revisionist histories of legal personality which suggest why its modern legal incidents, implicitly and explicitly, rely still on an ethically-suspect concept of "woman" who is always less than the full legal person and so remains a disabling status category.

The essay closes with some speculations about the sort of legal ontology which might augment, rather than diminish, the personhood of women in law. It draws on a range of philosophies of the person which serve to counter the dominant view of legal personality, in particular, by giving greater recognition to the temporal, corporeal and social dimensions of being.

II WHY SHOULD WE WORRY ABOUT LEGAL PERSONS? THE FEMINIST CASE FOR LOOKING AT PERSONALITY IN THE LIGHT OF THE MODERN DISAVOWAL OF ITS CONTINUING POLITICS

The more orthodox lawyer seems genuinely puzzled by contemporary feminist interest in the legal person. There are two conspicuous reasons why personality has ceased to be of particular ethical, theoretical and political concern within the mainstream of legal thought. One is that all human beings are now legal persons,[5] and so the concept appears to tell us little about the legal constitution, differentiation

Logico-Philosophicus (London, Kegan Paul, Trench, Trubner & Co Ltd, 1922) 189). However my intention is not to suggest that there is a natural woman who is obscured or trapped by legal woman. I have left it to the context of the discussion to distinguish the two different usages of "woman".

[5] As we will see, however, personhood is neither a stable nor constant concept and so while all human beings are legal persons for some purposes, some human beings are far more effective legal actors than others.

and allocation of human rights and obligations. On its surface, it is an all-embracing, and so apparently monolithic, term. When the concept had more obvious political purchase, when for example slavery was acceptable to American jurisprudence, the award and denial of legal personality served in a dramatic way to determine the constituency of those who could participate effectively in society: some human beings were persons who were allowed to own other human beings who were not themselves persons but property. The very limited legal life of married women, well into the nineteenth century, was also a function of the strategic deployment of the concept to secure a radically unequal social and economic order. Now it seems to many that the politics have largely gone out of the topic and, consequently, slight attention is now paid to the concept in most modern legal texts, including jurisprudential works. Corporate personality remains of interest to corporate lawyers as the means by which the artificial entity of the company comes into legal being and assumes legal rights and obligations. But personality as it applies to human beings has almost fallen into desuetude as a standard jurisprudential issue.[6]

A second reason why lawyers are likely to disavow the ethico-theoretical importance of personality is that they tend to see it as purely a neutral, technical enabling device which can be used in a variety of ways to achieve specifically legal ends. In his lectures on jurisprudence, for example, John Austin spent some time examining the meaning and location of person (and status) in law and concluded that there was little to it. It was mere legal convenience.[7] More recently Dias declared:

> "There is no 'essence' underlying the various uses of 'person'. . . . The application of it to human beings is something which the law shares with ordinary usage, although its connotation is slightly different, namely a unit of jural relations. . . . Neither the linguistic nor legal usages of 'person' are logical."[8]

To Richard Tur,

> "the concept of legal personality is wholly formal. It is an empty slot that can be filled by anything that can have rights or duties."[9]

In *The Pure Theory of Law*, Hans Kelsen examines the concept of the juristic person, terming it a "construction of legal science".[10] He too is impatient with any

[6] Its heyday seems to have been in the 1920s and 1930s with the publication of A Kocourek, *Jural Relations*, 2nd edn. (Indianapolis, Bobbs-Merill Co, 1928); C K Allen, "Status and Capacity" in C K Allen, *Legal Duties and Other Essays in Jurisprudence*, reprint of 1931 edn. (Verlag, Germany, Scientia, 1977) 28–70; A Nekam, *The Personality Conception of the Legal Entity* (Cambridge, Massachusetts, Harvard University Press, 1938); B Smith, "Legal Personality" (1928) 37 *Yale Law Journal* 238.

[7] J Austin, *Lectures on Jurisprudence, or the Philosophy of Positive Law* ed., R Campbell, 5th edn. (London, John Murray, 1885) 687. Here, Austin states: "The law of Persons is the law of *status* or conditions, detached for the sake of convenience from the body of the entire legal system."

[8] R W M Dias, *Jurisprudence*, 5th edn. (London, Butterworths, 1985) 270.

[9] R Tur, "The 'Person' in Law" in A Peacocke and G Gillett (eds.), *Persons and Personality: A Contemporary Inquiry* (Oxford, Basil Blackwell, 1987) 121–2.

[10] H Kelsen, *The Pure Theory of Law*, trans. Max Knight (Berkeley, University of California Press, 1967) 190–1.

suggestion that there are underlying politics to legal personality which must be grasped in order to make proper sense of the legal term. "That the human being is a legal subject (subject of rights and obligations)", according to Kelsen,

> "means nothing else . . . but that human behaviour is the content of legal obligations and rights—nothing else than that a human being is a person or has personality".[11]

For Kelsen:

> "A legal person is the unity of a complex of legal obligations and rights. Since these obligations and rights are constituted by legal norms (more correctly: *are* these legal norms), the problem of 'person' is in the last analysis the problem of the unity of a complex of norms. . . . It is not a natural reality but a social construction, created by the science of law—an auxiliary concept in the presentation of legally relevant facts."[12]

There is an important sense in which feminists would sympathise with Kelsen on the constituting, rather than simply responsive, nature of law, for feminist lawyers also tend to be socio-legal constructionists.[13] Thus they would agree that the legal person is a creation of law, a legal invention comprising a configuration of legal norms designed to enable someone or something to be, and to act, in law. However, they would be unpersuaded by the proposition that the legal person is fully intelligible within legal norms, without recourse to its larger political purposes, as Kelsen insists with his "pure theory". To Kelsen, the legal construct of the person is not to be understood by lawyers in terms of social, economic or political relations, for these are all extraneous to law. However, there is only a short step from this aggressively positivist assertion, designed to focus the legal mind on the internal norms of law, to the more overtly political statement, often made by even more orthodox lawyers, that there is no necessary coherence to the term at all, in its different manifestations.

Dias, for one, does not expect to discover a logic in the term, while to Salmond "[l]egal persons, being the *arbitrary* creations of the law, may be of as many kinds as the law pleases" (my emphasis).[14] By maintaining that the legal person is not only fully interior to law but also that he is only a sort of odd-job man who can do any task required of him by law,[15] rather than a figure of potentially considerable influence who assumes a quite particular character, the concept is shorn of moral and political significance. In reply to this jurisprudence of orthodoxy, feminists are likely to insist that the concept of the modern legal person takes its meaning from its political history, broadly defined, and that there remains a manifestly political dimension to its modern operations.[16]

[11] H Kelsen, *The Pure Theory of Law*, trans. Max Knight (Berkeley, University of California Press, 1967), at 173.

[12] *Ibid.*, at 173–4.

[13] See N Lacey, *Unspeakable Subjects: Feminist Essays in Legal and Social Theory* (Oxford, Hart Publishing, 1998).

[14] J Salmond, *Jurisprudence*, 7th edn. (London, Sweet & Maxwell, 1924) 306.

[15] His maleness, it will be argued, is still central to his characterisation.

[16] This point is made strongly in M Minow, *Making all the Difference: Inclusion, Exclusion and American Law* (Ithaca, NY, Cornell University Press, 1990).

Lawyers who concede the iniquitous history of personhood, and who resist Kelsen's (to my mind impossible) demand to remain within the arena of purely legal norms to make sense of the production of the concept, are likely to consign injustice to the past, hence the loss of juristic interest in the modern law of persons. They might agree that the former use of the concept was an overt means of establishing a social hierarchy, but that these days it is exclusively a response to natural human variation. Law now only deals with the already-constituted, and to this it applies liberal rights and duties. Law's treatment of children, for example, may seem to bear this out. Although they are persons in law, infants do not have the same legal capacity as adults because they do not have the same natural ability; and nor do those with mental impairments or diseases of the mind.[17] However, a mistake is being made here which Kelsen would be quick to seize upon. The necessary, but false, suggestion is that law now only responds to non-legal, natural difference and is not always constituting the natures of persons with their every invocation.[18]

Thus it is that modern legal personality itself remains naturalised and so often uninspected and non-suspect: it is conceded that the old divisions of persons were objectionable, but since they have largely been removed, they have left only the biological differences and they can hardly be blamed on law. It is therefore not uncommon to find references to the inappropriate indignities suffered by married women prior to the Married Women's Property Acts, which, happily, have now been removed.[19] As recently as 1991, the Australian High Court made such a manoeuvre in rejecting the spousal immunity from rape prosecution.[20] The Court dissociated itself from the shadowy past, regarding the immunity as anomalous and asserting the modern equality of all women. What it failed to cognise is the

[17] On the competence of children see D Price, "The Criminal Liability of Children" (1995) 69 *Australian Law Journal* 593; M Grove, "Are You Old Enough? In Defence of Doli Incapax" (1996) 70 *Law Institute Journal* 38; F Schoeman, "Childhood Competence and Autonomy" (1983) 12 *Journal of Legal Studies* 267; M Freeman, "Whither Children: Protection, Participation, Autonomy?" (1994) 22 *Manitoba Law Journal* 307; K Federle, "On the Road to Reconceiving Rights for Children: A Postfeminist Analysis of the Capacity Principle" (1993) 42 *De Paul Law Review* 983.

On the competence of persons with an intellectual disability or mental illness see J Dawson, "The Changing Legal Status of Mentally Disabled People" (1994) 2 *Journal of Law & Medicine* 38; Minow, *supra* n. 16; W Krais, "The Incompetent Developmentally Disabled Person's Right of Self-Determination: Right to Die, Sterilisation and Institutionalisation" (1989) 15 *American Journal of Law & Medicine* 333; J O'Sullivan, *Mental Health and the Law* (Sydney, Law Book Co, 1981); J Hall, T Payne and J Simpson (eds.), *Legal Rights and Intellectual Disability: A Short Guide* (Redfern, Intellectual Disability Rights Service, Redfern Legal Centre, 1986); G Ashton and A Ward, *Mental Handicap and the Law* (London, Sweet & Maxwell, 1992); B Hoggett, *Mental Health Law*, 3rd edn. (London, Sweet & Maxwell, 1990); J Williams, *The Law of Mental Health* (London, Format Publishing, 1990); J Blackwood, "Medical Treatment of the Intellectually Disabled Child" (1994) 1 *Journal of Law & Medicine* 252; C Witting, "Medical Decision-Making for the Incompetent" (1996) 3 *Journal of Law & Medicine* 377; J W Berg, P S Appelbaum and T Grisso, "Constructing Competence: Formulating Standards of Legal Competence to Make Medical Decisions" (1996) 48 *Rutgers Law Review* 345.

[18] There is nothing natural or inevitable about the limits and nature of childhood, for example, which determines that those designated children should assume only a certain level of legal responsibility. Thus the age of consent has undergone dramatic and sex-specific changes according to changing cultural assumptions about sexual maturity.

[19] See R H Graveson, *Status in the Common Law* (London, Athlone Press, 1953) 21.

[20] See *R* v. *L* (1991) 174 CLR 379.

continuing legal force of the term "woman", a legal concept whose compulsions and disabilities are most manifest when a woman is pregnant[21] but which shapes the lives of all women. Because the persisting sexual divisions in law are thought to come not from law, but from the sexes themselves, it seems that feminists who question the continuing legal use of the concept of "woman", and its relation to the concept of person, are simply being perverse.[22] They are trying to undo the work of God or nature; they are foolishly attempting the impossible.[23]

III FROM STATUS TO CONTRACT—FROM PERSONA TO PERSONALITY? WHO IS THE MODERN LEGAL PERSON?

To make sense of modern understandings of the legal person and their implications for women as a modern legal category, we need to know something of the antecedents of the concept. As Lon Fuller expressed it, "legal language of today is in part, at least, composed of the dead shells of former pretences".[24] There are two prominent orthodox histories of the concept, both of which describe the broad shifts in legal thought about the nature of the juridical person. In legal circles, the more familiar history is that sketched by Sir Henry Maine which depicts the movement of legal relations from those based on publicly-imposed status to those based on individually-chosen contracts. The other account traces the development of the etymology of the word person, a linguistic development which closely tracks the changes in legal meaning of the concept and so is often drawn on by lawyers to demonstrate changes in legal thought about the term. Perhaps the most celebrated account of this linguistic history is that supplied by the French anthropologist, Marcel Mauss. Both histories of the person are illuminating, though they stress slightly different aspects of his emerging character.

Maine's story of the rise of modern Anglo-American law is delivered as a tale of human progress and liberation. Maine describes a shift from medieval society, which was highly stratified, and in which status derived from custom, to modern society, in which relations are now based on personally-chosen contracts.[25] In the medieval world depicted by Maine, persons took their nature and their status from a place they were assigned by tradition and by law. Thus they were positively

[21] See discussion of the legal treatment of pregnant women, below, and also G Calabresi, "Do we Own Our Bodies?" (1991) 1 *Health Matrix* 5.

[22] See Minow, *supra* n. 16; Lacey, *supra* n. 13; K O'Donovan, *Sexual Divisions in Law* (London, Weidenfeld & Nicolson, 1985). On the way law continues to naturalise the category of woman see N Naffine and R Owens, "Sexing Law" in N Naffine and R Owens (eds.), *Sexing the Subject of Law* (Sydney, LBC Information Services, 1997) 3–6; Smart, *supra* n. 4. This is not to suggest that feminists necessarily wish to abandon the category of woman. It is to suggest that they continue to object to its current legal meaning and deployment.

[23] This is not to suggest a direct engagement by most jurisprudes with the writings of feminists. Although I have spelled out the implicit logic of their arguments, there are few jurisprudential critiques of feminism.

[24] L Fuller, *Legal Fictions* (Stanford, Cal., Stanford University Press, 1967) 20.

[25] H Maine, *Ancient Law* (London, John Murray, 1930).

obliged to assume relations of dependence. With the shift to contract, "[t]he individual [was] steadily substituted for the Family, as the unit of which civil laws take account".[26] Family ties and community obligations no longer encumbered the individual. The legal person was thus relieved of the suffocating relations of externally-imposed status and emerged as a sovereign individual—rational, self-determining and autonomous. Now he only ventured into society when he chose to do so, when he needed something done; when other people served a clear instrumental purpose. Otherwise, he was largely content with his own company and could manage well on his own.

A history of personality traced through its shifting etymology further accentuates the sense we have of the modern person as a particular social and psychological being, living in his own interior or private world, self-defined, not other-defined. In this account, the critical shift is one in which the person is released from the strictures of a public role or character—a *persona*—and is allowed to assume a private, distinctive individual *personality*: this being clearly bears a close relation to the self-defining man of contract. Here the point is not simply that made by Maine, that relations are now a matter of choice, rather than involuntary, externally-imposed obligation, but that a new type of mental being emerges who is not constituted in a social manner but who is self-knowing and so self-constituting and who asserts his individual personality against the rest of the world. The highly individualistic psychology of the person is more to the fore.

"The earliest traceable meaning of *persona*", according to Duff, "is a mask, such as Greek and Roman actors regularly wore on the stage".[27] As Keeton explains:

> "Originally it meant simply a mask. Later it denotes the part played by a man in life, and still later, the man who plays it. . . . Last of all, the term comes to denote a being capable of sustaining legal rights and duties."[28]

John Austin describes the linguistic process in terms of a series of metaphorical shifts:

> "It signified, originally, a mask worn by a player, to mark the character he bore in the piece: and is transferred by a metaphor to the character itself. By a further metaphor it is transferred from dramatic character to legal condition. For men as subjects of law are distinguished by conditions, just as players by the characters they present."[29]

In his influential study of the category of the person, Marcel Mauss questions the Latin origins of the term, speculating that they might be Etruscan, but concedes that "if it is not the Latins who invented the word and the institutions, at least it was they who gave it the original meaning which has become our own".[30] Mauss

[26] *Ibid.*, at 168.

[27] P W Duff, *Personality in Roman Private Law* (Cambridge, Cambridge University Press, 1938) 3.

[28] G W Keeton, *The Elementary Principles of Jurisprudence* (London, Sir Isaac Pitman and Sons, 1930) 117.

[29] Austin, *supra* n. 7, at 164.

[30] M Mauss, "A Category of the Human Mind: The Notion of Person; The Notion of Self" in M Carrithers, S Collins and S Lukes (eds.), *The Category of the Person: Anthropology, Philosophy, History* (Cambridge, Cambridge University Press, 1985) 15. In this volume, scholars from the three disciplines named in the title were asked to respond to Mauss's assessment of the concept.

documents the transformation in meaning from that of a mask or "superimposed image" to "the individual, with his nature laid bare and every mask torn away" and finally to the "psychological being" who is characterised by his "self-knowledge" and self-consciousness and who thus acquires moral status. While a sense of artificiality is integral to the first meaning of person, with its idea of a "role-player" or "man clad in a condition" (personage), as we move slowly towards the modern meaning we acquire a sense of "man, quite simply, that of the human person" and of "the innermost nature of this 'person' (personne)"[31] and then, ultimately, to the present, we have the person conceived of as inner or interior individual, as rational self-consciousness and pure reason. This final advance in our conception of the person Mauss attributes in part to Kant, but more importantly to Fichte, for whom "every act of consciousness was an act of the 'self' ".[32]

Mauss finds this final recognition of the person or self as an assertion of individual consciousness, an impressive accomplishment: he writes with pride of the modern person with his moral strength derived from his powers of reason; this concept is a "great possession" to be defended. He worries that,

> "the sacred character of the human 'person' . . . is questioned, not only throughout the Orient, which has not yet attained the level of our sciences, but even in the countries where this principle was discovered".[33]

There are therefore striking similarities between Maine, with his talk of the liberating effects of the shift to contract, and the emergence of the autonomous individual, and Mauss with his praise for the modern person conceived as "self-knowledge" and individual "psychological consciousness".[34]

Feminist and other legal critics have tended to give a less sanguine account of the modernisation of legal personality.[35] In this darker history of the law of persons, it was founded on, and is still reliant on, a binary view of human beings, as either normal or abnormal, and law's women have yet to accede to normality. Legal women are neither expected nor allowed to be the sovereign, private, rational subjects described variously by Maine and Mauss. Women's exclusion from the benefits of full legal personhood, and thus from the legal idea of normality, was once explicit. As John Dawson observes,

> "[c]hildren, married women, bankrupts, lunatics, Jews and foreigners have all been assigned a distinct legal status within the history of the common law, distinguishing their legal position from the norm of the adult, male, solvent, sane, Christian citizen".[36]

[31] M Mauss, "A Category of the Human Mind: The Notion of Person; The Notion of Self" in M Carrithers, S Collins and S Lukes (eds.), *The Category of the Person: Anthropology, Philosophy, History* (Cambridge, Cambridge University Press, 1985), *Ibid.* at 18–19, 22.

[32] *Ibid.*, at 22.

[33] *Ibid.*

[34] *Ibid.*, at 20.

[35] See for example Minow, *supra* n. 16.

[36] Dawson, *supra* n. 17, at 41.

Through a gradual legal process, involving the Married Women's Property Acts[37] and then the persons' cases,[38] all women were supposed to have become full persons in law—to have made the final move from status to contract. However, in the feminist account, the modernisation of legal personality did not entail a true relinquishing of the disabling status of the legal category of woman; nor did it abandon the concept of a human norm, and its necessary implication of abnormal types, with women firmly cast among them.

Proving that this is so has been difficult and the orthodox jurist is still far from convinced. One reason why it is not easy to discern the retention of a male norm within our jurisprudence is that the law of persons is so dispersed across the different parts of law, and so variable from human being to human being. One can not go to a single legal document to find an overarching, all-purpose definition of a legal person. Moreover, we lack a modern Blackstone who can supply us with a taxonomy of modern legal abilities and disabilities as they still apply to different human beings.[39] And of course it would be considered decidedly illiberal to produce such a manifestly discriminatory list. After all, the governing idea is that the law of persons does not so divide the populace.

Nevertheless it is possible, in the first instance, to make some fairly uncontroversial remarks about how the concept of the legal person works. Modern legal personality lacks a persistent character over time and place; even its beginnings and cessation are not easy to recognise.[40] Rather, legal personality is better regarded as a cluster of rights and duties which greatly varies according to such factors as age (regarded as a natural category), sex (also regarded as a natural category), mental ability (ditto), legal purpose and jurisdiction. For some purposes, an entity may have no or little ability to function in law, but for other purposes may be said to be in rude good health.[41] Thus a person with a mental disability may not be able to enter into an enforceable contract (if she is unable to appreciate its

[37] The dates of the first Married Women's Property Act are in the UK 1870, NSW 1886, Qld 1890, SA 1883, Tas 1884, Vic 1870, WA 1892. In the United States, the first State to pass a Married Women's Property Act was Mississippi in 1839.

[38] See the discussion in A Sachs and J H Wilson, *Sexism and the Law: A Study of Male Beliefs and Legal Bias in Britain and the United States* (Oxford, Martin Robertson, 1978).

[39] Blackstone's *Commentaries on the Laws of England*, reprint of 1st edn., 1765 (Chicago, Chicago University Press, 1979) endeavoured to bring together in one document the common law of England. Volume I contains a detailed taxonomy of persons.

[40] Although legal birth is supposed to be coterminous with biological birth, the foetus may be said to have a number of legal rights and so to exist as a legal person for certain purposes. For example it can be the beneficiary of a will, though this capacity only crystallises at birth. See *Wallis* v. *Hodson* (1740) 26 ER 472; *In Estate of K* (1996) 5 Tas R 365. Similarly legal death is supposed to be coterminous with biological death and yet the wishes of the deceased are respected in the will, leading some legal commentators (such as Tur) to suggest that biological death does not represent the complete termination of the legal person. See Tur, *supra* n. 9.

[41] As Richard Tur explains: "The law will ascribe legal personality to two entities even where they bear different clusters of rights and duties." Tur therefore describes legal personality as "a cluster concept, where in some cases a different cluster of rights and duties is present, and in other cases a different cluster of rights is present, perhaps somewhat overlapping with the first. . . . [I]t is conceivable that two entities, both of which are legal persons, might have no rights and duties in common at all." Tur, *supra* n. 9, at 116, 122.

terms),[42] but she may, with the aid of another, be able to sue for damages suffered as a consequence of a civil wrong. According to Salmond:

> "So far as legal theory is concerned, a person is any being whom the law regards as capable of rights or duties. Any being that is so capable is a person, whether a human being or not, and no being that is not so capable is a person, even though he be a man."[43]

Richard Tur explains that even the thinnest set of rights will constitute a legal person, because personhood is "a matter of degree".[44]

However, it is perfectly sensible to speak of a legal person in the full flush of legal existence, the person who is best able to act in law in his various legal capacities. And, as we will see, it transpires that the healthiest legal person is remarkably similar to the "normal" person of the former status societies described by Maine. This similarity may supply a further reason why orthodox theorists have found it difficult to discern this normal, ideal type of legal being: that is, he is positively characterised by his legal abilities rather than his disabilities, but it is the incapacity to act in law which has drawn particular legal attention and has been the subject of specific case and statute law. The absence of legal fetters is less easy to perceive than their presence.

How may this normal legal person be characterised? He is in the first instance manifestly an adult still. In law there is a fairly stark division between adults and children so that infancy remains an uncontroversial basis for diminishing a person's legal rights and duties.[45] He is also a rational adult: mental disease and disability are also associated with reduced legal ability and responsibility.[46] Neither of these statuses are perhaps particularly remarkable. There may seem to be obvious, practical and humane reasons for them, though they have also attracted criticism for their excessive applications and for their stereotyping. However, feminists and other legal critics would insist that modern status goes further than this: that the normal legal person is still sexed male. My aim in what follows is to identify just some of the ways in which feminists have sexed law's person. Feminist legal scholarship is of such breadth and depth, and is also now so specialised,[47] that this brief review of feminist theory will necessarily be selective. Its limited purpose is to demonstrate the deeply problematic nature of law's basic legal entity, as we currently understand it, as a means of securing legal equality for women.

[42] The ability of persons with an intellectual disability to make a contract depends on whether they understand the nature of each specific contract: *Gibbons* v. *Wright* (1954) 91 CLR 423. Intellectual disability also raises issues of undue influence and unconscionability.

[43] Salmond, *supra* n. 14, at 298.

[44] Tur, *supra* n. 9, at 122.

[45] See *supra* n. 17.

[46] See Minow, *supra* n. 16, and Dawson, *supra* n. 17, on the legal powers of the intellectually disabled.

[47] Thus there are feminist analysts of corporate law, international law and so on.

Explicit Sexing of the Legal Person

In the first instance, it has not been difficult for feminists to divine the various ways in which law still explicitly sexes. Despite the ostensible rejection of status and the insistence that modern identities and their constituting relations are now only acquired by choice, and despite the gender-neutrality of much legal language, the terms "man" and "woman" have retained a secure place within legal discourse as status categories.[48]

The sex status categories are perhaps most conspicuous within marriage laws which require one party to be a legal man and the other to be a legal woman. As the Australian High Court recently observed,

> "the institution of marriage and the status of husband and wife are inseparable from the connubial rights and obligations which are the incidents of the institution and which give content to the status".[49]

The form of marriage has changed little. It remains, as Lord Penzance described it in 1866 in *Hyde* v. *Hyde and Woodmansee*, "the voluntary union for life of one man and one woman, to the exclusion of all others".[50]

At first blush, it might appear that the explicit sexing of marriage laws is symmetrical, and therefore unobjectionable, for such laws not only invoke (legal) women, but they also invoke (legal) men. That is, marriage law could be said to give due recognition to *both* sexes, in liberal spirit, by imposing the same requirements on the two. As sex difference is generally thought to be natural, a pre-legal phenomenon, then this law is doing its best to accommodate such difference in an egalitarian, that is symmetrical, fashion. And certainly it is true that liberal ideals of equality and social and economic freedom have secured considerable legal benefits for married women. Within the modern law of marriage, women no longer automatically surrender their property to their husbands and the legal identities of husband and wives are now said to be separate and distinct; coverture has gone. Thus it might seem that the sexes within marriage are now legal equals who are free to engage in marital relations of their choice; they are in direct and unfettered relation with one another.

The most obvious liberal feminist objection to the sexing performed by marriage laws is that it is not truly liberal because it excludes legal men and legal women who may wish to marry their own sex. The underlying assumption is that a legal sexual relation of man-to-man or woman-to-woman is somehow against (pre-legal) nature and so cannot be accommodated by law. (Until recently, sex between men was explicitly outlawed; sex between women was unregulated because it was beyond the legal imagination.) The continuing exclusion of same-sex couples from the benefits of legal marriage reveals law's supposition that the status of woman is

[48] The classic work on these compulsory sexual divisions remains O'Donovan, *supra* n. 22.

[49] *R* v. *L* (1991) 174 CLR 379 at 397–8.

[50] *Hyde* v. *Hyde and Woodmansee* (1866) LR 1 P&D 130 at 133.

in some fundamental and natural way linked to and complementary with that of man. However, there is a second, and perhaps more fundamental, manner in which such sexing also represents an illiberal fixing of identity. The point is that one simply must assume the legal status of man or woman if one is to fit within these (or any) sexed laws. If nature fails to do its sexing job properly, if it fails to produce two clearly differentiated sexes, then law will step in, imposing the same obligations.[51] The legal woman of marriage laws is all-woman; the legal man is all-man.

Those who wish to opt out of this binary system of sexing are rendered unintelligible within these legal norms. Such people are invisible to such laws: they are other to, or outside, law. Every legal document which demands a disclosure of one's sex entails this explicit binary sexing. Such sexing starts with the birth certificate and ends with the death certificate.[52] It consigns to an existential limbo those who do not see themselves as unambiguously one sex or the other, or who endeavour to change sex through surgical intervention.[53] Sexed laws are therefore illiberal and unegalitarian. For no legal symmetry can obtain between those who are sexed and those who are unsexed. It is not just that the unsexed have a lesser legal status, though this is necessarily true. The point is that the unsexed have no legal life at all, whenever they are confronted by such laws which sex.

In England, sex status categories are also explicit in rape laws.[54] Rape is a crime which can still only be committed by a man and until 1994 only a woman could be his victim. There is an asymmetry here which is not so manifest in marriage laws. Like marriage laws, English rape laws explicitly sex in that they are still directed at legal men and legal women in legal relation with one another, adopting different legal/sexual positions. (The addition of legal men to the category of potential victims did not in any fundamental way alter the configuration of sex which has been developed by the common law.)[55] Only the man can offend and only in certain seemingly male-specific ways and, until recently, only a woman could be the victim and only in certain female-specific ways which are congruent with the sex of the man.[56] (The inclusion of men in the category of rape victim was done by the simple inclusion of non-consenting anal intercourse, rather than through a basic reconceptualising of the sex of rape law. In other words, traditional

[51] See M Davies, "Taking the Inside Out: Sex and Gender in the Legal Subject" in Naffine and Owens (eds.), *supra* n. 22, at 25–46.

[52] The particulars required when registering a birth or death in SA are set out in regulations under the Births, Deaths and Marriages Registration Act 1996 (SA), and in England in regulations under the Births and Deaths Registration Act 1953 (UK).

[53] See A Alston, "Legal Aspects of Gender Reassignment" (1988) 5 *Journal of Law and Medicine* 279.

[54] See Criminal Justice and Public Order Act 1994 section 142. In Australia such laws are now gender neutral.

[55] Moreover the dedication of a separate section for "male rape and buggery" in the Criminal Justice and Public Order Act 1994 (section 143) suggests that the main rape offence (section 142) is still framed with women in mind.

[56] Intercourse is not explicitly defined in the 1994 Act. Section 142 simply asserts that "It is an offence for a man to rape a woman or another man" and "A man commits rape if he has sexual intercourse with a person (whether vaginal or anal) who . . . does not consent to it" which suggests that the act still entails penetrative sex with a penis.

heterosexual sex supplied the basic, penetrative model of sex.)[57] The sexuality presupposed is therefore explicitly asymmetrical. This legal casting of sexual difference might again look like an innocent aping of nature by law. After all, it is men who have penises and it is women who receive them in the act of heterosexual intercourse, so this is the relation to which law should respond. But it is not difficult to see that law is not simply echoing nature here, but requiring us to see sex between men and women in a quite particular fashion, one which serves to diminish our freedom to cast our sexualities in more imaginative forms. (We will return to this problem of sexual type-casting later in the paper.)

There is an even more sinister sexing occurring here, however, which I will examine shortly. The woman of English rape law is not only being allocated a particular sexual position and function designed to complement the male, but she is also being unpersonned by this form of sexing, while the man retains his personhood. The asymmetries of sex in law, I will argue, implicitly operate in such a way that the sexed man can still be a legal person but the sexed woman can not.

Implicit Sexing

The implicit sexing of the legal person as male was early recognised by feminists. One of the first aspects of the legal person to be subjected to feminist scrutiny was his basic character or personality. It was noted that the legal person tended to think and act the way men were conventionally thought to think and act. Thus he was marked by his assertiveness (which enabled him to flourish in the setting of the adversarial trial), his self-interest (which motivated him to assert vigorously his legal rights), his essential individualism (he assumed individual legal responsibility for his behaviour and he pursued individual, rather than class, actions) and his disinterested objectivity (the blind maiden remains the metaphor for the way of law). Indeed he seemed to take his nature from the positive exclusion of those characteristics which have traditionally been associated with women and from the consignment to women of those qualities and activities which would represent a diminution of his person.[58]

Many feminist lawyers were persuaded by the arguments of American psychologist, Carol Gilligan, that a male "ethic of justice" consequently pervaded legal thought and method at the expense of an "ethic of care" associated with the feminine.[59] The abstract, interior, private rational being applauded by Mauss was thus by implication a man whose very rational being was defined and delimited by the affective and social female: what he was in essence was not-female. Catharine

[57] This argument is developed further in N Naffine, "Possession: Erotic Love in the Law of Rape" (1994) 57 *Modern Law Review* 10.

[58] See N Naffine, *Law and the Sexes: Explorations in Feminist Jurisprudence* (Sydney, Allen & Unwin, 1990).

[59] These ideas are expounded in Gilligan's enormously influential book, *In a Different Voice: Psychological Theory and Women's Development* (Cambridge, Mass., Harvard University Press, 1982).

MacKinnon indeed maintained that when law appeared to be most objective, to be most dispassionate, to be most itself, it was most male. She also insisted that this did tremendous violence to women and made her point most dramatically in a trenchant critique of American rape laws.[60] In this account, legal man realised his male autonomy by what was in effect a traffic in women. To MacKinnon, men were the only beings clearly present in law; women were objects of sexual trade between men and thus forced sex was only ever outlawed when it broke the male lore of sex right. Though MacKinnon's claims were to remain controversial, even among feminist theorists,[61] the immunity of husbands from rape prosecution supported a central plank of her argument.[62]

Feminists have observed also that the very form of the legal subject is male in that the legal person is always perceived as unitary, never multiple. He is a self-contained individual who asserts himself against other self-contained individuals. Mauss's interior private being, Maine's contractual individual, can and must be able to remove himself from society and commune only with himself in order to realise his freedom. And, when he withdraws, there is only himself. He is alone and singular, withdrawn from the world and immersed in his own singular privately-constituted thoughts. In this understanding of human being, the pregnant woman becomes a human curiosity. Law's response to the pregnant woman has been generally to assert that only she is present in law and that the foetus has no legal status. Law has thus imposed a unity on the woman so that the foetus becomes a property of, or part of, her, rather than a separate legal entity. The most-cited authoritative legal statement on the status of the foetus is to be found in the English case of *Paton* v. *Trustees of British Pregnancy Advisory Services* where it was said:

> "The foetus cannot, in English law . . . have any right of its own at least until it is born and has a separate existence from its mother. That permeates the whole of the civil law of this country . . . and is indeed the basis of the decisions in those countries where law is founded on the common law, that is to say, America, Canada, Australia, and, I have no doubt, in others."[63]

The Australian Family Court has confirmed also that a "foetus has no legal personality and cannot have a right of its own until it is born and has a separate existence

[60] See C MacKinnon, "Feminism, Marxism, Method, and the State: An Agenda for Theory" (1982) 7 *Signs* 515; C MacKinnon, "Feminism, Marxism, Method, and the State: Toward Feminist Jurisprudence" (1983) 8 *Signs*, 635.

[61] In particular there remained concerns about her claim that women's oppression was so thoroughgoing that it effectively silenced women, and MacKinnon's own declarations were taken as proof against it. See D Cornell, *Beyond Accommodation: Ethical Feminism, Deconstruction and the Law* (New York, Routledge, 1991) Chapter 3; D Cornell, "Sexual Difference, the Feminine, and Equivalency: A Critique of MacKinnon's Toward a Feminist Theory of the State" (1991) 100 *Yale Law Journal* 2247.

[62] The cases which only recently abolished this immunity are for Scotland: *S* v. *HM Advocate* [1989] SLT 469; for England: *R* v. *R* [1991] 4 All ER 481; for Australia: *R* v. *L* (1991) 174 CLR 379.

[63] [1978] 2 All ER 987at 989. Though we should note the unease recently expressed by the House of Lords at this existential erasure of the foetus at law, while at the same time confirming it: see *Attorney-General's Reference (No. 3 of 1994)* [1996] 2 All ER 10.

from its mother".[64] And yet, despite these firm declarations of the singularity and consequent autonomy of the pregnant woman, the law does not in truth maintain a consistent attitude towards her. Instead, it declares a powerful state interest in her physical being, through abortion laws which permit legal controls and interventions which would be unthinkable if women were full legal persons (for whom bodily autonomy is everything).[65] It renders the condition of pregnancy legally disabling and reduces the pregnant woman to an abnormal legal subject, with less than the full complement of rights—while maintaining all the time that pregnant women are autonomous and unitary legal subjects. While this duplicity is routinely exercised in the laws governing abortion,[66] its most dramatic manifestation has been in those English and American judicial declarations and decisions which have approved caesarean sections against the wishes of the pregnant woman.[67]

Further evidence of the pregnant woman's incongruity in law, of her abnormal status, comes from those cases in which women have positively endeavoured to have the specific effects of pregnancy recognised and legally accommodated. To fit themselves within the legal model of the person, they have been obliged to find a similarly-situated man with which to compare themselves. Pregnant women have therefore found it necessary to find parallels between female pregnancy and male sickness,[68] for legal persons do not reproduce and divide in this manner. Certainly they are never pregnant.

The unitary legal subject preserves his male integrity, not only by never being more than one, but also by never allowing others within himself or merging himself with others. Thus a common characterisation of the legal person, which draws heavily on liberal understandings of the autonomous individual, is as a self-owner. "To be a full individual in liberal society", as Katherine O'Donovan observes, "one must be an appropriator, defined by what one owns, including oneself as a possession, not

[64] *In the Marriage of F* (1989) 13 Fam LR 189, per Lindenmayer J. The Australian High Court has similarly stated that "a foetus has no right of its own until it is born and has a separate existence from its mother": *A-G (Qld) (Ex rel Kerr)* v. *T* (1983) 57 ALJR 285 at 286, per Gibbs CJ.

[65] This is not to recommend necessarily the removal of all laws governing abortion. The point is one about legal consistency.

[66] See Calabresi, *supra* n. 21.

[67] See especially *Jefferson* v. *Griffin Spalding County Hospital Authority* 247 Ga 86, 274 SE 2d 457 (Supreme Court of Georgia, 1981) and *In re Madyun* (DC Super. Ct. 26 July 1986) (114 Daily Wash. L. Rptr. 2233). But note that more recently the Appellate Court of Illinois (*In re Baby Boy Doe* 632 NE2d 326, 333 (1994)) refused to compel a woman to undergo a caesarean section, asserting that "the rights of the foetus should not be balanced against the rights of the mother". For the English approach see *Re MB (Medical Treatment)* [1997] 2 FLR 426, where the English Court of Appeal asserted the absolute right of a pregnant woman to refuse treatment but then approved a judicial declaration to proceed with a caesarean against her wishes, with the use of force if necessary. The woman in question had a chronic fear of needles and the Court decided that this fear rendered her incompetent. More recently, the English Court of Appeal disapproved a judicial declaration dispensing with the woman's consent to a caesarean section (the judge who issued the declaration deemed her incompetent despite a highly articulate written and verbal refusal of consent), but only after the caesarean had been performed. See *St George's Healthcare NHS Trust* v. *S* [1998] 3 WLR 913.

[68] See N Lacey, "From Individual to Group? A Feminist Analysis of the Limits of Anti-Discrimination Legislation", in Lacey, *supra* n. 13, at 24.

depending on others, free".[69] John Christman confirms that "[a] powerful way of expressing the principle of individual liberty is to claim that every individual has full 'property rights' over her body, skills and labour".[70]

To John Frow the very "form of the person" in Western liberal legal thought is one of "self-possession".[71] Or as Cohen, endorsing Nozick, expresses it, the person "possesses over himself, as a matter of moral right, all those rights that a slaveholder has over a complete chattel slave as a matter of legal right".[72]

Fundamental to self-ownership is self-control, the policing of clear personal territorial limits, and the exclusion of others. Integrity as a legal person characterised as self-proprietor thus depends on the preservation of one's physical boundaries. It is for this reason that American constitutional lawyer Jennifer Nedelsky has referred to the legal person as a "bounded self".[73] This "bounded" understanding of the person is conspicuous in the criminal and civil law governing human contact. As Lord Justice Goff declared in *Collins* v. *Wilcock*:

> "the fundamental principle, plain and incontestable, is that every person's body is inviolate. It has long been established that any touching of another person, however slight, may amount to a battery."[74]

In the common law tradition, this view may be traced to William Blackstone, who asserted that "every man's person being sacred . . . no other ha[s] a right to meddle with it, in any the slightest manner".[75]

A problem with this model of the person, as bounded self-proprietor, is that human beings do not maintain their body boundaries: for one thing, they periodically "meddle" with one another by engaging in sexual intercourse (and for another, as we have noted, humans are sometimes pregnant). A quite particular legal construction of sexual acts, however, has smoothed out this difficulty and ensured the compatibility of male sexual activity with self-proprietorship. At the same time, it has ensured the incompatibility of female sexuality with property-in-self. Thus sex has been interpreted in such a way that legal man does not lose his integrity in the act of intercourse with a woman, whether it is lawful or criminal. In blithe disregard of the actual diminutions and transformations in men's bodies when involved in (hetero)sex, somehow the legal male form manages to preserve its own distinctive nature.

[69] K O'Donovan, "With Sense, Consent, or Just a Con? Legal Subjects in the Discourses of Autonomy" in Naffine and Owens (eds.), *supra* n. 22, at 46.

[70] J Christman, "Self-Ownership, Equality and the Structure of Property Rights" (1991) 19 *Political Theory* 28 at 28.

[71] J Frow, "'Elvis' Fame: The Commodity Form and the Form of the Person" (1995) 7 *Cardozo Studies in Law and Literature* 131 at 149.

[72] G Cohen, "Self-Ownership, World-Ownership, and Equality" in F Lucash (ed.), *Justice and Equality Here and Now* (Ithaca, NY, Cornell University Press, 1986) 109.

[73] J Nedelsky, "Law, Boundaries and the Bounded Self" (1990) 30 *Representations* 162. See also M Davies, "Feminist Appropriations: Law, Property and Personality" (1994) 3 *Social and Legal Studies* 365.

[74] [1984] 3 All ER 374 at 378.

[75] Blackstone, *Commentaries on the Laws of England*, *supra* n. 39, III 120.

If we think of rape laws, for example, where sexual policing is to the fore, we can observe the workings of this two-sex system. When the legal vocabulary of rape laws assumed a more biblical form, it was easier to see how the man retained his identity and integrity in the act of sex, while the woman surrendered hers.[76] For rape was a man's "carnal knowledge" of a woman who was not his wife, against her will.[77] There was never any suggestion that the woman might know the man, lawfully or otherwise. The reason that a husband could not rape a wife, as Sir Matthew Hale explained, was that "by their mutual matrimonial consent and contract the wife has *given up herself* in this kind unto her husband, which she cannot retract".[78]

Indeed rape laws were originally devised as a means of preserving the sort of male property interests in women which were also the concern of the law of consortium—hence the right of the husband to the body of his wife, whatever her actual view of the matter.[79]

While modern rape laws have recently denied the husband this sex right,[80] the sexuality presupposed is little altered. Thus sex in the accepted English manner still entails the proposal of a man to "penetrate" a woman. The act is lawful when the woman agrees to be penetrated, or even just submits; it is rape when the woman refuses.[81] If considerable, even vigorous, persuasion is exercised to achieve this submission, but no direct force is applied or threatened, then the sexual act may still be interpreted as voluntary and normal, as no more than athletic seduction.[82] For normal sex is consistent with an active, appropriating male sexuality and a complementary passive and accommodating female sexuality.[83] The English laws of incest evince a similar view of sex. Thus it is an offence "for a man *to have* sexual intercourse with a woman whom he knows to be his grand-daughter [etc]" and "for a woman . . . *to permit* a man whom she knows to be her grandfather [etc] . . . to have

[76] For a fuller discussion of the possessive sexuality implicit in both the old and the modern laws see Naffine, *supra* n. 57.

[77] William Blackstone defined rape as "the carnal knowledge of a woman forcibly and against her will": *Commentaries on the Laws of England*, *supra* n. 39, IV 210. Edward Coke's definition was "the unlawfull and carnall knowledge and abuse of any woman above the age of ten years against her will, or of a woman child under the age of ten years with her will, or against her will": E Coke *The Institutes of the Law of England*, 15th edn. (London, E & R Brooke, 1797) III 60.

[78] M Hale, *History of the Pleas of the Crown*, reprint of 1736 edn. (London, Professional Books, 1971) I 629. (Emphasis added.)

[79] Australia, Model Criminal Code Officers Committee, *Model Criminal Code Chapter 5, Sexual Offences Against the Person: Discussion Paper* (1996) Introduction.

[80] The husband's immunity from rape prosecution endured late into the twentieth century. See *supra* n. 63.

[81] In jurisdictions which have rendered the crime gender-neutral, such as those of Australia, the sexual form has remained much the same. See Naffine, *supra* n. 57, and N Naffine, "Windows on the Legal Mind: Evocations of Rape in Legal Writing" (1992) 18 *Melbourne University Law Review* 741.

[82] The meaning of consent in Australian rape law has been subjected to critical scrutiny in V Waye, "Rape and the Unconscionable Bargain" (1992) 16 *Criminal Law Journal* 94.

[83] In Australia, this possessive form of sexuality was recently sanctioned by a current member of the South Australian Supreme Court. During a rape trial Bollen J approved the "no rougher than usual handling" of a husband by a wife, in order to persuade her to have sex. See *Case Stated by DPP (No 1 of 1993)* (1993) 66 A Crim R 259.

sexual intercourse with her by consent". The background understanding of conventional sexuality is one in which man retains the integrity of his person, his property-in-self, while he is "having" sex with a woman, while she allows herself to be had.[84] Such is the modest nature of her control over herself. While he preserves his bodily boundaries, his physical wholeness, her body walls are breached.

There is no sense that sexual congress entails the fusion or merging of man and woman or the engulfment of the man by the woman. Meanwhile sexual activities between women, where the self-contained man is entirely absent, have simply been rendered invisible by their omission from law.[85] They have no place in law's tacit sexual ontology. Thus is the sexual legal person as self-proprietor sexed male, while sexual woman is implicitly stripped of property-in-self and so unpersonned: this set of relations is not only built into law's appreciation of human sexuality, but it even manages to transfer its effects to men who choose to be "penetrated" by other men (by laws which have prohibited male homosexuality). The clear message of laws which proscribe sex between consenting men is that a man should not be unpersonned like a woman in the act of sex. A more risible example of law trying to keep the whole man whole and unfeminised is to be found in Tasmanian legislation which has outlawed men dressing like women after sundown.[86]

From this it follows that legal persons who engaged in sex in the highly variable ways people do, and according to their own lights,[87] would not be the persons we now recognise in law. There is good reason why orthodox legal theory has yet to elaborate an explicit and considered theory of sexual persons and has instead relied on disembodied abstractions of humanity (except when forced into the vulgar domain of sex laws with their crude couplings). The reason is that it would necessarily subvert the governing idea of a sovereign, abstract self-owning and implicitly male legal actor.

The compelling conclusion of this brief foray into feminist theory on the legal person is that legal women and legal persons are in many respects still mutually exclusive. The form of law's personification is to treat as paradigmatic person the autonomous, unitary (and therefore implicitly non-pregnant) rational contractual adult of full mental abilities.[88] To instantiate its ideal of the normal or proper person,[89] law sets up an individual who is apparently self-possessed, autonomous and

[84] Sexual Offences Act 1956 (UK) secton 10. For a brief analysis of the possessive language employed by English incest laws see N Lacey, C Wells and D Meure, *Reconstructing Criminal Law: Critical Perspectives on Crime and the Criminal Process* (London, Weidenfeld & Nicolson, 1990) 355.

[85] See R Robson, *Lesbian (Out)Law: Survival Under the Rule of Law* (Ithaca, NY, Firebrand Books, 1992).

[86] According to the Police Offences Act 1935 (Tas) section 8(1)(d): "A person shall not . . . being a male person, be in any public place at any time between sunset and sunrise, dressed in female apparel".

[87] For example, heterosexual women do not necessarily view the act as penetrative nor is penis to vagina sex necessarily the main act performed.

[88] This being has been described repeatedly in the critical jurisprudential literature, but see especially O'Donovan, *supra* n. 22.

[89] It is only quite recently that legal texts have ceased to refer to those who depart from this ideal as "abnormal". See for example T E Holland, *The Elements of Jurisprudence*, 11th edn. (Oxford, Clarendon Press, 1910) 137–8, 164–5, 334–52; Graveson, *supra* n. 19, at 2–3, 112.

sharply separated from other persons, even when engaged in the intimacies of sex.[90] As law currently understands its subject, legal women therefore simply cannot fulfil all the requirements of legal subjectivity (nor of course can many men) and in fact the case has been made by feminists for the positive dependence of the legal person, as currently conceived, on the negation and exclusion of women.[91] This means that women are constituted and positioned in law to perform a vital function of propping up the legal person and, from this position, they cannot be persons themselves. It can therefore be said that, in many ways, women are still mired in status—that they have not yet acceded to contract. This brings us to the question, Can the legal person do justice to women? Must we get rid of legal persons altogether? Do they have any redeeming features?

IV CAN WOMEN BE LEGAL PERSONS?

The progressive feature of the shift from status to contract and the idea of the self-legislating person has been emphasised by liberal feminists. It entails an apparent rejection of the fixing of identity by legal status categories and the emergence of the free, self-legislating individual. And it is true that women, as well as men, have derived considerable advantages from the liberal belief that persons should be permitted to choose their own relations and to define their own lives.[92] The point of this essay has been to show that this ostensible shift from status to contract, or, in Mauss's analysis, from public persona to private individual personality, has also operated in quite perverse, illiberal, and even counter-intuitive ways. Though I do not wish to deny the positive benefits that women and other status categories have derived through an appeal to liberal ideals, it must also be said that the modernisation of the law of persons has not led to the free negotiation of identity in law. In fact, in many respects it has served to conceal the different ways the state continues to impose forms of human being. With Blackstone's *Commentaries* and its legal taxonomy of persons now regarded as an historical curiosity, and the law of persons now largely a non-topic in contemporary jurisprudence, this persistent compulsory shaping of personality is rarely considered by lawyers, with the conspicuous exception of the inquiries of feminist (and some other critical) legal theorists.

What feminists have brought to light is not only the unethical retention of women as status category, but also the denaturing and diminution of human being within the legal subject—that is, the impoverishment of legal being. Once explicitly situated within, and constituted by, a complex network of socio-legal relations,

[90] Frances Olsen has described law's persons as "separated owners of their respective bundles of rights": "Statutory Rape: A Feminist Critique of Rights Analysis" (1984) 63 *Texas Law Review* 387 at 393.

[91] This has been the argument of much of this paper but see also Naffine, *supra* n. 57, and N Naffine, "Sexing the Subject of Law" in M. Thornton (ed.), *Public and Private: Feminist Legal Debates* (Oxford, Oxford University Press, 1995).

[92] Indeed feminists still take advantage of the liberal ideal of the autonomous legal subject to press their claims for the equal treatment of women.

the modern legal person has now been stripped of his social nature in such a thoroughgoing manner that he is barely recognisable as a social animal. The perverse effect of this wrenching from context, whose progressive purpose was to liberate, is that the legal person is thus disabled from negotiating and renegotiating his identity. In particular, he cannot change in ways that threaten or replace his contractual relations.

A mutable identity is only possible if, from moment to moment, I am not pinned down to a single persona but can be a particular being-in-process and in-relation. If I am allowed to be specifically responsive to you, as a human particular, if you are allowed to make your mark on me, and if I am correspondingly allowed to evoke responses in you to the particular which is me, only then do I have freedom of identity in relation. I am not just colliding with (or positively avoiding) others in the world, but engaging with them as an agent (and an object) of change. In this account of being human, I am constantly in transformation as I commune with others. However, if I cannot thus engage with others, if my self-understanding is not allowed to shape, and be shaped by others, if I am isolated from the transforming effects of the social world on me, then there is a certain fixity to my person. Law's bounded person is not only barred from social relations outside the impersonal contractual form, but he is also isolated from himself. He is denied access to the multiple characters which might otherwise form and enrich his public personae, for these are deemed to be always extraneous and threatening to the true self. They are merely inauthentic and potentially suffocating public roles. The authentic person must draw all his material for his own being from himself.

This person-in-relation has been theorised in various ways. Charles Taylor describes this more fluid understanding of personality, which he believes has been damaged with the privatisation of the subject, as one in which the individual is an interlocutor. To Taylor,

> "we have partly lost . . . the way in which we accede to the status of human subjects through being taken up as interlocutors in an exchange that pre-exists us. . . . And this may help to explain the importance of personae and names in some of the societies examined. Being given a name is being inducted into a linguistic exchange, being designated as an interlocutor. . . . To have the name, or perhaps the mask, is to be the interlocutor."[93]

To Drucilla Cornell:

> "Transformation is demanded of us precisely because there is no self-enclosed subject who can truly cut herself off from the Other. We are constantly being challenged by otherness, including the otherness which marks the boundaries of the self 'within', such as the unconscious."[94]

[93] C Taylor, "The Person", in Carrithers, Collins and Lukes, *supra* n. 30, at 279.

[94] D Cornell, "Convention and Critique" in D Cornell, *Transformations* (New York, Routledge 1993) 15.

Emmanuel Levinas has described a relational self which comes into being through an openness to the other.[95] Jennifer Nedelsky has theorised a legal person whose freedoms positively derive from enabling relations.[96]

The legal person has also been denied the remarkable transformations to his being wrought by time. Arrested in a perpetual adulthood, where he seems largely to be occupied with fairly dry and impersonal contractual negotiations, he is disallowed the movement and change (even joy and wonder) associated with human growth and maturation. What is missing from the orthodoxy of legal personality is therefore any sense of what Grant Gillett has called the "longitudinal form" of human being.[97] A number of philosophers have theorised the relation between the person and time. Heidegger regarded time as the essence of being—with the person engaged in the furious creative activity of projecting himself into a future in the light of his past.[98] William James recognised the temporal dimension of being, which he too depicted as a positive gathering up of the past though active imagination.[99] The legal person seems to lack the creativity and agency to see himself in all of his forms over time.

The sex life of the legal person is also a sad and stunted thing.[100] No transforming delights for him here as he engages in the crude mechanics of the thrust and withdrawal. Absent from legal understandings of the person is the corporeality of being; our extension in a world of other physical beings. In law we lack a sense of the ebb, flow, pulsation and fluidity of our physical natures. We may do well to draw on the insights of such philosophers of corporeality as Maurice Merleau-Ponty[101] and Elizabeth Grosz[102] who have sought to explore the existential significance of our physically being in the world.

So to the question, "Can the legal person do justice to women?" one would have to reply that, in his current form, he serves both sexes poorly but that he does a particular disservice to women. Moreover, it is unlikely that women would want to assume such an unattractive personality, with so little life in it. Paradoxically it is the lack of agency, the lack of creativity, the shrivelled being, of the normal person of liberal law that gives him such an undesirable nature. However, a legal person in relation is another thing—a legal person who is not in fact singular but equipped with many natures in transformation could well encompass women, who

[95] E Levinas, *Otherwise than Being or Beyond Essence*, trans. A Lingis (The Hague, Martinus Nijhoff, 1981).

[96] J Nedelsky, "Reconceiving Autonomy: Sources, Thoughts and Possibilities" in A Hutchinson and L Green (eds.), *Law and the Community: The End of Individualism?* (Toronto, Carswell, 1989) 230.

[97] G Gillett, "Ethics and Embryos" (1991) 17 *Journal of Medical Ethics* 62 at 63.

[98] M Heidegger, *Being and Time* (Oxford, Basil Blackwell, 1962).

[99] W James, *The Principles of Psychology* (London, Macmillan, 1890) and W James, *William James: A Selection from his Writings on Psychology*, M Knight (ed.) (Harmondsworth, Middlesex, Penguin, 1950).

[100] For an imaginative endeavour to enrich the legal understanding of sexual autonomy see N Lacey, "Unspeakable Subjects, Impossible Right: Sexuality, Integrity and Criminal Law" in Lacey, *supra* n. 13, at 98.

[101] M Merleau-Ponty, *The Phenomenology of Perception*, trans. C Smith (London, Routledge & Kegan Paul, 1962).

[102] E Grosz, *Volatile Bodies: Towards a Corporeal Feminism* (Sydney, Allen & Unwin, 1994).

might then even disappear as a significant grouping altogether, or assume new sexual forms. For the moment, we would do well to treat with suspicion every existing invocation of the legal woman in view of her unhealthy relationship with the man of law—she remains a suspect status category, with a bleak history of abuse and a current persona which often still serves the interests of others, not herself.

4

Feminism and the Promise of Human Rights: Possibilities and Paradoxes

STEPHANIE PALMER*

WE LIVE IN an era of human rights. The tradition of rights has become a fundamental element of our legal philosophy, our political life and imaginary aspirations: their moral authority cannot be easily dismissed. Human rights in the liberal legal system hold out the promise of emancipation through reason and law. They can form a vital bulwark against the arbitrary exercise of public and private power and a powerful discourse in both international and domestic law. The idea of human rights provides an ethical component to law, politics and international relations.

An affinity exists between human rights and feminism. On one level both operate as ideals, containing utopian elements with their commitment to progressive social change. Both place an emphasis on the concept of power and its influence on social relations. As movements seeking social transformation, theoretical developments have been entwined with demands for political change. Human rights are a powerful tool: they promise a world in which individuals are not oppressed or degraded. While a force for emancipation that can probably never be fully realised, they are a significant mechanism for judging the justice of rights in the liberal legal system.[1]

Feminist theory also provides a critical vantage point from which to assess the ethics of law. The primary focus of feminism is on the concept of "gender as a central organising principle of social life" and on attempts to understand the position of all oppressed groups.[2] Some would argue that women's rights are already protected by international and domestic human rights law. Civil and political rights, for example, include the concept of non-discrimination and equality.[3] Feminist

* I would like to thank Susan Marks, Leslie Turano and Pippa Rogerson for their comments on an earlier draft. The usual disclaimers apply.

[1] Some critics have claimed that human rights have now lost their critical edge. See C Douzinas, *The End of Human Rights: Critical Legal Thought at the Turn of the Century* (Oxford, Hart Publishing, 2000).

[2] S Millns and N Whitty, "Public Law and Feminism" in S Millns and N Whitty (eds.), *Feminist Perspectives on Public Law* (London, Cavendish, 1999) 1. Feminism itself is characterised by a multiplicity of approaches.

[3] See for example, Art. 26(1) International Covenant on Civil and Political Rights; Art. 14 European Convention on Human Rights and Protocol 12; Sex Discrimination Act 1975 and Art. 141 EC Treaty.

ideas, to some extent, have permeated thinking about human rights and led to the expansion of human rights concepts to encompass more effectively women's rights. For example, sex-specific rights concerning bodily integrity have been further developed by feminists and added to international legal instruments.[4] In spite of the overlapping concerns, women's rights have never been a central theme of human rights: women's rights discourse is usually positioned at the "periphery of human rights discourse".[5] Too often, there is a specific lack of recognition of women's rights as human rights where women's experience is distinct from that of men. Apart from the valuable but limited promise of formal equality, the application of international human rights norms to women have been largely ignored by "mainstream" human rights bodies.[6] Nevertheless, some feminists have cautiously argued that human rights may provide a viable avenue to achieve feminist objectives: a way to provide additional protection and rights for women and to give women a voice in the legal world.[7]

This chapter explores the possibility of drawing upon the shared aspirations of human rights and feminist theory to consider the strategic possibilities. The Human Rights Act 1998, incorporating the European Convention on Human Rights into domestic UK law, provides a possibility of reframing debates and challenging existing legal categories. Feminists should not ignore the opportunities provided by such legal changes. Yet puzzles remain to be considered. On the one hand, feminists demand that law respect the dignity and human rights of women while on the other, many feminist theorists are sceptical of the individualist premise of liberal theory. Ultimately, the concept of human rights remains entrenched in the world of liberal legalism. Some feminists have argued that the articulation of political demands in terms of rights is misguided in a legal world antipathetic to feminist concerns: the institutionalisation of rights results in a loss of their transformative effect. These paradoxes reflect the problem inherent in building a theory and practice that combines respect for individual freedom and recognises the social nature of human beings. To what extent then can feminism deploy the concept of human rights to achieve its own objectives?

[4] See for example, Declaration on the Elimination of Violence Against Women, G.A. Res. 104, UN GAOR, 48th Sess., UN Doc. 1/49/104 91993). See also K Hevener, "An Analysis of Gender Based Treaty Law: Contemporary Developments in Historical Perspective" (1986) 8 *Human Rights Quarterly*. 70 at 87–8.

[5] K Engle, "International Human Rights and Feminism: When Discourses Meet" (1992) *13 Michigan Journal of International Law* 517 at 519. See also H Charlesworth, C Chinkin and S Wright, "Feminist Approaches to International Law" (1991) 85 *American Journal of International Law* 613; and C Bunch, "Women's Rights as Human Rights: Toward a Revision of Human Rights" (1990) 12 *Human Rights Quarterly* 486.

[6] H Charlesworth, "What are Women's Human Rights?" in R Cook (ed.), *Human Rights of Women: National and International Perspectives* (Philadelphia, University of Pennsylvania Press, 1994) 58.

[7] J Nedelsky, "The Practical Possibilities of Feminist Theory" (1993) 87 *Northwestern University Law Review* 1286; S Palmer, "Critical Perspectives on Women's Rights: The European Convention on Human Rights and Fundamental Freedoms" in A Bottomley (ed.), *Feminist Perspectives on the Foundational Subjects of Law* (London, Cavendish, 1996); and S Millns, "'Bringing Rights Home': Feminism and the Human Rights Act 1998" in Millns and Whitty, *Feminist Perspectives on Public Law*, *supra* n. 2.

This chapter initially explores some feminist scholarship and its uneasy engagement with law. It will then analyse some of the European Convention rights secured in the United Kingdom through the Human Rights Act 1998 and the potential for feminist approaches.

THE LEGAL SUBJECT AND RIGHTS

Feminist engagement with human rights raises questions about the space within legal discourse for feminist voices. Historically, women were invisible in law as they had no standing as persons who could possess legal rights.[8] They were excluded from the systems that created, interpreted and applied the laws.[9] Early feminism aimed to achieve equality through the admission of women to those spheres of public life from which they had been excluded, including the legal world. During the twentieth century, much of the struggle by women in the UK and the rest of the Western world concerned extending the "rights of man" to include women. It was assumed that that the inclusion of women would transform existing structures.

The androcentric nature of human rights law has only relatively recently been the subject of feminist analysis. Although human rights instruments are universal, historically women's rights have not been accommodated in the international law context. Burrows notes that:

> "Human rights discourse has traditionally been male dominated in the sense that, in what is essentially a man's world, men have struggled to assert their dignity and common humanity against an overbearing state apparatus. Attempts to define a body of civil and political rights were made from the eighteenth century onwards in societies that were organized by men and, predominantly, for men."[10]

She concludes that civil and political rights are not inherently male, but that the rights were designed to regulate the relations between men and the state. "Declarations of the rights of man reflected exactly that perspective."[11] In parallel with attempts to accommodate women in the national laws, legislative reforms in the international law context sought to place women in the same situation as men.[12]

As long as women as a group were considered to be ineligible for equal status with men because of the perceived "natural" difference between men and women, it was logical to challenge exclusion through demands for equal rights that were blind to gender differences.[13] In order for women to be included within legal

[8] N Naffine, "Can Women be Legal Persons?", *supra* 69 chap. 3 at 69 .

[9] See C Pateman, *The Sexual Contract* (Cambridge, Polity Press, 1988).

[10] N Burrows, "International Law and Human Rights: The Case of Women's Rights" in T Campbell et al. (eds.), *Human Rights: From Rhetoric to Reality* (New York, Basil Blackwell, 1986) 80.

[11] *Ibid.*, at 41.

[12] See the United Nations Convention on the Political Rights of Women 1953 and the United Nations Convention on the Nationality of Married Women 1957.

[13] This section draws upon S Palmer, *supra* n. 7.

discourse, it was in terms of sameness not difference: there was no accommodation for any difference between men and women.[14] Equality for women came to mean equality with men: the benchmark for comparison and the means to assess success or failure. Yet, gradually it became clear that the comparison was constructed on the basis of specific male attributes. Unsurprisingly then, norms of formal equality (that women should never be treated differently from men) have sometimes impaired, rather than advanced, the claim for equality in substantive terms. Law's promised objectivity masks the privileging of male perspectives. The language of "equal rights" merely serves to reinforce the status quo: women are given access to a world already constituted. Once formal equality has been attained, gender is no longer perceived as a problem. Formal equality in the law means that gender as an explicit category of political decision and distribution has been dismantled with the subsequent loss of its critical foothold.[15]

These insights concerning the social specificity of the subject have led to further theoretical and practical "riddles" for feminists and feminist theory. The first, is the problem of essentialism. Once it is illustrated that the universal subject of the legal world is constructed on the basis of male attributes, the feminine is constructed as the "other". If, however, feminism seeks to construct a universal woman as "subject", then that figure will inevitably be just as partial as her male opposite. This postmodernist view suggests that feminist theory cannot speak on behalf of the essential universal "woman".[16] Rather, feminism must embrace differences between women taking into account factors such as race, class, ethnicity, age and sexual orientation and accept that only limited knowledge is ever possible. This scepticism of universal claims poses difficult questions for law, as women are analysed as a category, and for any political claim made on behalf of women as a group. If sexual difference is no longer the central feature of women's identity, then how can any feminist legal strategy be possible? How can feminist theory hold onto the category of "woman" and respect diversity? Rosi Braidotti asks: "By what sort of interconnections, sidesteps, and lines of escape can one produce feminist knowledge without fixing it into a new normativity?"[17] Braidotti's work suggests one avenue to escape this impasse. She argues for the need to retain the use of the category or "political fictions", for strategic purposes. She uses the image of the nomad who is both situated and possessing a critical consciousness resisting incorporation. This metaphor suggests a way in which theory can emphasise the fragmentary nature of identity while retaining the insights of postmodernism. Such

[14] W Williams, "The Equality Crisis: Some Reflections on Culture, Courts and Feminism" in K Bartlett and R Kennedy (eds.), *Feminist Legal Theory: Readings in Law and Gender* (Colorado, Westview, 1991).

[15] E Fraser and N Lacey, *The Politics of Community* (London, Harvester Wheatsheaf, 1993) 79.

[16] E Spelman, *Inessential Woman: Problems of Exclusion in Feminist Thought* (London, Women's Press, 1988). See also J Conaghan, "Reassessing the Feminist Theoretical Project in Law" (2000) 27 *Journal of Law and Society* 351.

[17] R Braidotti, "The Exile, the Nomad, and the Migrant: Reflections on International Feminism" (1992) 15 *Women's Studies International Forum* 7; and R Braidotti, *Nomadic Subjects: Embodiment and Sexual Difference in Contemporary Feminist Theory* (New York, Columbia University Press, 1994).

theorising permits feminist work to frame the discussions while recognising that only partial knowledge is possible. If feminism discards for all purposes the category of woman, a legal strategy or any political or social action cannot be pursued. It threatens the very possibility of a feminist theory. While no universal "women's point of view" can be assumed, there are also shared concerns among women which suggests that it may be worthwhile persisting with the category in law for strategic purposes.[18]

The second conundrum concerns the utility of rights discourse in the struggle for civil and human rights for women. Equal rights exist in law but equality is not always recognised in practice. There is a striking gap between the existence of law and the experience of women's lives. It is hardly surprising then that some feminists should be sceptical about the difference that more rights would make to their everyday lives. They point to legislation such as the UK Sex Discrimination Act 1975 and the principle of equal pay for male and female workers under Article 141 of the EC Treaty which has failed to deliver the promised equality between men and women.[19] These legal instruments embody notions of procedural justice which do not guarantee substantive equality.[20] The liberal legal world ignores the gender inequalities which are built into the very definition of the system. Men and women cannot compete if the gender neutral rules are established to suit the apparent interests and needs of a man's world.

Some feminists have concluded that a rights-based strategy is misguided in a liberal legal world hostile to feminist ideals. Understandably, experience of the limitations of rights-based discrimination statutes has led to doubts about the wisdom of exploiting law as an essential strategy in achieving equality.[21] Feminists, such as the sociologist Carol Smart, have even concluded that the use of rights discourse to achieve equality has been counterproductive; it has led to false hopes and perhaps even been detrimental to women's claims.[22]

The abortion debate, which has been highly contentious in the USA and Canada, is often used as the example to expose the potential pitfalls of rights discourse. One perceived drawback is that the effects of open-textured human rights guarantees are incapable of any accurate prediction.[23] Claims to a right inevitably attract counterclaims: a "woman's right to choose" could be challenged by the

[18] See also A Bunting, "Theorizing Women's Cultural Diversity in Feminist International Human Rights Strategies" in A Bottomley and J Conaghan (eds.), *Feminist Theory and Legal Strategy* (Oxford, Blackwell Press, 1993) 6.

[19] Note also the Equal Pay Act 1970 and the Equal Treatment Directive 1976. See S Fredman, *Women and the Law* (Oxford, Clarendon Press, 1997) and N Lacey, "Legislation against Sex Discrimination: Questions from a Feminist Perspective" (1987) 14 *Journal of Law and Society* 411.

[20] There have been attempts to develop concepts of substantive equality. See S Fredman, "A Critical Review of the Concept of Equality in UK Anti-Discrimination Legislation", Working Paper No. 3 (Cambridge Centre for Public Law and Judge Institute of Management Studies, 1999) paras. 3.7–3.19.

[21] C Smart, *Feminism and the Power of Law* (London, Routledge, 1989) 143–4.

[22] *Ibid.*, at 158.

[23] E Kingdom, "Citizenship and Democracy: Feminist Politics of Citizenship and Radical Democratic Politics" in S Millns and N Whitty (eds.), *Feminist Perspectives on Public Law* (London, Cavendish, 1999) 149, 168.

"right to life" of the foetus or the "right to private, family and home life" of the potential father. Nor are rights automatically a progressive force. Even if the state permits lawful abortion, the right is an empty promise for many women if the state refuses to fund abortions or abortion clinics.

The feminist critique of rights has several related aspects. It demonstrates the difficulties of including feminist insights in the legal context. One facet of this critique is that rights are inherently individualistic, competitive and indeterminate. Women's experience is not easily translated into this narrowly accepted language of rights.[24] The most extreme example is the pregnant woman who "does not fit law's conception of the legal person as a bounded unitary self".[25] Rights rhetoric can simplify complex power relations but it fails to overcome existing structural inequalities which are woven into women's daily lives.[26] The socialised conception of the subject contrasts sharply with the individualistic understanding of the "man" in law. The discourse of rights limits possibilities by ignoring "the relational nature of social life".[27]

Another facet of the critique of rights rests on their inapplicability in the private sphere. The public world of state, market, politics and men is perceived as superior to the private realm of women and the family. In the USA and Canada, the public/private dichotomy has been at the centre of the argument concerning the ineffectiveness of rights in the national sphere. The reasoning is that rights discourse takes for granted that there is or should be a division between the public world, that enforces rights, and a private world of family life in which individuals pursue their diverse goals, relatively free from state interference.[28] The limitation of rights usage to the public sphere is a special disadvantage to women and children who may face oppression in the hidden private sphere. Some feminists have argued that the human rights movement can only accommodate women if the conceptual problem of this public/private divide is overcome.[29]

On a more pragmatic level, many feminists fear that by diverting attention away from political reform and into legal disputes, rights-based strategies will limit aspirations by merely reframing debates within the dominant discourse and increasing reliance upon a predominantly male judiciary. Thus, this emphasis on rights will inevitably be at the expense of other aspects of women's situation. As the legal system is skewed in favour of those whose interests are already protected in the law (the prevalent norms are based on male attributes), then rights discourse is unlikely

[24] H Charlesworth, *supra* n. 6, 58 at 61. The feminist critique of rights draws upon other critical inquiries including the critical legal studies movement. See R Gordon, "New Development in Legal Theory" in D Kairys (ed.), *The Politics of Law* (New York, Pantheon Books, 1990) 413.

[25] K Savell, "The Mother of the Legal Person", *supra* chap. 2 at 64.

[26] C Smart, *supra* n. 21, at 138–44.

[27] M Tushnet, "Rights: an essay in informal political theory" (1989) 17 *Politics and Society* 403 at 410.

[28] W Williams, "The Equality Crisis: Some Reflections on Culture, Courts and Feminism" in K Bartlett and R Kennedy, *supra* n. 14 at 15.

[29] N Burrows, *supra* n. 10, at 86. See also K Engle, "After the Collapse of the Public/Private Distinction: Strategizing Women's Rights" in D Dollmeyer (ed.), *Reconceiving Reality: Women and International Law* (Washington DC, American Society of International Law, 1993) 143.

to change the structural inequalities of power.[30] Indeed, it may have the perverse result of reinforcing the most privileged groups in society.[31] Moreover, the discourse may not allow women to address the fundamental issues underlying inequality, questions of the feminisation of poverty, inequality in earnings, and the provision of child care. A primary concern, then, is that rights may be appropriated by the powerful and women's concerns will continue to be marginalised.[32] Some rights, for example the right to respect for family life or freedom of religion, have been used by both international and domestic institutions to justify the oppression of women.[33]

On the basis of this critique of rights, should feminists be wary of the promise of rights? There are persuasive arguments which suggest that women should cautiously support a formal declaration of rights. First, the potential to exploit the immense political power of a rights-oriented framework cannot be ignored or discarded as irrelevant. Given the power of law in society, women cannot afford to abandon law as a potential medium for change. Rights rhetoric has played an important part in improving the lives of subordinate groups in society, including women.[34] The language itself offers a recognised mechanism through which to frame political and social wrongs. Second, rights can be an effective means of harnessing political demands for progressive change. They can influence the general terms of the political debate and potentially contribute to wider social change. Third, they could provide an opportunity to introduce perspectives and experiences into the courts which have been consistently excluded or marginalised in national law. It provides greater scope for the inclusion into law of feminist insights gained from experience. Catherine MacKinnon has recently argued that international law is a way to provide new grounds for theory and action where national law has failed to address adequately sex-based violations.[35] Fourth, feminist theorists, such as Jennifer Nedelsky, have advocated constructive ways of understanding rights. She suggests that we need to recognise the "reality of rights as relationships and make it central to our interpretations". [36] Rights, she argues, define and structure relationships of power. The challenge is to foster interpretations that promote relations of equality.

Finally, the symbolic power of rights cannot be easily dismissed. Patricia Williams states that she is uncomfortable with that part of the Critical Legal Studies movement which rejects rights-based theory, in particular that part of the critique

[30] M Minow, "The Supreme Court, 1986 Term Foreword: Justice Engendered" (1987) 101 *Harvard Law Review* 10 at 10–17.

[31] D Kairys, *supra* n. 24, at 413.

[32] C Smart (1989), *supra* n. 21, at 145.

[33] H Charlesworth, C Chinkin and S Wright, *supra* n. 5, at 635–8.

[34] The attack on liberalism by critical feminists has been more ambivalent than that of their critical male colleagues. They have been more willing to acknowledge that in the past liberalism has proved to be a progressive political doctrine. See D Rhode, "Feminist Critical Theories" (1990) 42 *Stanford Law Review* 617 at 627.

[35] C MacKinnon, "Disputing Male Sovereignty: On United States v. Morrison" (2000) 114 *Harvard Law Review* 135 at 177.

[36] Nedelsky, *supra* n. 7, at 1290.

which relates to the black struggle for civil rights.[37] In a powerful statement she provides some indication of the power of rights claims:

> "'Rights' feel so new in the mouths of most black people. It is still so deliciously empowering to say. It is a sign for and a gift of selfhood that is very hard to contemplate restructuring . . . at this point in history. It is the magic wand of visibility and invisibility, of inclusion and exclusion, and of power and no power."[38]

The empowering nature of rights discourse is too important to overlook as one tactic, among others, to challenge gender subordination.

It is suggested that rights claims could be used in a strategic way to empower oppressed groups although the feminist critique outlined above cannot be disregarded; feminists should be wary of the concealed traps posed by such a tactic. Rights are a double-edged sword in that they operate within the existing discourse. In Canada, feminists fought hard to have equality rights included in the Canadian Charter of Rights and Freedoms. Yet more men than women have successfully resorted to this equality guarantee in order to resolve their equality claims.[39] There is a risk in using legal rights to achieve feminist goals within "the realm of legality which is embedded within a deliberately obtuse masculinist culture".[40] Experience of reforms suggests that entering the liberal world of legality exposes contradictions and throws up paradoxical results.[41]

A feminist strategy in law cannot exist without accepting some aspects of liberalism even though feminists have demonstrated that law's liberalism is premised on women's inequality. Does the recognition of the paradoxical relationship between law and feminism provide a window of opportunity to reconsider the relationship? The Human Rights Act 1998 may be a key to rethinking as it is a tool to challenge or at least unsettle the liberal categories that have developed by and through the ideological exclusion of women. These new rights may enable feminists to seek access to law without being silenced by it. Perhaps rights discourse could be viewed as an ongoing conversation rather than as closure. Yet feminism must still maintain its critical stance and requires the adoption of an ethical standard. One such aspect of this practice might simply be the continual evaluation of strategies deployed to improve the conditions of women's lives. In this strategic approach, the possible use of rights discourse is not to be simply accepted or abandoned but carefully examined and cautiously adopted for its possibilities.[42] Nicola Lacey also warns against an unqualified commitment to any philosophical analysis of the relation

[37] P Williams, "Alchemical Notes: Reconstructed Ideal from Reconstructed Rights" (1987) *Harvard Civil Rights—Civil Liberties Law Review* 401 at 404.

[38] *Ibid.*, at 431.

[39] See A Cote, "Canada Kills the Court Challenges Programme" in J Kerr (ed.), *Ours By Right* (London, Zed Books, 1995) 68–71.

[40] M Thornton, "Feminism and the Contradiction of Law Reform" (1991) *19 International Journal of the Sociology of Law* 453 at 467.

[41] See also M Eberts, "Canadian Charter: A Feminist Perspective" in P Alston (ed.), *Promoting Human Rights through Bills of Rights* (Oxford, Oxford University Press, 1999) 241 at 278–9.

[42] See A Bottomley and J Conaghan, *Feminist Theory and Legal Strategy* (Oxford, Blackwell Publishers, 1993) 1–5.

between ethics and law. She advocates that feminists should adopt a pragmatic approach to theorising in order to further the interests of women.[43]

HUMAN RIGHTS IN THE UNITED KINGDOM

It is against the background of these debates within feminism, that I now turn to consider the Human Rights Act 1998. Although the Human Rights Act only partially incorporates the European Convention on Human Rights (ECHR), the influence of this legislation will be wide ranging. The Act makes it possible for individuals to argue their Convention rights in any national court or tribunal. Even before the Human Rights Act came into force, Lord Hope commented that:

> "It is now plain that the incorporation of the European Convention on Human Rights into our domestic law will subject the entire legal system to a fundamental process of review and, where necessary, reform by the judiciary".[44]

This potentially revolutionary change to the UK constitutional system will transform the way in which legislation is drafted and politics is conducted.

The ECHR described as the "jewel in the crown" of the Council of Europe, is a treaty ratified by the post-war Labour Government in 1951 and came into force in 1953. It protects traditional civil and political rights, sometimes referred to as "first generation" rights. The Convention guarantees include the right to life (Article 2), the right not be subjected to torture or inhuman or degrading treatment (Article 3), freedom from slavery or forced labour (Article 4), personal liberty (Article 5), fair trial (Article 6), freedom from retrospective criminal offences and punishment (Article 7), respect for private and family life (Article 8), and freedom of thought, conscience and religion (Article 9). Article 10 protects freedom of expression, Article 11 guarantees freedom of assembly and Article 12 the right to marry and found a family. The Protocols include the protection of property, right to education and free elections (Protocol 1). Protocol 6 abolishes the death penalty. Article 14 secures the right to non-discrimination but it is not a free-standing right. It is an ancillary protection to those rights and freedoms guaranteed by other substantive provisions of the Convention. Rather than securing additional rights, it ensures the effective exercise of the substantive rights set out in the earlier provisions.

Since 1966, individuals in the United Kingdom, who claim to have suffered because of an alleged breach of the Convention, have been able to petition the Commission and may ultimately have their case heard by the European Court of human rights.[45] The system of individual petition has been one of the reasons for the great success of the European Human Rights system.

[43] N Lacey, "Violence, Ethics and Law; Feminist Reflections on a Familiar Dilemma" *infra* at 134.

[44] *R* v. *DPP, Ex p. Kebilene* [2000] A C 326 at 374–5.

[45] The Commission was abolished and a full-time court was established by Protocol No. 11 which entered into force on 1 November 1998.

On many occasions, the European Court of Human Rights has found that the United Kingdom has breached the Convention. As a consequence, the United Kingdom has been required to change its laws and policies on a wide range of issues among them the rights of prisoners,[46] refugees and asylum seekers,[47] newspapers and the contempt law[48] and the criminalisation of homosexual relations.[49] The right of an individual to petition to the Strasbourg organs remains unchanged by the Human Rights Act but it is expected that the number of successful applications to Strasbourg from the United Kingdom will be substantially reduced.

In a number of significant ways, the ECHR is a flawed and outdated human rights instrument. The Convention is limited to civil and political rights and does not directly tackle social and economic injustices.[50] From a feminist perspective, the relatively weak protection from discrimination and the lack of an explicit clause guaranteeing equality are serious disadvantages. Yet the rights secured in the Convention do create a new opportunity for feminist engagement with law. In particular, they could provide greater protection for women in the private sphere.

The Convention rights are only partially incorporated into domestic law through the Human Rights Act 1998. The UK Government claims that the Act achieves the dual role of preserving parliamentary supremacy as well as effectively protecting the Convention rights.[51] The Government has fashioned a unique solution to the democratic dilemma posed by the protection of fundamental rights: is democracy best protected by leaving power in the hands of the elected legislature or should fundamental rights be protected by a judiciary who limit the power of the democratically elected majority?[52] The judiciary have been given considerable freedom to develop domestic law in line with the Convention principles while the supremacy of Parliament is preserved as the courts will be unable to strike down any primary legislation which is incompatible with the Convention. The courts have the power "to make a declaration of incompatibility".[53] Such a declaration will not affect legal rights and obligations but it is a signal to Parliament and the public that in the court's view a violation of fundamental rights has occurred. The Human Rights Act also provides for a parliamentary "fast-track" procedure for amending any offending legislation.[54]

The Human Rights Act introduces two distinct mechanisms for incorporating these international law Convention rights into domestic United Kingdom law. The first is an interpretative obligation imposed on the courts.[55] Section 3 of the Human Rights Act provides that:

[46] *Silver* v. *UK* (1983) 5 EHRR 347; *Thynne, Wilson and Gunnell* v. *UK* (1990) 13 EHRR 666.

[47] *Chahall* v. *UK* (1996) 23 EHRR 413.

[48] *The Sunday Times* v. *United Kingdom* (1979) 12 EHRR 245.

[49] *Dudgeon* v. *UK* (1981) 4 EHRR 149.

[50] Note that the First Protocol includes the right to education, the only social and economic right in the ECHR.

[51] See "Rights Brought Home: The Human Rights Bill", Cm 3782 (1997) para. 2.13.

[52] See S Fredman, "Bringing Rights Home" (1998) 114 *LQR* 538 .

[53] Human Rights Act, section 4 .

[54] Human Rights Act, section 10.

[55] Human Rights Act, sections 3–5.

> "so far as is possible to do so, primary and subordinate legislation must be read and given effect in a way which is compatible with the Convention rights."

It is likely that the courts, if at all possible, will devise imaginative ways to avoid finding any conflict.

The second mechanism provided in the Act to give effect to Convention rights is in section 6. This section makes it unlawful for a public authority to act in a way that is incompatible with one or more of the rights protected under the Convention. The question of whether a body is a public authority is pivotal as the Human Rights Act creates new direct remedies for any breach of section 6. The Act does not define the term but according to the Lord Chancellor, it should be interpreted broadly to provide as much protection as possible.[56] The section does state however that courts and tribunals are considered public authorities. This is significant because the duty on public authorities to act compatibly with the Convention is imposed regardless of whether all of the parties to legal proceedings are private individuals or entities.

The Human Rights Act does not specifically address the position of the common law and its compatibility with the Convention but the courts are utilising Convention rights as a device for the future development of the common law.[57] This approach is hardly novel, as it is not solely dependent upon the Human Rights Act: the Convention has been influencing the development of the common law, directly and indirectly, for a number of years.[58]

Human rights guarantees, such as those set out in the European Convention on Human Rights, do not avoid the interpretative difficulties confronting decision-makers that must assign a meaning to constitutional rights. Rights are capable of being given a wide range of interpretations, not least because such charters are formulated at a high level of abstraction. In some ways this elasticity is an advantage, allowing flexibility in decision-making and adaptation to novel circumstances, yet there are times when consequential choices need to be made. Inevitably, these broad and open-textured guarantees can lead to uncertainty when these general rights are applied in specific contexts. There has been little discussion of the interpretative analysis that the courts are likely to use when articulating rights that contain no obvious fixed meanings. The courts will also draw upon the Strasbourg jurisprudence and the traditions in other jurisdictions. The Human Rights Act requires the courts to have regard to the jurisprudence of the European Court of Human Rights, the Commission and the decisions of the Committee of Ministers; but they are not bound by it. [59]

One consequence of the lack of interpretative guidance will be the heavy reliance on the judiciary to give rights meaning. This has led to disquiet about the

[56] See the Lord Chancellor's comments at HL Deb. vol. 582, col. 1232 (3 November 1997).

[57] See for example, *Douglas* v. *Hello! Ltd* (2001) 9 BHRC 543 and *Venables* v. *News Group Newspapers Ltd* (2001) 9 BHRC 587.

[58] See for example, *Derbyshire County Council* v. *Times Newspapers Ltd* [1992] QB 770 (Court of Appeal).

[59] Human Rights Act, section 2.

lack of diversity of members of the judiciary in the United Kingdom and the socially exclusive and secretive process of judicial selection. The issue of women's exclusion from the decision-making process has already been raised before the House of Lords. The recently enacted Youth Justice and Criminal Evidence Act 1999, section 41 stipulates that a complainant's sexual history cannot be introduced in evidence, except in specific circumstances. The law was designed to protect women in rape cases from humiliating cross-examination about their sexual history unless absolutely relevant to the case. This law has been challenged as a violation of human rights.[60] The argument is that the "rape shield law" may prevent men accused of rape from receiving a fair trial as demanded by Article 6 of the Convention. Yet, as recognised by Parliament, victims in rape trials also have a countervailing right to respect for their privacy and dignity (Article 8), and not to be subject to inhuman and degrading treatment (Article 3). The Director of the Fawcett Society points out:

> "Not surprisingly, how to strike this balance is a question on which there has been a strong divergence of views between men and women. Yet, when the Court of Appeal decided this case, the three male judges appealed to 'common sense' and 'human nature' to justify their decision."[61]

In a unique legal action, the Fawcett Society asked the House of Lords for permission to intervene in the case to argue that it should not be decided by a court comprised exclusively of men. The challenge was quickly dismissed although the Society was permitted to submit written arguments. Nevertheless, one of the most striking aspects of the House of Lords is that all of the judges are white men. Given that the freedoms articulated in the Convention are open to varying interpretations then the role of the judiciary becomes immensely important. Our present senior judiciary are not representative of the community.

Some of these misgivings could be overcome by making changes to the way that judges are appointed and trained. The Lord Chancellor has already made some changes and, for example, solicitors are now eligible for appointment to the bench. It is clear that adding a few token women or minorities to the bench will not necessarily mean that the silenced communities will have a representative. Far more radical alterations are needed to achieve a judiciary that is more representative of the community as a whole.[62]

[60] *Regina* v. *A* (House of Lords, 17 May 2001). The House of Lords decided that the "rape shield law" was a violation of Art. 6 ECHR. Their Lordships did not, however, issue a declaration of incompatibility. The decision of the House of Lords was handed down too late to be included in the above analysis.

[61] Mary Anne Stephenson, "Bad Judgment" *The Guardian*, 27 March 2001.

[62] See discussion in K Ewing, "The Bill of Rights Debate" in K D Ewing, C A Gearty and B A Hepple (eds.), *Human Rights and Labour Law: Essays for Paul O'Higgins* (London, Mansell, 1994) 147 at 170.

THE JURISPRUDENCE OF THE EUROPEAN COURT OF HUMAN RIGHTS AND THE HUMAN RIGHTS ACT 1998

As the Human Rights Act directs the courts to take into account the Strasbourg jurisprudence if it is relevant to the proceedings,[63] it is necessary to examine the approach of the European Court of Human Rights to cases concerning violations of women's rights. The next section will analyse some of the Convention rights that have been used to promote the rights of women.

In recent years, the European Court of Human Rights has shown increased sensitivity to violations of women's human rights. A number of recent cases have specifically linked violence against women with abuse of human rights. In *Aydin* v. *Turkey* [64] the applicant was detained blindfolded, stripped naked, hit, placed in a tyre and hosed with high-pressure water and raped over a period of three days. The Court considered that rape of a detainee by a state official was "an especially grave and abhorrent form of ill treatment" that leaves "deep pyschological scars on the victim".[65] The Court concluded that the "accumulation of acts of physical and mental violence inflicted on the applicant and the especially cruel act of rape to which she was subjected" constituted torture and a violation of Article 3 of the European Convention on Human Rights. The Court also considered that the failure of the Turkish authorities to carry out any effective investigation into the applicant's allegations was a further Convention violation. In *Jabari* v. *Turkey*,[66] the European Court of Human Rights found that it would be a violation of Article 3 of the Convention, to force a woman accused of adultery to return to Iran. Punishment of adultery by stoning still remains on the statute book in Iran. In reaching its decision, the Court relied upon the conclusions of the United Nations High Commissioner for Refugees and the findings of Amnesty International.[67]

The European Court of Human Rights has also considered the human rights implications of the judicial decision to overturn the marital rape exemption that was a part of the UK common law. Until 1991, a wife's lack of consent was legally irrelevant in English law. This rule encapsulated some of the problems that women have identified in relation to law: the gendered nature of law and the disempowerment of women. The House of Lords in *R* v. *R*[68] decided that rape by a husband of his wife was always a criminal offence. Although this decision was greeted with relief by many, some academics expressed strong reservations on the basis that the Law Lords had created a retrospective crime in breach of the principle of legal certainty. [69] This decision of the House of Lords in *R* was then

[63] The Act does not impose any duty on the domestic courts to follow the Strasbourg jurisprudence but the petition to Strasbourg remains.
[64] (1997) 25 EHRR 251.
[65] *Ibid.*, para. 83.
[66] Application No. 40035/98 (11 July 2000).
[67] *Ibid.*, para 41.
[68] [1992] 1 A C 599.
[69] See G Williams, "The Problem of Domestic Rape" (1991) *New Law Journal*, 205–6, 246–7.

challenged as a violation of Article 7 ECHR which prohibits retrospective changes of the criminal law. In Strasbourg, where the cases were called *CR* v. *UK* and *SW* v. *UK*[70], the European Court of Human Rights concluded unanimously that there was no violation of the Convention. Article 7 ECHR permitted the gradual clarification of the rules of criminal liability through case-by-case evolution, provided it was consistent with the essence of the offence and was reasonably foreseeable. The abolition of the marital rape exemption was considered to be foreseeable. In reaching this conclusion, the European Court of Human Rights endorsed the appellate English courts' conclusion that "a rapist remains a rapist subject to the criminal law, irrespective of his relationship with his victim".[71] Importantly, it acknowledged that this evolution of the common law was in accordance with the fundamental objectives of the Convention, the very essence of which is respect for human dignity and human freedom. This strong affirmation by the European Court of the Human Rights of women makes this a vital decision in European human rights law jurisprudence.[72]

In sum, these decisions of the European Court of Human Rights have made some advances for women's rights. They have specifically acknowledged that the dignity and freedom of women's human rights is protected by the European Convention. These are important statements in international law where women's rights, to a large extent, have been marginalised.[73]

HUMAN RIGHTS AND THE PUBLIC/PRIVATE DIVIDE

The European Convention has proved to be an accessible area of international human rights law for women by providing a mechanism to challenge the power of the state. Its success as a human rights treaty can be largely explained by the fact that it gives individuals the right to bring an application directly to the courts. The relatively recent integration of women's human rights into the mainstream of the Convention jurisprudence is especially welcome.

Yet there are only few occasions when the European Court has addressed women's human rights. The explanation lies in the types of rights that are protected by the Convention. The European Convention protects certain fundamental civil and political rights. The assumption is that these stipulated human rights are universal and held by all people regardless of their gender: the rights of men have been extended to include women who are placed, theoretically, in the same situation as men in the public sphere. Traditionally these rights have been given prominence as protection for men within the public sphere and their relationship with government.

[70] (1995) 21 EHRR 363.

[71] Para. 40.

[72] See also *Open Door and Dublin Well Women* v. *Ireland* (1990) 15 EHRR 244. (Women's right to information about abortion services upheld, in spite of strong Irish laws against the dissemination of such material).

[73] H Charlesworth and C Chinkin, *The Boundaries of International law: A Feminist Analysis* (Manchester, Manchester University Press, 2000) 218–20.

While civil and political rights, in the traditional sense, are important for all people, economic, social and cultural rights may offer even more to women's everyday lives. It is hardly surprising then, that European Union law has had a far greater direct influence on the lives of women in those states that are Community members. The realisation of sex equality has been the most highly developed pillar of the European Community's social policy.[74]

A further critique of civil and political rights, as discussed above, focuses on the gendered public/private distinction in human rights law. As a result of their historical development, civil and political rights are directed towards the protection of men within the public sphere. One feminist argument is that violations of these rights are not the harms from which most women need protection.[75] The emphasis placed on the protection of individuals in public life side steps the fact that many women spend all, or at least a major part of their lives, within the non-political private sphere, the realm of the family and domestic life. Traditionally this area of private life has been considered inappropriate for human rights and civil liberties protection.[76] This private sphere, which includes major sites for the oppression of women—home, family and religion—- has been immune from scrutiny [77]

Although, as shown above in the *Aydin* case, women can be victims of rape in the "public" sense (rape may be used as a weapon of the state to achieve political objectives), the greatest amount of violence against women occurs in the "private" non-governmental sphere. In line with other international law treaties, the application of the European Convention emphasises state actors. Yet, the case law of the European Commission and Court of Human Rights has exposed the fluid nature of the public/private boundary. There are a number of European Court decisions where states have been held responsible for a violation of an individual's Convention rights by a non-state actor. In some circumstances, the Strasbourg institutions have recognised that certain of the Convention Articles (2, 3, 5, 8 10 and 11) require member states to take positive action to protect individuals against Convention rights violations by other private individuals. It includes a duty on the relevant authorities to put in place a legal framework that secures the effective protection of Convention rights. This jurisprudence is highly relevant in the domestic UK context since, as noted above, courts and tribunals must take into account the Strasbourg case law if it is relevant to the proceedings.

Marckx v. *Belgium*[78] is the source of the Court's jurisprudence of positive state action. In that decision, the Court considered that the state's duty not to interfere with the right to "respect for family life" in Article 8 imposed positive obligations,

[74] C Barnard, "Gender Equality in the EU: A Balance Sheet" in P Alston (ed.), *The EU and Human Rights* (Oxford, Oxford University Press, 1999) 215.

[75] Charlesworth and Chinkin, *supra* n . 73, at 233.

[76] See C Pateman, "Feminist Critiques of the Public/Private Dichotomy" in S Benn and C Gaus (eds.), *Public and Private in Social Life* (London, Croom Helm, 1983) 281, 285.

[77] Charlesworth and Chinkin, *supra* n. 73, at 233–7.

[78] (1979) 2 EHRR 330. D J Harris, M O'Boyle and C Warbrick, *Law of the European Convention on Human Rights* (London, Butterworths, 1995) 19–22. See also A Clapham, *Human Rights in the Private Sphere* (Oxford, Clarendon Press, 1993).

requiring an enactment of legislation in order to safeguard the individual's Convention rights. In later decisions, the Court established that this positive obligation includes a requirement to protect an individual against infringement of their Convention rights by other private parties. This positive obligation has applied even within the context of the family unit, the very heart of the private sphere. In *A* v. *United Kingdom*,[79] the state was found to have violated Article 3 for failing to provide adequate legal safeguards for a child beaten by his stepfather. Although a prosecution had been brought, the stepfather had successfully pleaded the defence of reasonable chastisement and was acquitted at the trial. These decisions on positive state obligations are significant because the state can be held responsible at Strasbourg for failing to control the behaviour of private individuals. This was clearly stated by the Court in *X* v. *Netherlands*:

> "The Court recalls that although the object of Article 8 is essentially that of protecting the individual against arbitrary interference by the public authorities, it does not merely compel the State to abstain from such interference: in addition to this primarily negative undertaking, there may be positive obligations inherent in an effective respect for private or family life. These obligations may involve the adoption of measures designed to secure respect for private life even in the sphere of the relations of individuals between themselves."[80]

A state cannot hide behind a claim of "private relations" in order to avoid securing the Convention rights of victims of abuse. The obligation on public authorities to adopt positive measures to protect the Convention rights of individuals is a potentially powerful avenue to address violence against women in the private sphere. The Convention rights secured in the Human Rights Act could play an important role in changing attitudes and altering the way in which the law and police deal with issues such as protecting women from domestic violence and forced marriages. Laws that inadequately protect the security of women or the systematic failure by, for example, the police, to enforce existing laws are likely to be Convention violations. This duty is strictest where fundamental rights are at stake, including protection of the public from violent crimes.[81] Nevertheless, according to *Osman* v. *UK*,[82] in order to show a violation of a positive obligation, the applicant must establish that the authorities failed to do all that could reasonably be expected of them to avoid a real and immediate risk to life of which they have or ought to have knowledge. In the *Osman* case the facts were quite extreme. It concerned the alleged failure by the police to protect the applicants and their families from an obsessed schoolteacher. The European Court concluded that there was no violation despite a number of worrying signals and "the half-hearted efforts of the police to exercise control" over the schoolteacher.[83] As Charlesworth and Chinkin point out:

[79] (1998) 5 BHRC 137.
[80] (1985) 8 EHRR 235 at 239–40 (para. 23).
[81] *T* v. *UK* and *V* v. *UK* (1999) 30 EHRR 121, para. 98.
[82] (2000) 29 EHRR 245.
[83] See the partly dissenting opinion in the Commission decision of Mr S Trecshsel, *ibid.*, at 293.

"In the context of violence against women, the concealed nature of many acts of domestic violence committed by men who otherwise do not appear to pose any threat may make it difficult to establish such failure."[84]

The Human Rights Act falls short of providing a specific cause of action against private individuals for violating Convention rights. Yet the Human Rights Act, as confirmed by the Court of Appeal,[85] has an indirect horizontal effect. In some circumstances individuals will be able to rely on Convention rights indirectly in proceedings against private parties. As the courts and tribunals are included within the definition of public authorities,[86] the public/private boundary that has traditionally rendered much abuse against women and discriminatory practices invisible has shifted. The horizontal indirect effect of the Human Rights Act will permit the infiltration of Convention standards through the interpretation of statutes, and the future development of the common law, even in proceedings between private parties. It is possible, then, that the Human Rights Act could provide one avenue to redress the harms suffered by women in the private sphere. This is an exciting prospect for feminist lawyers as it opens the possibility of a strategic and contextual approach to issues of women's rights.

As outlined above, the European Court has already taken the opportunity in *SW* v. *UK* and *CR* v. *UK* [87] (the rape in marriage cases) to articulate that "the very essence" of the Convention's fundamental objectives is "respect for human dignity and human freedom".[88] Arguably, this clear statement of values is not at odds with our existing public law standards and it could become the touchstone for evaluating both public and private actions.[89] The importance of this decision also lies in the shift in the boundary between the public and private spheres. This conclusion is in stark contrast to the recent decision in the United States where the Supreme Court struck down federal legislation which attempted to buttress inadequate state laws concerned with domestic violence and sexual assault. They sought to provide a civil sex discrimination action that victims could initiate directly against perpetrators.[90]

Article 8 of the Convention, protecting the "right to respect for private and family life, home and correspondence", has been a dynamically interpreted provision of the Convention. It is perhaps the most likely Article to serve as a residual guarantee of liberty.[91] David Feldman has pointed out that "privacy-related rights have extended beyond their original concern—threats to private space, especially the

[84] Charlesworth and Chinkin, *supra* n. 73 at 150.

[85] *Venables and Thompson* v. *News Group Newspapers Ltd* (2001) 9 BHRC 587.

[86] Human Rights Act, section 6(3).

[87] (1995) 21 EHRR 363.

[88] *Ibid.*, para. 42.

[89] See S Palmer, "Rape in Marriage and the European Convention on Human Rights: *CR* v. *UK*, *SW* v. *UK*" (1997) 5 *Feminist Legal Studies* 91; and S Millns, *supra* n. 7, at 200.

[90] C MacKinnon (2000), *supra* n. 35. See also J Fudge, "The Public/Private Distinction: The Possibilities of and the Limits to Charter Litigation" (1987) 25 *Osgoode Hall Law Journal* 445.

[91] D Feldman, "The Developing Scope of Article 8 of the European Convention on Human Rights" [1997] EHRLR 265.

home—to encompass personal security, self-fulfilment and identity, [and] sexual mores".[92] The potential breadth of this article provides considerable scope for imaginative litigation and an opportunity to insert feminist values into human rights cases. For example, it is widely accepted that the law governing property rights of cohabitants, or unmarried partners, is inadequate and inconsistent. Indeed, it is widely accepted that the common law and equitable principles applied to determine property rights on the breakdown of an unmarried partnership perpetuate a gender bias. As the law stands, when a cohabiting but unmarried couple part, the rules which decide how any communally enjoyed property is to be allocated are those which govern the allocation of property between strangers. A number of problems arise in applying strict rules of property to a dispute between formerly cohabiting partners. Women are often placed in a disadvantageous position, as their ability to contribute financially to the acquisition of property is prejudiced in a number of ways. They typically earn less than men[93] and if they bear children and take on the greater part of primary care, they reduce their chance of full-time employment outside the home. Moreover, when the courts examine the motive of the parties, the bias against the non-owning party puts women at a disadvantage. Where there is an intimate relationship, the courts will attribute activities such as housekeeping, gardening and maintaining and improving the property to the "love and affection" that exists between partners, and this will displace any presumption that such activities were undertaken because of any proprietary interest. It may be possible using Article 8 in conjunction with Article 14 (right to non-discrimination) to argue that the unsatisfactory domestic law dealing with financial affairs on the termination of a relationship should be developed to take account of these Convention rights.[94] The Human Rights Act requires the domestic courts to give appropriate effect to Convention rights: it could be the catalyst that enables the English courts to reconsider this problem afresh and modify the common law. Alternatively, consideration of the human rights issues raised by this institutional discrimination could persuade Parliament to provide some legislative protection of the financial and property rights of unmarried couples who cohabit.

EQUALITY, NON-DISCRIMINATION AND THE CONVENTION

Although the right of women to equal treatment and non-discrimination on the basis of sex is part of the traditional canon of human rights, the protection against discrimination in the European Convention is limited.[95] Article 14 of the

[92] D Feldman, "The Developing Scope of Article 8 of the European Convention on Human Rights" [1997] EHRLR 265.

[93] Women earn over 25 per cent less than men in full-time employment: National Statistics : *Labour Force Statistics: Quarterly Supplement*, No. 11, November 2000, Table 33.

[94] See S Palmer and L Turano, "Love and the Law: Cohabitants and Human Rights" in M McCabe and M Rae (eds.), *Human Rights and the Family* (Oxford, Hart Publishing, 2002) (forthcoming).

[95] Compare the Universal Declaration of Human Rights, Art. 7 and the International Covenant on Civil and Political Rights, Art. 26.

Convention provides that the rights and freedoms in the Convention shall be secured without discrimination on any grounds including, among others, sex. There are a number of widely accepted limitations with the interpretation of this Article. First, Article 14 does not establish a right to non-discrimination independent of the rights and freedoms guaranteed by other substantive rights of the Convention. Rather than securing an additional right, it represents a commitment to ensure the effective exercise of the substantive rights set out in the earlier provisions.[96] Article 14 will apply where the facts in issue "fall within the ambit" of one or more of the Convention guarantees.[97] The "parasitic" nature of this right has resulted in relatively few cases based on discrimination before the European Court and an undeveloped discrimination jurisprudence.[98]

Convention caselaw has established that some grounds of different treatment, including differential treatment on the basis of sex, are more difficult to justify. The European Court has stated that:

> "[T]he advancement of the equality of the sexes is today a major goal in the Member States of the Council of Europe. This means that very weighty reasons would have to be advanced before a difference of treatment on the ground of sex could be regarded as compatible with the Convention."[99]

In spite of this strong commitment to equality, the restricted nature of the substantive rights protected means that most of the social and economic discrepancies between men and women are not addressed by the Convention.

The concept of non-discrimination, as we have seen, raises complex issues. In order to establish differential treatment pursuant to Article 14, an applicant must show that he or she has been treated less favourably than others who are in an analogous or similar situation. Many complaints are rejected on the basis of a lack of similarity in the situations invoked.[100] As it is essentially a comparative concept, the question arises in relation to whom should the comparison be made. The answer usually appears to be that a woman has the right to be treated the same as a man. The discrimination standard demands a comparison of the victim's treatment with the "normal", that is, male, standard. The formulation assumes that there exists an objective neutral test that can be applied to determine when men and women are similarly situated. Disadvantages suffered by women are redressed by equal treatment with men and the value of any specifically female life experiences is inevitably marginalised. Equality is promised only to those women who can conform to a male model. The torturous search for a "true comparator" has caused considerable

[96] See A H Robertson and J G Merrills, *Human Rights in Europe* 3rd ed. (Manchester, Manchester University Press, 1993) chap. 5.

[97] *Rasmussen* v. *Denmark* (1984) 7 EHRR 371.

[98] See *Abdulaziz, Cabales and Balkandali* v. *UK* (1985) 7 EHRR 471. See also Harris, O'Boyle and Warbrick, *supra* n. 78, at 463.

[99] See *Abdulaziz, Cabales and Balkandali* v. *UK* (1985) 7 EHRR 471, para. 78.

[100] S Grosz, J Beatson and P Duffy, *Human Rights: The 1998 Act and the European Convention* (London, Sweet and Maxwell, 2000) 329. On occasions the Court has avoided the issue altogether by deciding that the question of comparability is just one facet of the wider question whether the difference of treatment is justified.

difficulties in UK discrimination laws. This approach, as Nicola Lacey has observed, assumes,

> "a world of autonomous individuals starting a race or making free choices [which] has no cutting edge against the fact that men and women are simply running different races."[101]

Recently, the European Court of Human Rights has extended its understanding of the discrimination principle. In *Thlimmenos* v. *Greece*[102] the European Court concluded that:

> "the right not to be discriminated against in the enjoyment of the rights guaranteed under the Convention is also violated when States without an objective and reasonable justification fail to treat differently persons whose situations are significantly different."[103]

This new gloss on the principle may give greater leeway for feminist arguments and provide the opportunity for more subtle arguments.

The nature of the non-discrimination principle raises further issues. Although the principle demands consistent treatment between men and women, it provides no guarantees of substantive rights. Article 14 rights are secured whether rights are "levelled up" or "levelled down". A clear example is found in the European Court decision of *Abdulaziz, Cabales and Balkandali* v. *United Kingdom*. Under the immigration rules in force in the UK at that time, non-national husbands of women who had been granted indefinite leave to remain in the UK would not normally be granted the same immigration status. Yet foreign men with indefinite leave to remain in the UK could normally bring their non-national wives and fianceés into the country on the basis of indefinite leave to remain. This was found to be a breach of Article 14 in conjunction with Article 8 (right to respect for family life), as the same right was denied to women without justification. The United Kingdom Government responded by changing its immigration law so that neither spouses of male nor female applicants would normally be granted a favourable immigration status. Some feminists conclude that there is no point fighting expensive and lengthy legal battles which fail to lead to positive changes.

As the scope of Article 14 is so limited, it has proved difficult to use it to challenge inequalities in the provision of resources such as jobs and housing. This is in stark contrast to the development of European Community law: the Article 14 guarantee of equal pay for men and women and the subsequent equality directives have proved to be a fruitful legal avenue to challenge sex discrimination.[104] In spite of its restricted scope, Article 14 has had some impact and its invocation has served

[101] N Lacey, *supra* n. 19, at 420.

[102] Application No. 34369/97 (Decision 6 April, 2000) unreported.

[103] *Ibid.*, para. 44.

[104] See for example, Council Directive No. 75/117/ EEC (OJ 1975 L 45/19) on the principle of equal pay for men and women: Council Directive No. 76/207 (OJ 1976 L 39/40) on the implementation of the principle of equal treatment for men and women as regards access to employment, vocational training and promotion and working conditions; Council Directive No. 86/613/EEC (OJ 1986 L 359/56) on the application of equal treatment between men and women engaged in an activity, including agriculture, in a self-employed capacity, and on the protection of self-employed women during pregnancy and motherhood.

to expand the ambit of other substantive Convention rights. The European Court of Human Rights in *Schuler-Zgraggen* v. *Switzerland*[105] considered an issue of indirect discrimination. This form of discrimination is where a rule, apparently neutral on its face, impacts adversely on a particular group. In this particular case, the female applicant's appeal against refusal of a disability pension had been dismissed without a hearing as the relevant social security tribunal had concluded that the woman, who now had a child, would have been unlikely to be seeking work anyway. The Court found that the tribunal had relied upon "stereotypical assumptions" and this was a violation of Article 14, taken in conjunction with Article 6. Although the burden of proving indirect discrimination is heavy, there is some scope to invoke Article 14 in conjunction with substantive rights to challenge rules or court decisions that rely on discriminatory assumptions. Some observers have suggested that criminal law self-defence and provocation standards, whose operation discriminate against women, could be challenged via this route.[106] This optimistic assessment depends on the willingness of the judiciary to recognise the gender dimension in the operation of the criminal law.

The Council of Europe has proposed a new Protocol in order to remedy the deficiencies in Article 14. Protocol 12 provides that "the enjoyment of any right set forth by law shall be secured without discrimination" on any arbitrary ground.[107] Such a change will bring the Convention guarantees into line with other international human rights instruments by providing for an independent right to non-discrimination and equality. Although it has been signed by twenty-five of the Council of Europe's member states, the UK is not yet among them. Although the UK Government states that it is in principle in favour of an independent discrimination right, it is not prepared to sign the new Protocol. The Government has explained that the Protocol is "unacceptably open-ended and uncertain".[108] It may also be that the Government is concerned that the flawed domestic discrimination legislation currently in place will not measure up to this new standard.

The Convention rights, as secured in the Human Rights Act 1998, do not include any positive affirmation of equality between men and women, such as the equality guarantee in the Canadian Charter of Rights and Freedoms, section 15. The Canadian Supreme Court has stated that the purpose of section 15(1) is:

> "[T]o prevent the violation of essential human dignity and freedom through the imposition of disadvantage, stereotyping, or political or social prejudice, and to promote a society in which all persons enjoy equal recognition at law as human beings . . . equally capable and equally deserving of concern, respect and consideration."[109]

105 (1993) 16 EHRR 405.

106 S Livingstone, "Article 14 and the Prevention of Discrimination in the ECHR" [1997] 1 EHRLR 25 at 34.

107 G Moon, "The Draft Discrimination Protocol to the European Convention on Human Rights: A Progress Report" [2000] EHRLR 49.

108 P Hain, Home Office Minister, *Hansard*, Written Answers (28 November, 2000).

109 *Law* v. *Canada (Minister of Employment and Immigration* [1999] 1 SCR 497, para. 88.

The Supreme Court has adopted a contextual approach to equality rights which requires a court to examine the historical disadvantage of a group and consider substantial inequality.[110] Through the adoption of this approach, women have a voice and their stories can be presented to the court. According to the Women's Legal Education and Action Fund (LEAF):

> "Women must get their stories into court to develop a body of evidence about women's poverty, physical vulnerability and social and legal inequality in order to force the courts to respond."[111]

The Supreme Court has specifically rejected the Aristolelian formulation that,

> "things that are alike should be treated alike, while things that are unalike should be treated unalike in proportion to their unlikeness."[112]

According to the Court, the promotion of equality has a more specific goal than the mere elimination of distinctions, because "for the accommodation of differences, which is the essence of true equality, it will frequently be necessary to make distinctions",[113] and "identical treatment may frequently produce serious inequality".[114] In contrast, the rights set out in Article 14 of the European Convention dictate a role of non-interference rather than a positive guarantee by the state to promote equality. It is far more difficult to rely on Article 14 to empower women.

Without an equality clause in the Human Rights Act, can women gain a foothold in order for their perspectives to be presented and considered? When the courts come to balance up conflicting interests, those rights secured in domestic law through the Human Rights Act are likely to be given priority, to trump those that are excluded. For example, in the United States of America, the First Amendment, which guarantees freedom of speech, has been defined to include the right to make, use and distribute pornography. In *American Booksellers' Association Inc* v. *Hudnut*,[115] an Indianapolis ordinance that restricted pornography was found to have violated First Amendment guarantees. The ordinance at issue imposed restrictions on pornography, which was defined to mean the graphic sexually explicit subordination of women, whether in pictures or in words in a number of defined situations such as: women being presented as sexual objects who enjoy pain or humiliation or women being presented in scenarios of degradation, injury, abasement or torture. The Court struck down the ordinance emphasising that the definition of pornography had created a constitutionally impermissible viewpoint which the court likened to "thought control".[116] The judges were unable to accommodate these new feminist principles that addressed the status and dignity of women within their Constitution and attempted to rectify an imbalance in speech. Advocates of

[110] *Ibid.* para. 63. and *R* v. *Morgentaler* [1988] 1 SCR 30.
[111] Leaf Equality Symposium (1992) 5 *Leaf Lines* 3.
[112] *Andrews* v. *Law Society of British Columbia* [1989] 1 SCR 143 at 166.
[113] *Ibid.*, at 169
[114] *Ibid.*, at 171
[115] (1985) 771 F 2d 323.
[116] *Ibid.*, at 328.

the legislation had argued that pornography silences women and prevents them from playing a full and active role in the community. This measure could then be justified as a means of empowering women in the market place of ideas.[117] But such notions could not compete with the powerful First Amendment jurisprudence.

In contrast, when the Canadian Supreme Court, in *R* v. *Butler*,[118] was called upon to consider whether the Canadian obscenity law contravened the Charter guarantee to freedom of expression, it focused on the risk of anti-social behaviour, and in particular, the threat to the integrity and safety of women. According to Sopinka J, such material was obscene not because it offends against morals but because it is contrary to the "equality and dignity of all human beings", and is perceived as a social harm, in particular, to women.[119] He stated:

> "If true equality between male and female persons is to be achieved, we cannot ignore the threat to equality resulting from exposure to audiences of certain types of violent or degrading material."[120]

The importance of this decision is that Charter issues were approached in a manner which centrally locates harm to women, as well as addressing the threat posed to other Charter values, such as physical integrity and equality. The Court was attempting to balance the objective of protecting freedom of expression as against securing the goals of ending victimisation and promoting substantive equality. In a more recent challenge to the Canadian obscenity law, the Supreme Court has robustly defended its decision in *Butler*.[121] The Court affirmed that the *Butler* test related to harm and not taste or morality: "harm that rises to the level of being incompatible with the proper functioning of Canadian society".[122]

In spite of the apparent willingness of the Supreme Court Justices in *Butler* to redress social and sexual inequality, there are mixed views on whether the Charter has produced positive advantages for women. Some commentators suggested that the results generally under the Charter regime have been, at best, ambiguous,[123] while others take a more positive view.[124] A distinctive feature of Canadian constitutional cases affecting women's rights is that the vast majority of them have been brought by men, or raised Charter arguments invoked by men in proceedings taken against them by the state. Perhaps the most notorious example is the striking down of the rape-shield laws, which imposed certain restrictions on evidence concerning the sexual activity of victims in sexual assault cases.[125] Nevertheless, the equality

[117] See C MacKinnon, Feminism Unmodified: Discourses on Life and Law (Cambridge, Mass. Harvard University Press, 1987) 193–5.

[118] (1992) 8 CRR (2d) 1.

[119] *Ibid.*, at 20.

[120] *Ibid.*

[121] *Little Sisters Book and Art Emporium and others* v. *Minister of Justice* (2001) 9 BHRC 409.

[122] *Ibid.*, 431.

[123] J Fudge, "The Public/Private Distinction: The Possibilities of and the Limits to Charter Litigation" (1987) 25 *Osgoode Hall Law Journal* 445 at 485.

[124] M Eberts, *supra* n. 41, at p. 278 and J Nedelsky, *supra* n. 7, at 1286.

[125] See *R* v. *Seaboyer* (1991) 83 DLR (4th) 193.

guarantees in the Canadian Charter have provided a powerful political symbol around which feminist groups can unite. For the first time the Court has placed women in the central position in judicial reasoning: it has acknowledged that pornography can harm women, the value of the child-bearing role of women, the real dynamics of wife-abuse and the power imbalances inherent in sexual harassment.[126]

CONCLUSION

The partial incorporation of the European Convention of Human Rights into domestic United Kingdom law may not to lead to a radical transformation of our legal system. It fails to cover many of the social and economic rights that would make a dramatic difference to the everyday life of women. Although sex is a prohibited ground of discrimination in the Convention, the limitations inherent in Article 14 may still render systemic disadvantage invisible. Although a few European Court decisions have shown sensitivity towards the position of women, the vast majority of cases do not address the experience of women.

Nevertheless, the adoption of the Human Rights Act has created an opportunity for feminist engagement with public law and new ground for theorising and strategy-making. The concepts traditionally invoked by law to demonstrate its neutrality in relation to the sexes—concepts such as "impartiality", "objectivity" and "rationality" can now be tested against human rights standards. Feminist insights together with human rights principles may contest the unspoken assumptions inherent in the apparently neutral legal principles. There is a unique opportunity to unsettle existing discourses and to ask previously unasked questions.

Relying on law as a means of achieving social change remains a high risk strategy. It is understandable that feminists do not agree on the utility of law reform in domestic legal systems as it has the potential for gains and losses.[127] As well as being expensive, litigation also requires considerable emotional support and many individual litigants report the experience as a disempowering one.[128] Nor can there be any certainty that the judiciary will be sympathetic to feminist ideals. In the Canadian Supreme Court, there have been two or three women judges who have been willing to argue forcefully and persuasively from a feminist perspective. Yet even in Canada, feminists have found that significant conceptual constraints exist which limit attempts to achieve social change through litigation.

It seems unwise, however, to abandon the potential of rights to those unsympathetic to feminist ideals. Whether or not women look to law, the law will continue to have a profound effect on our everyday lives. Rights could provide a weapon to challenge previously hidden gender based harms. The reception of amicus briefs,

[126] M Eberts, *supra* n. 41, at 278.

[127] S Millns, *supra* n. 7, at 208.

[128] See M Thornton, *The Liberal Promise: Legislation Against Sex Discrimination in Australia* (Oxford, Oxford University Press, 1990).

expanded submissions to the Court which set out a diversity of perspectives, should enhance the Court's deliberative process and provide a mechanism to give women a voice in the legal system. Rights claims, then, may be one tactic in seeking to reconstruct our legal system and give validation to the insights of women.

Law and its language can be a critical frontier for feminist change. Legal discourse is a site of political struggle over sex differences.[129] The language of rights has the potential to mobilise movements, to influence political debate, and, perhaps, to contribute to social change. While cautiously adopting rights discourse as one strategy to improve the condition of women's lives, feminist theory must still retain its critical vantage point on gender subordination. The challenge lies in giving meaning to rights that are imaginative and responsive to the realities of women's lives.

[129] M J Frug, "A Postmodern Feminist Legal Manifesto" (An Unfinished Draft) in F. Olsen (ed.), *Feminist Legal Theory* (Aldershot, Dartmouth, 1995) 491, 492.

5

Violence, Ethics and Law: Feminist Reflections on a Familiar Dilemma

NICOLA LACEY*

THE PARADOXICAL RELATIONSHIP between law and violence is a familiar puzzle in legal and political theory. On the one hand, the legitimating ideology of modern law—most obviously in purportedly liberal-democratic systems—is founded on two aspirations. First, law aspires to distinguish, among actions which on their face appear to constitute "violence", the authorised from the unauthorised, the legitimate from the illegitimate. Second, law purports to underpin an institutional framework which allows both governmental and (within strictly defined limits) non-governmental actors[1] to act, in a variety of ways, against illegitimate violence and, on occasion, the threat of such violence.

To put the aspirations of modern law in this way is already to suggest the dilemma referred to in my title. For, on the other hand, law itself may plausibly be understood as founded in—even as a system of—violence, since it can carry within itself no account of its own legitimacy. This point is perhaps made most graphically in Derrida's well known essay "Force of Law";[2] but it is at the heart of a long tradition

* I should like to thank Henrietta Moore, Renata Salecl and Mariana Valverde for their very helpful comments on an earlier version of this paper. I am also grateful to participants in seminars at the University of Cambridge and the International Institute of the University of Michigan to which the paper was presented, and to my colleagues at the Law Program in the Research School of Social Sciences of the Australian National University, which provided an ideal environment in which to complete work on it.

[1] It is often said that the constitutional state claims the monopoly of violence, but this is an exaggeration: rather, it claims a monopoly in defining the circumstances under which violence is legitimate; see J Raz, *The Authority of Law* (Oxford, Clarendon Press, 1979) chap. 2.

[2] J Derrida, "Force of Law: the 'Mystical Foundation of Authority'" in D Cornell, M Rosenfield and D Gray Carlson (eds.), *Deconstruction and the Possibility of Justice* (New York, Routledge, 1992). The intimacy of law and violence is often associated with Robert Cover's claim in the opening paragraph of "Violence and the Word" that legal interpretation takes place "in a field of pain and death" (1986) 95 *Yale Law Journal* 1601. In fact Cover's argument depends upon a significant distinction between "the word" of law and the violence which marks its implementation. For further discussion, see P Fitzpatrick, "Why the Law is also Non-Violent" (Manuscript, 1999). Another source for debates about law's violence is Pierre Bourdieu's idea of the "symbolic violence" involved in the imposition of symbolic representations—including languages—on people who have little nor no choice as to whether to adopt them. For a general discussion of the relevance of Bourdieu's ideas for legal theory, see P Bourdieu, "The Force of Law: Toward a Sociology of the Juridical Field", translated by Richard Terdiman (1987) 38 *Hastings Law Journal* 805. The fact that both Bourdieu and Derrida deploy the concept of violence in relation to law does not, however, imply any deeper connection: for a taste of Bourdieu's views on deconstruction, see for example Bourdieu *supra* n. 2, at 819 n. 27.

within legal theory which engages with the fact that "positive law" can, by definition, generate no explanation of its own foundations and hence has to be understood as a distinctively institutionalised system of force.[3]

The unpalatable taste of this conclusion, with its apparently devastating implications for the supposed normativity of law, tends to call forth one of two general responses among legal theorists. The first response, sticking to its positivist guns, as it were, side-steps the problem of violence by espousing an "internal" or "legal" point of view which focuses on the capacity of legal discourse to generate a system of norms which is coherent on the basis—or presupposition[4]—that a particular agent such as a judge has adopted that perspective. In effect, this banishes the problem of violence to another discipline—to sociology, moral or political philosophy, economics, psychology, psychoanalysis or political science. Everything turns on the espousal of the legal point of view,[5] yet legal theory is excused from the task of producing an account of why agents should (or do) adopt such a perspective. [6] Law's violence—and with it, one horn of the dilemma—simply disappears, and "external" questions about the force of law become questions for the social and human sciences.

The second response is that of the natural law tradition. This response has a more inclusive and ambitious approach to legal theory, in that it denies that the question of violence can be banished to another realm of inquiry, and insists that the (moral) legitimacy of law is internally related to law's validity. On the natural lawyer's view, law is a moral system and not merely an institutionalisation of force: the idea of law as violence is roundly rejected in favour of the idea of law as an institutionalisation of practical ethics.

Neither of these responses, of course, is likely to satisfy anyone who takes the sort of position espoused by Derrida in "Force of Law". The positivist response is Derrida's more obvious target, and its inadequacies from his point of view hardly need any restatement here. Though in some moments positivism is prepared squarely to face the problem, its consistent espousal of the normativity of law (not to mention the implicit alliance of much positivism with political liberalism) amounts to an (ideological) suppression of the brutal view of law as an institutionalisation of force.[7] The limitations of the natural law response are somewhat more

[3] See M Davies, *Delimiting the Law* (London, Pluto, 1996).

[4] As, respectively, in the positivist theories of H L A Hart's *The Concept of Law* (Oxford, Clarendon Press, 1961) and H Kelsen's *General Theory of Law and State* (Cambridge, Mass., 1945).

[5] See Raz, *supra* n. 1, chaps. 4 and 7.

[6] Interestingly, there is a significant structural similarity between this positivist move and the sociological view of law as an autopoietic system which reflexively determines its own conditions of validity (N Luhmann, *A Sociological Theory of Law* (London, Routledge and Kegan Paul, 1985); G Teubner, *Law as an Autopoietic System* (Oxford, Basil Blackwell, 1993)). Since systems theory does not purport to offer an account of law's normativity except from the point of view of law itself, the problem of law as violence disappears, albeit exiting by a somewhat different route than in the positivist account. See further Bourdieu, *supra* n. 2, at 816.

[7] In one recent version, which announces itself as "ethical positivism", legal positivism is simply reinterpreted as a branch of liberal political theory (see T Campbell, *The Legal Theory of Ethical Positivism* (Aldershot, Darmouth, 1996)). This version has the great merit of wearing its normative credentials on its sleeve, but it continues to assert the separability of law and political morality at the level of legal reasoning and legal judgment.

complex. For this response implies that legitimate laws are not "violent" in any morally relevant sense, and many of its proponents would dismiss the Derridean argument as an analytically dubious (indeed obfuscating) inflation of the concept of "violence"—an inflation which threatens to rob it of its critical force in normative thinking.

Interestingly, the idea that law's violence can be tempered by an ethics has now begun to emerge in the context of a different genre of legal theory. In recent postmodern and critical legal theory, there has been a marked focus on ethics.[8] Conversely, writers on what one might loosely call "postmodern ethics"[9] are taking a renewed interest in the juridical sphere. Law's violence, and its ethical limits and possibilities have, in short, provided a productive seam of enquiry in contemporary social theory.[10] Yet the sense of the ethical which is invoked here appears to be significantly different from that in ancient or modern natural law traditions. Indeed, the relevant debates are clouded by movements back and forth between ideas of the ethical as "good", "right" or "desirable" (in a sense which either echoes the natural law tradition or evokes modernist moral and political theory) and of the ethical as "open" or "beyond" (as invoked by those taking deconstructionist or postmodern approaches).[11] Not only the idea of ethics, but also the relationship between the ethical, the just and the moral, are being used in very different senses.

Another distinctive feature of this recent literature is its tendency to associate the ethical or the just with the feminine or with sexual difference.[12] Given the persuasive feminist interpretation of law's masculinity, and the fact that both ethics and justice are often defined by contrasting them to law, this tendency to feminise the ethical is perhaps understandable. It also ties up with the postmodern conception of the ethical as "open" or "beyond", via the Lacanian argument that woman's jouissance escapes representation in language, and hence symbolises that which lies beyond violent or difference-repressing institutionalisation. Yet, as I shall argue, this feminisation of the ethical puts an undue theoretical burden on the concept of sexual difference, and one which threatens not only to collapse into a form of essentialism but also to confer upon the *feminine* a set of associations or responsibilities which

[8] See for example C Douzinas, R Warrington and S McVeigh, *Postmodern Jurisprudence: The Law of Texts in the Texts of Law* (London, Routledge, 1991); C Douzinas and R Warrington, *Justice Miscarried: Ethics and Aesthetics in Law* (Hemel Hempstead, Harvester, 1994); and C Douzinas and R Warrington, "The Face of Justice: A Jurisprudence of Alterity" in A Young and A Sarat (eds.), *Beyond Criticism: Law, Power and Ethics*, Special Issue (1994) 3 *Social and Legal Studies*. Douzinas and Warrington's interpretation of ethics is drawn from Levinas, and hence explores the responsibilities generated by radical alterity.

[9] See for example Z Bauman, *Postmodern Ethics* (Oxford, Basil Blackwell, 1993).

[10] See Young and Sarat (eds.) *supra* n. 8; J Butler, *Excitable Speech* (New York, Routledge, 1997).

[11] See L Irigaray, *An Ethics of Sexual Difference*, translated by C Burke and G Gill (London, Athlone, 1993).

[12] This is true not only of feminist work such as Irigaray's, *ibid*. For example, Douzinas and Warrington *supra* n. 8, invoke the figure of Antigone to symbolise the commitment to justice in contrast to law. See also P Goodrich's, *Law in the Courts of Love* (London, Routledge, 1996) exploring medieval texts describing laws created and administered by women and, significantly, repressed within the canon of legal history.

bear a striking resemblance to those imposed on *woman* in nineteenth and early twentieth-century anti-feminist or separatist discourse.[13]

Similar difficulties attend the use to which the concept of violence is being put on the other side of this theoretical coin. In researching this paper, I have found myself increasingly bemused about just what is meant by "violence"; more and more troubled by the need to unpick the analytic and rhetorical aspects of the claim that law may—or must?—be understood as violence, or as founded in violence, or as having violent aspects; and occasionally affronted by the potential trivialisation of the sorts of violence perpetrated by legal institutions upon, for example, criminal defendants within an inflated rhetoric of law's *generally* violent or objectifying method. Nevertheless, in what follows, I shall remain within the framework of violence and ethics, while interrogating and adapting it as my argument develops. For, even as I have struggled with the problems just rehearsed, I have found that a more differentiated conception of violence and ethics indeed provides a useful interpretative framework within which to assess some of the central issues of contemporary legal theory.

LAW'S VIOLENCE

So far, I have focused on the difficulty of distinguishing legitimate from illegitimate force as the key to the paradoxical relationship between law and violence. But from Derrida's point of view, and in particular in the context of the distinction which he wants to emphasise between law and justice, the issue of law's violence is not merely to do with the legitimacy of legal force. Rather, it has to do with the nature of legal judgment and legal subjectivity. In fixing subjects and events within a particular framework, and in drawing practical and ultimately—at least internally—unchallengeable conclusions, the enforcement of law (anticipated, inevitably, in law itself) closes off the "possibility of justice": in applying general rules to specific cases, the irreducible particularity of the human world is foreclosed. This, as much as the violent foundations of law which reverberate in the moment of judgment, lies at the heart of Derrida's argument, and it relates to the social practice of law understood in either positivist or naturalist terms.

The same is true of another, rather different way of thinking about law as violence. This is the idea, central to socio-legal studies, that the social practice of law has disciplinary effects—effects which stretch beyond the juridical and sovereignty aspects of legal power.[14] Like law's violence in Derrida's sense, these aspects of legal or quasi-legal power—including the power to shape the kinds of social subjects

[13] For further discussion, see below. See Also M Valverde, "Life and Death Questions: Gender, Justice and Irony" (Manuscript, 1999).

[14] See M Foucault, *Discipline and Punish*, trans. A Sheridan (London, Penguin, 1977); M Foucault, *The History of Sexuality* vol. 1 (London, Penguin, 1981); for further discussion, see N Lacey, *Unspeakable Subjects: Feminist Essays in Legal and Social Theory* (Oxford, Hart Publishing, 1998) chap. 8; see also, from a different point of view, I M Young's conceptualisation of violence as one aspect of power: *Justice and the Politics of Difference* (Princeton, Princeton University Press, 1990).

which we may become—are difficult to rationalise within either the liberal accounts of law's legitimacy espoused by positivists or in terms of naturalist accounts of law's moral credentials. I mention this argument because it expands the horizon of Derrida's argument. For it implies that we may usefully interrogate the violence of law's determinations well beyond the obvious forum of judicial decision. And in doing so, as I shall argue below, it opens up the possibility—indeed necessity—of theorising law not merely as a body of doctrine but also as a social practice, deploying and enacting various different forms of power.

Derrida's claim about law's violence is not, of course, advanced so as to engage in what we might call "modernist normative theory". That is, to paraphrase from C Northcote Parkinson's famous satire on textbook history, *1066 and all that . . .*, Derrida's project is not to make the direct claim that violence is "a bad thing"(!). Rather, he maintains that it is a significant aspect of law or of the social world of which the social theorist should take note. On the other hand, however, he uses a technique of articulating the aspects of legal (or other) practices which he wants to emphasise in terms which have an undoubted rhetorical force. In the political and social culture of contemporary Europe or North America, for example, it would be absurd to claim that "violence" is a neutral concept, and it seems fair to assume that Derrida's deployment of that resonance is an entirely conscious one.

I want to focus on this debate about the contours of "violence", because I think that it helps to shed light on some crucial issues in contemporary legal theory. For the position which we take on law's violence—how we conceptualise it, whether we think it is inevitable and, if so, whether we think it is interesting or problematic—makes a decisive difference to our position on the relationship between the ethical and the legal. If it is the case not only that law is founded in (by definition unlegitimated) violence but also that the practice of law—the force of law anticipated and enacted by the enunciation of legal standards—implies violence, then the consequences for what we might call the "utopian" voice in legal theory seem significant. If violence is located within the deep structures of, for example, language or law, difficult questions arise about how to construct strategies of opposition (indeed even of critique). To put it in another way, equally familiar in recent critical legal theory, if law inevitably ("violently") flattens out or represses difference and particularity,[15] fixing subjects in pre-given identities, the project of finding some ethical space within law seems destined to find its terrain only on the margins of legal practice, in law's failures and incompletenesses rather than its (possibly reconstructed) successes. This, of course, is one way of reading the Derridean project of celebrating the "play of différance"; it is also one way of looking at reception within some critical legal theory of the Lacanian assertion of an excess which

[15] As A Norrie has recently noted ("Three Dialectics in Search of a Subject: Law and the Critique of 'Identity Thinking'" (1999) *Social and Legal Studies*), this aspect of Derrida's argument reveals his retention of a primarily analytic, rather than socio-historical, approach to legal critique. I shall take up later in this paper the question of whether such analytic generalisations are an appropriate method for critical appraisal of either law's violence or the ethical possibilities of the legal.

escapes language (or law).[16] The logical impossibility of challenging linguistic or legal violence *through language or law* therefore pulls in the direction of the postmodern notion of the ethical as "beyond". And, as I shall argue, this link has important implications for the relationship between critique and the progressive political interventions from which even Derrida is reluctant to distance himself.

My particular interest in these questions of violence and ethics in legal theory derive from my engagement with feminist legal theory.[17] Feminist scholars have been among the most rigorous and forthright critics of the substance and structure of law in modern societies, and feminist legal theory has drawn on Derridean deconstruction, Foucauldian conceptions of power and a Lacanian analysis of the sexual dynamics of language—the necessary role of the repressed "other" in the constitution of legal subjectivity—to produce an analysis of law's violence. Yet much feminist thought is also preoccupied to a significant degree by the idea that law might be otherwise than it has been and is: that we might imagine (and institutionalise?) a law capable of delivering sexual justice, or at least a law significantly less sexually unjust than contemporary law has been shown to be. This sort of "ethical" voice in feminist legal theory is perhaps most obviously represented by the substantial tradition of feminist legal reformism, much of it located within liberal or marxist political values.[18] The contrasting, postmodern vision of the "ethical" (or perhaps utopian) in relation to law is exemplified by Luce Irigaray's engagement with the question of special rights for women[19] and by Drucilla Cornell's idea of an "ethical feminism".[20] These feminist writers draw on the techniques of critique and deconstruction to produce an analysis of law's specifically sexual violence. In Cornell's case, this analysis is premised on broadly Lacanian view of sexual difference; Irigaray's philosophy, though critical of aspects of Lacan's account of sexual difference, also has a substantially psychoanalytic orientation. And both make an explicit link between the deconstruction of law's sexual violence and "ethics".

Does it make sense at once to espouse a broad deconstruction of law's violence and to entertain utopian dreams about either an ethical law or an ethical space within and around law? And how, if at all, do these utopian feminist projects relate to the tradition of reformist scholarship? With these general questions in mind, I want to step sideways to examine one influential set of debates within feminist legal

[16] See D Cornell, *Beyond Accommodation: Ethical Feminism Deconstruction and the Law* (London, Routledge, 1991); D Cornell, *The Philosophy of the Limit* (London, Routledge, 1992).

[17] Lacey, *supra* n. 14.

[18] See, in different veins, C MacKinnon, *The Sexual Harassment of Working Women* (New Haven, Yale University Press, 1979); S Fredman, *Women and the Law* (Oxford, Clarendon Press, 1998).

[19] L Irigaray, *J'aime à toi Esquisse d'une felicite dans l'histoire* Paris, Grasset (translated as *I Love to You*, trans. A Martin) (London, Routledge, 1996); L Irigaray *Je, Tu, Nous: Towards a Culture of Difference*, trans. A Martin (London, Routledge, 1993); L Irigaray, *Thinking the Difference*, trans. by K Montin (London, Athlone, 1994); for the philosophical background to Irigaray's specific interventions in law, see her *Marine Lover of Friedrich Nietszche* (Columbia, Columbia University Press, 1991); L Irigaray, *Speculum of the Other Woman* (Ithaca, Cornell University Press, 1985); L Irigaray, *This Sex which Is Not One* (Ithaca, Cornell University Press, 1985).

[20] Cornell, *supra* n. 16; see also D Cornell, *Transformations: Recollective Imagination and Sexual Difference* (London, Routledge, 1993) and *The Imaginary Domain* (London, Routledge, 1995).

theory. These have to do with the (re)conceptualisation of the subject of law in less sexually exclusive—and hence violent, in Derrida's sense—terms. I shall review some of the most familiar moves within this debate, before moving on to consider the general lessons to be learned about both the theoretical utility of deploying the notion of law as violence and the promise of the search for an ethical space in law.

CONCEPTUALISING THE SUBJECT OF LAW

In this section, I want to set out some of the main themes in feminist legal theory which might plausibly be concerned with the critique of the violence of legal judgment or legal power more broadly conceived. Perhaps the most fundamental issue in this context is the debate about how modern law conceptualises its subjects. Though taking different forms in different feminist traditions, a key concern has been to develop a critical analysis of the ways in which law conceptualises its subjects as autonomous, self-identical and (in some versions) purportedly disembodied individuals.[21] This is an ambitious argument, because it tries to locate sexual difference in the very conceptual framework out of which law is constructed. Moreover, it connects directly with the questions of violence and ethics, in that the feminist critique suggests that legal subjectivity is a site of violent sexual exclusion. However, a significant strand of feminist theory has also argued for a reconstruction of the legal subject in less violent—and hence more ethically appealing—terms; and it is this ambivalence about the *inevitability* of law's violence, and the shifts between different senses of the ethical, in feminist legal theory which are of particular interest to the project of this paper.

Synthesising from a wide range of feminist work, we could put the main contours of the debate about the legal subject in the following way. First, it has been argued that modern law conceptualises its subjects as pre-social individuals; in other words, it takes itself to be *responding* to persons pre-legally constituted as individuals with certain "natural" characteristics, interests, needs. The important point about this is that it disguises the dynamic role which law itself plays in constituting social and legal subjects in specific ways. In other words, law is one important social institution or practice which constitutes us as subjects. Of course, this argument is not distinctively feminist but more broadly constructionist. For example, the debate about corporate liability for crime takes place against a backcloth of assumptions about the "fictitious" nature of corporate personality as opposed to "natural" human personhood. Yet from a constructionist perspective, the way in which we are constituted as subjects for the purposes of criminal law is neither natural nor given: law itself decides/selects which features of our lives are relevant for the purposes of interpreting us as full subjects of criminal law.

[21] See for example N Naffine, *Law and the Sexes* (Sydney, Allen & Unwin, 1990); J Nedelsky, "Reconceiving Autonomy" (1989) 1 *Yale Journal of Law and Feminism* 7.

This constructionist argument does, however, have some very striking feminist applications. For example, and most vividly, the law of rape constitutes us as subjects sexed in particular ways; and the particular ways in which rape law constitutes sexed subjects provides an excellent example of the varieties of legal power. It is not just a question of the "violent" exclusion of the rape victim's experience—her (or his) constitution as an "unspeakable subject"—with its direct consequences for criminal law's capacity to respond to sexual violence. It is also a question of sexual offences' disciplinary power—the capacity of a range of criminal laws to making it possible or impossible, easy or difficult to live certain kinds of lives. This set of arguments connects closely with an important group of debates in contemporary feminist philosophy—particularly those concerned with the constitution of the body in social practices.[22]

Secondly, and following on from this, it has been argued that legal subjects are typically conceptualised in terms of distinctive characteristics which are culturally associated with the masculine. This argument generally takes off from the analysis of a number of dichotomies in Western thought, male/female; public/private; reason/emotion/ active/passive; individual/community; form/substance—which are interpreted as both hierarchised and sexualised.[23] To the extent that this interpretation is convincing, we can construct arguments about the "sex" or "gender" of social institutions. In legal terms, and staying for the moment with the analogy of criminal law, the argument goes something like this: The subject of criminal law is defined, doctrinally, in terms of a particular set of capacities. Three sorts of capacities are of particular importance: the cognitive capacities of reason and understanding; the volitional capacity to control one's behaviour; the moral capacity to know right from wrong. These capacities are in turn associated with the masculine in Western culture: they are the capacities of the mind and of reason rather than emotional or embodied attributes. In substantive offences such as rape, this cashes out in terms of a conceptualisation of both wrongdoing and harm in primarily mental, rational or proprietary terms.[24]

Thirdly, it has been argued that the legal subject, particularly in civil or public law, is typically interpreted as the bearer of individual rights, and that both rights themselves and rights-based reasoning are constructed in ways which are either culturally marked as masculine or inimical to women's interests or both. For example, drawing on Carol Gilligan's work, feminist legal theorists have noted the marginalisation of relational reasoning in deductive legal reasoning; the cultural celebration of the "sharpness" and "rigour" of analytic, deductive reasoning in both legal practice and legal education; the cultural inferiority of the "feminine voice" in moral reasoning and its silencing in law; the marginalisation of emotion, commitment,

[22] See for example J Butler, *Gender Trouble* (New York, Routledge, 1990); J Butler, *Bodies that Matter On the Discursive Limits of "Sex"* (New York, Routledge, 1993); M Gatens, *Imaginary Bodies* (London, Routledge, 1996); E Grosz, *Volatile Bodies* (Sydney, Allen & Unwin, 1994).

[23] See F Olsen, "Feminism and Critical Legal Theory: An American Perspective" (1990) 18 *International Journal of the Sociology of Law* 199.

[24] See Lacey, *supra* n. 14, chaps. 4 and 7.

relationship; and the interpretation of anything approaching an "ethics of care" as impossible or difficult to articulate within law.[25] This strand of analysis has generated a huge debate about the "feminine" voice in adjudication and legislation,[26] as well as a controversy about whether Gilligan's gender-association of the two voices really holds up to further empirical scrutiny. But whatever one's view of the general adequacy of Gilligan's approach, there can be no doubt that her argument has been of great importance in pointing up features of legal reasoning which may have exclusionary effects along a number of different lines.

This kind of analysis has been associated with a widespread feminist critique of rights. In a range of feminist work,[27] rights have been criticised as competitive, individualistic, and ultimately indeterminate.[28] Significantly from the point of view of our question about violence and ethics, this has led, in the work of writers from such different traditions as Jennifer Nedelsky[29] and Luce Irigaray, to a feminist move to reconstruct or reconceptualise rights in less atomistic, competitive and more intersubjective, relational terms.[30] Renata Salecl's argument about the location of rights within an empty space of Kantian universalism, while differing significantly from the "standard" feminist critique of rights and of the Cartesian conception of subjectivity, suggests why rights have constituted a figure of promise as well as an object of critique in recent feminist thought.[31] From her Lacanian perspective, the discourse of universal human rights represents the "fantasy scenario in which society and the individual are perceived as whole, as non-split": but the discourse also allows us to discern an alternative "feminine" or "postmodern" logic of rights which moves beyond an idea of rights as a form of property, as something which can be possessed. I will return to these debates later in my analysis of "utopian" projects in feminist legal theory.[32]

[25] C Gilligan, *In a Different Voice: Psychological Theory and Women's Development* (Cambridge, Mass., Harvard University Press, 1982); see also M J Frug, *Postmodern Legal Feminism* (London, Routledge, 1992); N Noddings, *Caring: A Feminist Approach to Ethics and Moral Education* (Berkeley, University of California Press, 1984); S Sevenhuisen, *Citizenship and the Ethics of Care* (London, Routledge, 1998).

[26] See for example S Sherry, "Civic Virtue and the Feminine voice in Constitutional Adjudication" (1986) 72 *Virginia Law Review* 543.

[27] Similar arguments are of course to be found in the Marxist and socialist traditions: see T Campbell, *The Left and Rights* (London, Routledge and Kegan Paul, 1983); J Waldron, *Nonsense Upon Stilts: Bantam, Burke and Marx on the Rights of Man* (London, Methuen, 1987); some of them may even be argued to derive from Jeremy Bentham; see N Lacey, "Bentham as Proto-Feminist?" (1998) *Current Legal Problems* 441.

[28] See for example J Fudge, "The Effect of Entrenching a Bill of Rights on Political Discourse" (1988) 17 *International Journal of the Sociology of Law* 445; J Fudge and H Glasbeek, "The Politics of Rights: A Politics with Little Class" (1992) 1 *Social and Legal Studies* 45; E Kingdom, *What's Wrong with Rights? Problems for a Feminist Philosophy of Law* (Edinburgh, Edinburgh University Press, 1991).

[29] J Nedelsky, "Reconceiving Rights as Relationship" (1993) *Review of Constitutional Studies* 1.

[30] There is an interesting contrast here between feminist critique of rights and critical race theorists' more pragmatic approach: see for example P Williams, *The Alchemy of Race and Rights* (Cambridge, Mass., Harvard University Press, 1991).

[31] R Salecl, *The Spoils of Freedom* (London, Routledge, 1994) chap. 8.

[32] R Salecl's argument about rights, *ibid.* and accompanying text, though it concludes by contrasting modern and postmodern logics, seems to me to gesture at a framework which might be used to challenge the dichotomy. On the capacity of pragmatism to disrupt aspects of the modernist/postmodernist opposition, see further below.

Summing up, constructionist ideas about the nature of human being have been invoked as part of the conceptual framework out of which feminist legal theory has begun to shape what we might call the project of "sexing the subject of law".[33] This project has three distinct senses. First, it may be regarded as providing a critical analysis geared to unearthing law's gendered assumptions about the ideal–typical legal subject—i.e. interpreting the law as sexed (in its most ambitious forms, at a conceptual level), and revealing the "violent" exclusion of the (feminine) "other" whose identity is the necessary underpinning of the phantasmatic, self-identical legal subject. Second, it may be regarded as working towards an understanding of the dynamic role of law in producing sexed identity, and sexed social subjects—i.e. interpreting the law as a sexing practice. Third, it may be regarded as implicitly utopian; as moving towards the horizon of "resexing" law—i.e. changing the shape of its assumptions about sexed and sexual identity. It is this third sense which reveals most clearly the split between different senses of the ethical and of violence and which tracks feminist theory's ambivalent stance *vis à vis* modernist and (non-pragmatist) postmodernist perspectives. This is not always apparent, however, because the three different senses of the "sexing" project have not always been carefully distinguished in contemporary feminist thought.

SPECIFIC DEBATES EMERGING FROM THE "SEXING" ANALYSIS

I now want to discuss some more specific debates within the "sexing" project which illustrate the elision of critical, reformist or utopian projects. As I shall argue, unacknowledged shifts in conceptions of the violent and the ethical appear to be one of the main symptoms—or perhaps causes—of this elision.[34]

I shall set out from the basic premise of the feminist critique of the legal subject: modern law assumes a rationalistic conception of the person as individual abstracted from its social, bodily and affective contexts, and this conception of the person is implicitly marked as male. This leads to two kinds of feminist legal strategy. The first, which may be called "*contextualisation as critique*", engages in a critical analysis which aims to show that this conceptualisation of the legal subject is itself a contextualisation, a construction; that law is not "innocently" acting as "the mirror of nature"; [35] that the construction of legal subjectivity is a contextualisation which represses "the other"; and, finally, that the shape of this specific contextualisation is in any case inconsistently realised in law. For example, the shaping of the time frame in rules of criminal law and evidence shifts in arbitrary ways:[36] an array of defences broaden the legal subject in terms of pre-existing factors (the experience

[33] See N Naffine and R Owens (eds.), *Sexing the Subject of Law* (Sydney, Allen & Unwin, 1997).

[34] It is illustrated, albeit in different ways, in both MacKinnon's work on pornography C Mackinnon, *Toward a Feminist Theory of the State* (Cambridge, Mass, Harvard University Press, 1989)) and Irigaray's work on rights (*supra* n. 19); for further discussion, see below.

[35] R Rorty, *Philosophy and the Mirror of Nature* (Princeton, Princeton University Press, 1979).

[36] See M Kelman, "Interpretative Construction in the Substantive Criminal Law" (1981) 33 *Stanford Law Review* 591.

of long-term domestic violence, for instance) which amount to conditions under which subjectivity is realised.[37] Similarly in the law of contract, the recognition of losses caused by one party's reliance on the other as grounding a claim for damages has broadened out the concept of the contractual relationship in certain areas: for certain purposes, yet not others, the contracting subject is seen not just as an agent making a bargain at a particular moment, but also as part of a web of social and economic relationships which generate legal responsibilities.[38] This immanent critique of law's shifting framework is once again a way of emphasising law's dynamic role in shaping our conceptions of the world: it reveals the stereotype of the rational, atomistic legal subject to be not a seamless ideological fiction but a form which is unevenly realised in legal doctrine.

Our perception of the unevenness of law's conceptualisation of subjectivity is sharpened if we widen our perspective to look beyond legal doctrine to the broader legal and social discourses which shape women's and men's insertion into the doctrinal framework. And it is surely important to do so if—as a social theorist must be—we are interested in law not merely as an articulated body of doctrine but as a developing social practice. Certainly, we can find doctrinal examples of the abstracted legal subject. We can also find telling doctrinal examples of the subject contextualised in sexual and bodily terms: English criminal law's incest provisions, which differentiate the sexual position of woman and man as, respectively, passive and active, is an obvious one.[39] But this does not mean that we can get an adequate feminist analysis of the law of incest, rape or anything else just by looking at legal rules. We also need to look at the broader interpretative frames which shape the impact and meaning of doctrine: rules of evidence, enforcement practice and so on. The examples which we have considered suggest that even within its current conceptual limits, law is nonetheless capable of contextualising—indeed does contextualise—its subjects in "embodied" or "situated" ways, albeit not consistently. So there is always a risk of overplaying the ambitious conceptual claim in feminist legal theory. Again, it may be helpful to think about the analogy with corporate criminal liability: it is not just law which is important in marginalising corporate liability, but also broader social discourses of responsibility, conduct, agency and blame which underpin legal arrangements.[40]

The second kind of feminist project proceeding from the sexing analysis may usefully be called "*contextualisation as strategy*". Again, drawing on Carol Gilligan's work, it sometimes seems to be assumed that if we were to broaden the ways in which the legal subject is contextualised—bringing in a wider array of social relationships, bodily attributes or states, emotional experiences as relevant evidence contemplated by legal rules, broadening the context in which legal disputes can be framed—we might break down the association of the legal subject with the masculine and hence make

37 A Norrie, *Crime, Reason and History* (London, Weidenfeld and Nicolson, 1993).

38 H Collins, *The Law of Contract*, 3rd ed. (London, Butterworths, 1998).

39 Sexual Offences Act 1956 sections 10 and 11.

40 See N Lacey, "*Philosophical Foundations of the Common Law: Social not Metaphysical*" in J Horder (ed.), *Oxford Essays in Jurisprudence (4th Series)* (Oxford, Oxford University Press, 2000).

law more accessible/sensitive to women's concerns. In other words, we could have an impact on this particular aspect of law's exclusionary violence, rendering law more open and flexible, and hence more ethically sensitive to multiple subject positions, capable of moving closer to the "possibility of justice". In this argument, crucially, the two rather different senses of the ethical mentioned above—the ethical as "good" and the ethical as "open" or "beyond"—are elided. And with this elision, an important distinction between what I shall call—tracking my earlier distinction between critical, reformist and utopian projects—"institutional reformist strategy" and "utopian rhetorical strategy" is lost.

Another example of such elision might be drawn from the widespread debates about alternative dispute resolution. To paint with broad brush strokes, it has been argued that if we made the legal process more polycentric and less adversarial, horizontal rather than vertical, this would be an advance from a feminist point of view, and from the more general point of view of diluting law's violence.[41] This argument speaks directly to the assertion that legal judgment is inevitably violent in its binary, determinate categorisations: in moving towards a more open-ended conception of legally relevant standards, a less hierarchical and more participatory view of the dispute-resolving process, and a more powerful role for legal actors, it is argued that we would be not only breaking down law's hierarchical method but also increasing law's capacity to respond to particularity and hence to approach justice.

Each of these two examples of "contextualisation as strategy" makes the same move: it aspires, by reshaping the conceptual or procedural framework of law, to achieve ethical or political advances. Furthermore, this kind of argument has had a real effect on legal policy. In the criminal law field over the last decade, one striking example is that of the gradual (and partial) reception of evidence of phenomena such as "battered women's syndrome", and "pre-menstrual syndrome" in the articulation of criminal defences (and hence in the constitution of legal subjectivity). Similarly, recent years have seen significant experiments and developments in informal justice, mediation, conciliation and arbitration, not only in employment and commercial contexts, but also in the fields of family disputes and even criminal justice. In certain areas of English criminal law, there has been a significant recontextualisation of subjects within long-term relationships, emotional experiences and bodily states.[42] Is there a certain paradox to finding this apparent germ of emancipation or gender justice in the very body which has been the object of the denigration of women? This touches on a general dilemma for the strategy of (re)contextualisation.

[41] See B Santos (ed.), "State Transformation, Legal Pluralism and Community Justice" (1992) Special Issue, Vol. 1, No. 2, *Social and Legal Studies*; B Santos, *Toward a New Common Sense* (London, Routledge, 1995); for further discussion, see Lacey, *supra* n. 14, chap. 5.

[42] For further discussion, see Lacey, *supra*, n. 14, chap. 7.

DILEMMAS OF CONTEXTUALISATION

The strategy of contextualisation which elides reformism and utopianism is, however, double-edged, and this feature of the strategy holds some cautionary insights for the critical focus on "law's violence". I now want to illustrate this difficulty, before returning to consider how feminist social theory might most usefully deploy appeals to different conceptions of the ethical.

When understood as recontextualising a violent encounter in terms of, for example, the effect of long-term violence within a relationship, the impact of gendered stereotypes on sexual behaviour, or the effects of shock on the demeanour of witnesses in criminal trials, the criminal law developments which I have sketched undoubtedly expand law's capacity to accommodate particularity and to avoid violent exclusions. But—as becomes clear once we move from legal rules to legal discourse, from law as a body of doctrine to law as a social practice—their tendency to be interpreted in ways which are closely related to prejudicial stereotypes about male and female bodies and sexualities ("woman as victim of her hormones", for example . . .) suggests that the strategy has its dangers. It suggests, significantly, that law's violence is a product not only of its own dispositive method, but also of the surrounding relations and vectors of power which shape and characterise the totality of social practices. Much the same has been observed about the apparent panacea of informal dispute resolution, which, in the family context in which it has most frequently been implemented in Western Europe and North America, has often been shown both to disguise and to reinforce pre-existing power differentials precisely through the informalisation which was intended to reduce law's hierarchical and excluding method. This suggests that a critique of law's violence which is too narrowly focused on the conceptual framework of legal subjectivity risks—like the long tradition of analytical jurisprudence—evacuating the environment of historically specific power relations from the realm of legal theory.[43]

It is perhaps helpful to divide these pitfalls of contextualisation into the pragmatic and the intellectual. From a pragmatic feminist viewpoint (and, as I shall argue below, there are strong reasons for a feminist viewpoint to be pragmatic . . .), contextualisation within broader kinds of social knowledge will only favour women if they are less marked by (in the broadest sense) sexual violence than is law. There is little reason why we should believe this of, say, psychiatric medicine—one of the discourses most often invoked in recontextualising, for example, women's crime as pathology.

However, the lessons for our general puzzle about "law as violence" and the "ethical space in law" lie rather in the intellectual questions raised by the strategy of contextualisation. In terms of the violence of judgment—of closing off challenge and enquiry, of imposing binary structures, of repressing difference—it seems obvious

[43] See J Balkin, "Being Just with Deconstruction" in Young and Sarat (eds.), *supra* n. 8, and G Rose, "Athens and Jerusalem: A Tale of Three Cities" in Young and Sarat (eds.), *supra* n. 8 at 333, 393.

that the "ethical appeal" of recontextualisation depends not merely on the nature of the specific recontextualisation proposed, but also on the sense in which we are deploying the idea of the "ethical". On the "postmodern" notion of the ethical, any legal recontextualisation will be "violent" because of the features of legal judgment already noted. This may be logically persuasive, but it does not take forward the political concern implied by the rhetorical invocation of "violence". On the "modern" notion of the ethical, by contrast, any potential recontextualisation demands a further substantive assessment of the "pros and cons" of the particular strategy. The same is true of a third, "pragmatist" notion of the ethical, according to which we may continue to espouse and pursue ideals, values and commitments even once we have let go of the "modernist illusion" that they have metaphysical foundations or transcendent status.[44]

We can illustrate this with examples drawn respectively from what would probably be regarded as modernist and postmodernist camps. Starting with the former, an obvious example would be the feminist argument for the embrace of an embodied, relational (feminine) subjectivity in law. There is an analogy here with the communitarian critique of liberalism in political theory, which uses a social constructionist approach to subjectivity not only to criticise but also to move beyond the partiality of liberal individualism.[45] Charles Taylor, for example, argues in his essay on multiculturalism that women should be allowed access "to their own culture".[46] As many commentators have noted, this move risks replacing one "logic of identity" with another,[47] as well as romanticising its central recontexualising frame of "community" (a characteristic which one might argue also applies to some postmodern invocations of "the ethical").[48]

There is an interesting—and troubling—analogy here with the controversy about so-called "cultural defences" in criminal law. Should evidence of white Anglo-Saxon protestant, or African-American, or Asian-American, or Hispanic culture be taken into account in deciding, for example, whether a particular defendant reacted in a "reasonable" way, or in deducing what they actually intended or foresaw? If so, are we committed to the view that, for example, the male rape defendant who says that he genuinely thought a dissenting woman was consenting because of the sexist culture in which he was educated has a presumptive cultural defence? Are we to take "expert evidence" on "special" cultures? And, if so, how are we to avoid the implication that the legal process is reifying these

[44] Both Bauman (*supra* n. 9) and Rorty describe their positions as "postmodern" because of their anti-foundationalism (see in particular Rorty's paper "Postmodern Bourgeois Liberalism" in his collection R Rorty, *Objectivity, Relativism and Truth* (Cambridge, Cambridge University Press, 1991)). The pragmatist position differs, however, from the postmodern (or perhaps deconstructionist) evocation of the "ethical" as "open", in that it envisages a substantive debate about values and ideals and a political struggle to realise them.

[45] See E Frazer and N Lacey, *The Politics of Community A Feminist Analysis of the Liberal–Communitarian Debate* (Hemel Hempstead, Harvester, 1993).

[46] See C Taylor's contribution in A Gutman (ed.), *Multiculturalism and "The Politics of Recognition"* (Princeton, Princeton University Press, 1992).

[47] See in particular Young, *supra* n. 14.

[48] On this point, see Rose, *supra* n. 43.

"cultures", fixing defendants and plaintiffs alike in their cultural pigeonholes as part of the complex fabric of the case—well removed from the more obviously "violent" decision, yet equally "violent" in their effects, particularly once the constitutive, normalising power of law and legal processes is taken on board? There is a real worry here about fixing women within a sexually-based culture which feminism has always struggled to redefine. It is this kind of problem which gives the postmodern conception of the ethical as "open" or "beyond social practice" its critical bite in contemporary legal theory. And yet it is arguably a strength of both modernist and pragmatist approaches that they allow for a debate about the substantive ethics or politics of specific recontextualisations—a debate which appears to be closed off or at least inhibited by these "postmodern" conceptions.

Let us turn now to a rather different example: Luce Irigaray's argument for women's access to a distinctive culture, a distinctive subjectivity. Irigaray's argument is that a recognition of special rights for women is a precondition for women's being treated as fully human subjects rather than merely as "other" to the self-identical masculine ego. Irigaray's analysis goes to the core of the problematic way in which dominant liberal discourse represses difference, and in particular of the way in which it excludes the feminine from subject status. Her argument is that a relational conception of rights would have to be premised on the recognition of irreducibly different subjectivities which relate in an intransitive way to one another.[49] Until women, in other words, are recognised as full subjects, those of us with female bodies will never be either citizens or rights-bearers. But if women were accorded special rights appropriate to the feminine genre—including rights to virginity and motherhood, to guardianship of the home, as well as rights to equal institutional representation and access to economic resources—this would itself represent a recognition of our subjectivity, which would in turn change the nature of our possible relations with men and with one another.

Irigaray's argument is distinctive because it is explicitly premised on the idea that human identity is made up not of one but of two poles; masculine and feminine; and that discourses and institutions such as law must accommodate these two genres of human being if they are to break out of the repressive (violent) exclusion of the (female) other. Hers is a strategy of metaphor and mimesis. The aim is to disrupt conventional metaphorical associations, and to effect a revaluation—indeed a humanisation—of the feminine by mimicking, ironically, the masculine construction of the feminine and changing its meaning in the process. It is a reading and speaking against the grain of contemporary institutions, whether legal, political, or linguistic. As such, it is a philosophy whose conception of ethics is literally utopian. Hence sexual difference—like the unrepresentable feminine in Lacanian thought—becomes the metaphor for an ethics of "becoming" rather than an ethics of moving towards—let alone arriving at—a fixed destination.

[49] See Irigaray, *J'aime à toi Esquisse d'une felicite dans l'histoire*, Paris, Grasset, *Je, Tu, Nous: Towards a Culture of Difference*, and *Thinking the Difference*, *supra* n. 19.

Yet, notwithstanding her ironic method, I would suggest that the rhetorical impact of Irigaray's case for special rights for women risks, in her own terms, doing just as much "violence" as does the more generally criticised elision of femininity with a condition of victimisation.[50] There are two main reasons. First, the implicit prioritisation of sexual over other differences might itself be argued to entail a form of difference-repressing violence: indeed, this would be one way of viewing critical race theory's critique of feminism. One way of understanding Irigaray's argument is that it replaces one universalism—a universalism which has been effectively deconstructed as totalising and excluding—with two. These two are mapped onto the masculine and the feminine. They take no account of the many other differences which structure subjectivity and experience.[51] There is a liberatory potential in Irigary's thought that "je suis sexué(e)" implies "je ne suis pas tout(e)". But this depends on our reading her analysis of sexual difference as a metaphor for difference more generally. We need, in other words, to resist the binarism which her analysis of sexual difference as fundamental reasserts, and to locate the ethical impulse to "attend to otherness" not just within the vector of sexual difference but within those of racial, ethnic, national, class and other differences too.

The second difficulty with Irigaray's position on rights, and one which is of particular relevance to this paper, is that in constructing an argument which is a blend of critique and of what might be called postmodern ethics, Irigaray borrows (unusually within her work) the language of a very different project—that of institutional reform in the modernist sense. In doing so, she apparently espouses a curiously naive and instrumental optimism about legal reform and takes up a position which assumes a dubious autonomy of law. Read literally, she also invites a policy response which, in the current political, economic and legal conditions of either France or Britain, would be retrogressive. Understood as political rhetoric, the replay of sexual stereotypes is already problematic.[52] Understood as a programme for reform, it is potentially disastrous. We have only to think of actual instances of "special rights" for women—those surrounding pregnancy are the best example—to see their adverse implications for women in a world in which activities such as child-rearing have not been effectively economically or culturally valued. In the world of real politics, irony may not be the best policy.

The utopian strategy of contextualisation sets out to tap the resources of the imagination: to read and speak against the cultural grain, and hence to make possible the impossible task of thinking beyond the present towards a different future. Yet, however radical its theoretical credentials, is easily (mis)read as a standard reformist project which risks obscuring the full range of law's violence by focusing

[50] This is a criticism frequently voiced in relation to Catharine MacKinnon's radical feminism (*supra* n. 34); for discussion of this aspect of MacKinnon's work, see W Brown, *States of Injury* (Princeton, Princeton University Press, 1995).

[51] Hence it may be argued that, in the final analysis, such arguments re-essentialise sexual difference: see Valverde, *supra* n. 13.

[52] For a defence of Irigaray as concerned with "remetaphorising the feminine" as opposed to "describing women", see P Deutscher, "Luce Irigaray's Sexuate Rights and the Politics of Performativity" (manuscript 1999).

on one of its aspects—an aspect which is unevenly realised in actual legal arrangements. By losing sight of the varying ways in which legal practices currently contextualise their subjects, the argument makes it seem as if everything about law's violence turns on the repression of difference in the moment of judgment or formal classification. And this emphasis occludes our perception of law's more pervasive—and, at least rhetorically, equally violent—disciplinary power, not to mention the material "field of pain and death" within which law operates.[53]

Of course, one could argue that every recontextualisation entails its own logic of identity, and hence its own excluding violence. This is logically impeccable, but it has the disadvantage that it blunts our perception of real shifts in the mode of contextualisation—shifts which we may have pragmatic and political reasons for wanting to track. More fundamentally, it trivialises the argument about law's violence both because it is generalisable and because it directs attention away from all the other—extra-legal as well as legal—factors which block the "possibility of justice" in more historically contingent—and hence potentially tractable—ways. If the impossibility of justice through law is a matter of logic, then all radical lawyers can go home, or take early retirement, or retrain as poets or freedom fighters. But if law's violence is not—as Derrida suggests—such as entirely to close off progressive legal analysis and political action, we need some framework for distinguishing between its different aspects. Such a framework must be grounded in a socio-historical analysis of the conditions of particular social orders at particular points in time, and in applying it, we must show a willingness to argue for our ethical commitments.

CONCLUSION

This review of feminist work on the legal subject confirms some of the difficulties of any attempt to convert a critical, deconstructive argument about the shape of legal subjecthood into a utopian argument about opening law to "the play of difference". When a further elision is made with reformist arguments for policies such as informalising legal processes, widening laws of evidence, and making explicit law's accommodation of certain kinds of difference, the difficulties multiply. Yet this review also demonstrates that feminism's political impulses will tend to draw it—in crude terms—from the deconstructive to the reconstructive. Inevitably, legal methods select among the plurality of social practices, emotional, bodily and social associations, in relation to which individual subjectivity may be constructed. Feminist critique is justified in asserting that the sexual assumptions underlying this selection should be open to political and moral assessment. And it is surely open to feminism to argue for a more flexible approach to constructing legal subjectivity in ways which are sensitive to the most important associations in terms of which people live their lives, and which recognise the interaction between gender, ethnicity and other differences in constructing social identity.

[53] See Cover, *supra* n. 2.

But we must recognise that these feminist issues may be approached from a number of different points of view. How laws construct subjectivity is a question of legal theory, of the sociology of law and of social theory, and it is a question to which critical techniques such as deconstruction have undoubtedly made an important contribution to our understanding. The question of how laws might or should construct subjectivity may be seen as a reformist question, raising technical and political issues about legal change. It may be seen as moral and a political/democratic issue, as taken up in normative mode by modernist versions of feminism which deploy a notion of the ethical as "good" or "desirable", and in persuasive mode by pragmatist versions of feminism which conceive the ethical in terms of human ideals and commitments.[54] Or it may be seen as a "utopian" issue in postmodernist mode: a valuable imaginary space which deploys the idea of the ethical as "open" and as always "beyond" social practices; and which reminds us of the futility of law's attempts to fix or to determine; of the incompleteness of law's "violence".

From this postmodern perspective, we cannot go further without simply reproducing the problems of law's excluding violence which are the objects of its own critique. But this perspective risks effacing political action. As soon as—like Irigaray—the postmodernist is drawn back into the field of political action, she must confront if not modernist then at least pragmatist ethical questions: what will be the effects of this (rhetorical) strategy; what are the recommendations of the likely outcome?

Throughout this paper, I have argued for a focus on the influence of extra-legal discourses in shaping the excluding force of law, and insisted on the need for a certain pragmatism in assessing the recommendations of particular recontextualisations. These arguments imply that the Derridean focus on law's violence suffers from much of the formalism, the ahistoricism, the focus on power as sovereignty to the exclusion of power as discipline, and the doctrinal orientation which characterises analytic legal theory. The violence of judgment which Derrida locates in law infects, on his own analysis, any discourse, just as any linguistically articulated practice will contain, in the logic of the Derridean system, the shifting play of difference and hence the possibility of justice. While Derrida's analysis of the force of law is highly suggestive, its invocation of law's violence and its evocation of justice (like, one might add, "the ethical space" in so much contemporary legal philosophy) remain rhetorical rather than substantial. They are hence of limited interest to those who, while accepting in large part the proposition that law can never attain justice, would nonetheless like to think that the degree of injustice perpetrated by law can gradually be affected by critical analysis and pragmatic political action.

Critical legal theory remains fundamentally ambivalent about its own utopian pretensions. This ambivalence relates to the reversion within postmodern critique of law's violence to a utopian vision whose emancipatory potential often runs along

[54] See R Rorty, "Feminism and Pragmatism" (1990) 59 *Radical Philosophy* 3.

lines adapted from liberal reformism.[55] In shifting between ideas of the ethical as "good" and the ethical as "open to critique", "transformable", "unfixed", "indeterminate", "infinite", or indeed "feminine"—taking up a burden one would have thought women in the late twentieth century might be spared . . .—feminist thought reveals its uneasy stance *vis à vis* the modernist/postmodernist opposition.[56] From a postmodern perspective, the deconstruction of law's violence is succeeded by a rhetorical ethics which invokes a future or space beyond modern law.

Here many feminists hesitate, drawn by the assertion of the contingency and openness of social arrangements but suspicious of the indeterminacy of the vision. Feminism is generally—and in my view rightly—reluctant to ignore the senses in which the "violence" of modern law may be mitigated or counterbalanced by its actual and potential social advantages. It is also reluctant to give up the project of institutional reform, to the extent that real gains for those currently marginalised or disadvantaged by current legal arrangements are to be made.[57] This might be thought to imply that ethical feminism must keep its feet in the modern world even if its eyes are looking towards the postmodern horizon. But I would prefer to argue that contemporary feminism should resist this aspect of the modernist–postmodernist dichotomy. Feminism, in short, should be pragmatic in its deployment of a range of critical and reformist arguments, while being pragmatist in its espousal and pursuit of the commitments which define it. And for both pragmatic and pragmatist reasons, it needs to handle the undifferentiated rhetoric of "law's violence" with care.

[55] A particularly instructive example of this is the shift of gear is to be found in Drucilla Cornell's work as between her earlier, deconstructive and Lacanian approach (*supra* nn. 16 and 20) and her more recent work, which focuses on substantive areas of legal analysis and which engages primarily with contemporary liberal political theory (see for example *The Imaginary Domain*, *supra* n. 20).

[56] See L J Nicholson (ed.), *Feminism/Postmodernism* (London, Routledge, 1990).

[57] These references to "feminism" should not be taken to imply that it is a unitary tradition: I make merely the minimal assumption that a feminist theory is one which regards sex/gender (i) as a key variable in the explanation of social life and (ii) as, presumptively, an axis not merely of differentiation but also of injustice or oppression: see Lacey (*supra* n. 14), Introduction.

6

Sexual Difference and Collective Identities: The New Global Constellation

SEYLA BENHABIB

POSTMODERNISM AND GLOBALISATION

IN RETROSPECT, THE term *postmodernism*, which dominated discussions in the humanities and social sciences in the 1980s and announced a new spirit of the epoch, appears to have captured a play at the level of surfaces only. Postmodernism heralded the end of history, understood as a cumulative, progressive, coherent sequence; postmodernism announced the end of man and reduced the anthropological subject to a vanishing face in the sand, a disappearing signifier, a fractured, centreless creature; postmodernism trumpeted the end of philosophy and of master narratives of justification and legitimation. Certainly, there were distinctions between postmodernism and poststructuralism. While the former designates a movement with wide currency in many different fields, the latter refers to a specific moment in the evolution of high theory, in the European—but particularly French—context, when Marxist and psychoanalytic paradigms, as well as the models of Claude Lévi-Strauss and Ferdinand de Saussure, which had dominated French theory construction from the early 1960s onwards, came to an end. Judith Butler[1] and Chantal Mouffe[2] are correct in remarking that one should not lump

Reprinted from *Signs: Journal of Women in Culture and Society* (1999) vol. 24, no. 2. 335.

This article has been a long time in the making. Versions of it were delivered at a National Endowment for the Humanities Seminar on Ethics and Aesthetics organised by Anthony Cascardi and Charles Altieri at the University of California, Berkeley, in the summer of 1993. My discussion of Virginia Woolf and Charles Taylor formed part of a lecture delivered at the Northwestern Humanities Institute Series in the spring of 1994 titled "Sources of the Self in Contemporary Feminist Theory". Most recently, versions were read as a plenary address to the conference "Virtual Gender: Past Projections and Future Histories," organised by the Interdisciplinary Group for Historical Literary Study and the Women's Studies Program at Texas A & M University in April 1996; at the New School for Social Research Graduate Faculty Women in Philosophy Colloquium in the spring of 1996; and at the Cambridge University Interdisciplinary Feminist Philosophy Colloquium in March 1998. My thanks go to participants on all those occasions for their criticisms and comments. I owe special thanks to Bonnie Honig, Lynn Layton, Doris Sommer, Jill Frank and Melissa Lane for commenting on versions of this article at various stages of its evolution.

[1] J Butler, "Contingent Foundations: Feminism and the Question of 'Postmodernism'" in J Butler and J W Scott (eds.), *Feminists Theorize the Political* (New York, Routledge, 1992).

[2] C Mouffe, "Feminism, Citizenship, and Radical Democratic Politics" in Butler and Scott, *ibid.*

together Michel Foucault, Jean-François Lyotard, and Jacques Derrida, as if they all represented the same philosophical tradition. Nonetheless, each of these thinkers, in different ways, contributed to the set of cultural sensibilities that were associated with the term *postmodernism* in the 1980s.

Frederic Jameson[3] was one of the few social and cultural critics to point out that postmodernism's fixation on incommensurabilities, conflicts, and antagonisms at the level of surfaces was failing to account for processes of uniformisation and homogenisation occurring at deeper levels. Jameson sought to establish links between late capitalism's developmental stage and postmodernism. Contingency at the surface is necessity at a deeper level, he argued; antagonism at one level is subservience to the same forces at another, less visible level. Jameson was right. There is little question that the surface antagonisms, conflicts, and agonisms noted by postmodernists were accompanied by deeper forces of economic, military, technological, and communications and information integration—in short, by what we have come to call *globalisation* in the 1990s. If *fragmentation* was the code word of the eighties, *hybridity* is the code word of the 1990s; if *incommensurability* was a master term for the 1980s, *interstitiality* is one for the 1990s; if the *clash of cultures* was the horison of the 1980s, *multiculturalism* and *polyglotism* are the framework of the 1990s.[4]

It is my thesis that the new constellation formed by the coming together of global integration and apparent cultural fragmentation is the contemporary horizon against which the project of contemporary feminism must be rethought. Our contemporary condition is marked by the melting down of all naturalistic signifiers in the political and cultural realm and a desperate attempt to recreate them. The decline of superpower polarism and the end of the Cold War have brought with them a dizzying reconfiguration of the map of Europe. But elsewhere in the world as well, contradictory pulls are at work: as globalisation proceeds at a dizzying rate, as a material global civilisation encompasses the earth from Hong Kong to Lima, from Pretoria to Helsinki, worldwide integration is accompanied by cultural and collective disintegration. India and Turkey, among the earliest and oldest democracies of the Third World, are in the throes of religious struggles and ethnic strife that at times call into question the very project of a secular representative democracy. Need one mention the civil war in the former Yugoslavia and the simmering nationality conflicts in Chechnya, Azerbaijan, Macedonia, and Rwanda? As the markers of certainty at the economic, geopolitical and technological spheres decline and can no longer be used to create hierarchies among nations and cultures, new signifiers are generalised to fill their place—signifiers that seek to renaturalise historical and cultural identities by presenting them as if they were racially and

[3] F Jameson, *Postmodernism, or The Cultural Logic of Late Capitalism* (Durham, NC: Duke University Press, 1991) 37–8, 48ff.

[4] "Political empowerment and the enlargement of the multiculturalist cause", writes Homi Bhabha, "come from posing questions of solidarity and community from the interstitial perspective". In *The Location of Cultures* (London and New York, Routledge, 1994) 3.

anthropologically deep-seated distinctions.[5] The worldwide resurgence of ethnic and nationalist movements, at a time of the decline and weakness of nation-states everywhere, is a further testimony to this process. What does this mean for contemporary feminism? How can we think of sexual difference in the context of new struggles around collective identities?

Debates around identity, which have always played a crucial role in the women's movement, are now dominating nationalist, separatist aspirations worldwide. The purpose of this article is to engage in a retrospective analysis of identity debates within feminism of the past two decades, while keeping in mind the insights and dangers inaugurated by the new global constellation. The "paradigm wars" of feminist theory, which have raged among critical and poststructuralist feminist theorists in particular, lead me to draw some general analytical conclusions about identifiers, be they personal, gender, or national. I propose a narrative model for conceptualising identity at all these levels, and, by toggling back and forth between global political considerations and the concerns of feminist theory, I hope to outline a viable model for thinking about identities in the context of radical democratic politics.

THE PROBLEM OF THE SUBJECT REVISITED

In my view, the most important theoretical issue to emerge from the feminism/postmodernism debates of the 1980s remains the problem of the subject. This problem comprises several others: first, how do we reconceptualise subjectivity in light of the philosophical contributions of feminism? How does feminism alter our understanding of the traditional epistemological or moral subject of Western philosophy—the *cogito ergo sum* of Descartes or the Kantian rational moral agent who is free only insofar as he can act in accordance with a universal law that he, as a rational being, legislates to himself? Has the feminist emphasis on embodiedness, intersubjectivity, caring and empathy, sexuality and desire subverted the categories of the tradition? If so, what has it brought in their place?[6] Second, what is the relation between subjectivity and political agency? Can we think of political/moral/cultural agency only insofar as we retain a robust conception of the autonomous, rational, and accountable subject, or is a concept of the subject as fragmentary and riveted by heterogeneous forces more conductive to understanding varieties of resistance and cultural struggles of the present?

[5] The new literature on Islamic movements and, in particular, the use of terms such as "Jihad", to designate all aspirations in the contemporary world for ethnic, religious, and cultural particularisms, even if well-intentioned, unfortunately contribute to the portrayal of "Islam" as the enemy of the West. After the end of the Cold War, Islam has become the new archenemy. For instance, the title, when not the substance of Benjamin Barber's well-known book, *Jihad* v. *McWorld How Globalism and Tribalism are Reshaping the World* (New York, Ballantine Books, 1995) succumbs to these tendencies.

[6] See Louise M Anthony and Charlotte Witt's important collection of works by analytically-oriented feminist philosophers: *A Mind of One's Own: Feminist Essays on Reason and Objectivity* (Boulder, Westview Press, 1993).

These issues have been at the heart of my ongoing public disagreement and dialogue with Judith Butler over the processes of identity formation, an exchange that has been reproduced in the volume *Feminist Contentions: A Philosophical Exchange.*[7] My position was that in *Gender Trouble*[8] at least, Butler subscribes to an overly constructivist view of selfhood and agency that leaves little room for explaining the possibilities of creativity and resistance. I objected that the term *performativity* appeared to reduce individuals to masks without an actor or to a series of disjointed gender enactments without a centre. Butler clarified subsequently that she had meant *performativity* to invoke not a dramaturgical but a linguistic model. She writes in *Bodies That Matter,*

> "Performativity is . . . not a singular 'act', for it is always a reiteration of a norm or a set of norms, and to the extent that it acquires an act-like status in the present, it conceals or dissimulates the conventions of which it is a repetition".[9]

Relying on Derrida's appropriation of speech-act theory, Butler sees perfomativity as a reenactment, as an iteration that in the process of enunciation also transforms what it iterates or enunciates. Repetition and innovation, necessity and contingency are brought together in an interesting fashion here. I have little quarrel with this view of linguistic agency; however, I think that one needs a stronger concept of human intentionality and a more developed view of the communicative–pragmatic abilities of everyday life to explain how speech acts are not only iterations but also innovations and reinterpretations, be it of old linguistic codes, communicative or behavioural.

[7] S Benhabib, J Butler, D Cornell and N Fraser, *Feminist Contentions: A Philosophical Exchange* (New York, Routledge, 1995). One of the more exciting and incisive contributions to our exchange is a recent article by Amanda Anderson titled "Debatable Performances: Restaging Contentious Feminisms" (1998) 16 (1) *Social Text* 54, 1–24. Anderson passes some unfortunate judgments about the motives as well as the context of the publication of this work, naming us "an elite 'gang of four'" (1). Despite some unwarranted rhetorical side-flourishes, Anderson defends a "more capacious model of dialogue, one that can accommodate different forms of political practice, particularly disruptions of spectacle, performance" (2). Defending Habermas against me, or my earlier work against my exchanges with Butler, Anderson attempts to show how communicative ethics can be made compatible with processes "of radical *disidentification*" (2). I find this an interesting argument; however I remain sceptical on two counts. First, as I argue in the body of this article, disidenttification only works against a background of identification constituted through narrative. Otherwise, disidenification may not be in the service of the self, but it can further the dissolution of a strong sense of self. Second, I am sceptical about the "transformative-political" potential of such performative disidentifications. As Anderson notes, I am a civil libertarian on a whole range of issues relating to pornography, sadomasochism, etc., but I do not share the optimism of the artistic avant-garde of the modern period, since the Dadaist movement of this century, that the performative disruptions of artistic life must also produce good politics. The politics of culture must always be judged against the background of the culture of politics in any given country. The United States, since the 1960s has managed to produce an avant-garde artistic culture in arts, theatre, dance, music, and literature that is the envy of the world without managing to solve the problems of corrupt campaign financing, blockages in legislative processes, misguided foreign policy, and lack of universal healthcare coverage, parental leave, decent housing, and education for all who live in this polity. It is my sense of these discontinuities and contradictions between culture and politics, and not some "cultural purism", that leads me to be sceptical about the "cultural politics of the performative".

[8] J Butler, *Gender Trouble: Feminism and the Subversion of Identity* (New York, Routledge, 1990).

[9] J Butler, *Bodies That Matter: On the Discursive Limits of "Sex"*(New York, Routledge, 1993) 12.

This philosophical disagreement concerning the nature of language and human intentionality was not always at the forefront of my earlier exchanges with Butler. Her recent work in *Excitable Speech* helps articulate these differences more sharply. In this work, Butler explores, among other issues, Derrida's critique of J L Austin's theory of speech acts.[10] What she fails to note, and what is of crucial importance in our dispute, is that Derrida and Jürgen Habermas agree that the Austinian theory of speech acts is too conventionalist, that is, it identifies performativity with the fulfilment or satisfaction of a given social code or norm.[11] Derrida and Habermas concur that the most interesting aspects of language-in-use occur in situations in which there are no stipulated social rules or codes. Such situational understanding is quite distinct from fulfilling a norm or following a convention. In his critique of John Searle, Derrida complains that Searle's "speech act" theory cannot account for the "surfeit of meaning" that transcends the boundaries of mere conventionality. There is always "more" in language. Derrida writes:

> "I do not believe that iterability is necessarily tied to convention, and even less, that it is limited by it. Iterability is precisely that which—once its consequences have been unfolded—can no longer be dominated by the opposition nature/convention. It dislocates, subverts, and constantly displaces the dividing line between the two terms. It has an essential rapport with the forces (theoretical and practical, 'effective', 'historical', 'psychic', 'political', etc.) deconstructing these oppositional limits".[12]

For Habermas, this "more" in language comes about through the communicative competence of social actors in generating situational interpretations of their life-world through communicative acts oriented to validity claims. For Derrida, this "surfeit" of meaning, the subversions that transform iterations, are part of the bounty of language itself. For Habermas, this surfeit is part of the bounty of communications—not merely of language, but of language-in-use. The crucial issue is this: can there be resignification without communication among members of a language game? If, as Derrida argues and Habermas concurs, speech acts are acts not only, or not primarily, because they reproduce a set of established norms and conventions but because they reinterpret and resignify, modify, and discursively challenges such norms and conventions, then how does anyone know that such resignification and reinterpretation have taken place?[13] In the Derridian model of

[10] J Butler, *Excitable Speech: A Politics of the Performative* (New York and London, Routledge, 1997) 146–55.

[11] J Habermas, "Excursus on Leveling the Genre Distinction between Philosophy and Literature" in J Habermas, *The Philosophical Discourse of Modernity: Twelve Lectures*, trans. F Lawrence (Cambridge, Mass, MIT Press, 1987) 194–9.

[12] J Derrida, *Limited Inc a b c .... In Limited Inc.* (Evanston, Ill., Northwestern University Press, 1988) 102.

[13] Martin Jay, "The Debate over Performative Contradiction: Habermas versus the Poststructuralists" in A Honneth, T McCarthy, C Offe, and A Wellmer (eds.), *Philosophical Interventions in the Unfinished Project of Enlightenment* (Cambridge, Mass., MIT Press, 1992), sees these different orientations to language as the central issue of contention among critical theorists and poststructuralists. For an exploration of the complex issues of understanding (*Verstaendigung*), reaching understanding (*Einverstaendnis*) and consensus (*Konsens*) in universal pragmatics, see the exchange between myself and David Hoy on Habermas' theory of universal pragmatics (S Benhabib, "The Local, The Contextual

speech as enunciation, the surplus of meaning seems to reside in the almost oracular quality of utterances themselves. In the model of communicative pragmatics, by contrast, the same proposition—let us say, "The moon is made of green cheese"—can be treated as incorporating different speech acts depending on the validity claims raised by the speaker and accepted or rejected by the hearers. For example, is this statement to be understood as a scientific claim about the material composition of the moon or as an expressive–poetic claim about one's emotions concerning the moon? Or is it a normative statement, exhorting us to accept as correct that we should view the moon as if it were made of green cheese? In communicative pragmatics the intentions of the speaker and the negotiations about these intentions between speaker and hearer are articulated through the various validity claims that the same proposition can embody. These are the claims to truth or falsehood, rightness or wrongness, sincerity and deception, and intelligibility. The validity claims of propositions cannot be identified independently of the intentions of their speakers.

As Butler's *Excitable Speech* makes admirably clear, views of political agency and legal accountability are inextricably bound up with our philosophical understandings of linguistic activity. Nevertheless, this account still offers no explication of how regimes of discourse/power or normative regimes of language and sexuality both circumscribe and enable the subject. As Allison Weir observes:

> "What's lost here is any recognition of the perspectives of the participants in these performances, and hence, any meaningful differentiation among unreflective, deliberate, dogmatic, defensive, anxious, ironic, playful, and parodic performances of gender, and any understanding of the ways in which these interact and conflict in specific performances and particular subjects. What's lost then, is any meaningful concept of agency, and any meaningful concept of subversion".[14]

I would like to suggest a "narrative" model of subjectivity and identity-constitution in place of the "performativity" model.[15] My contention is that the narrative model has the virtue of accounting for that "surfeit of meaning, creativity and spontaneity" that is said to accompany iteration in the performativity model as well but whose mechanisms cannot actually be explained by performativity.

I will introduce this narrative model first by an excursus into Virginia Woolf's *Orlando* and, second, through a detailed examination of Charles Taylor's views on

and/or Critical" (1996) 3 (1) *Constellations: An International Journal of Critical and Democratic Theory* 83; D Hoy, "Debating Critical Theory" (1996) 3 (1) *Constellations: An International Journal of Critical and Democratic Theory* 104).

[14] A Weir, *Sacrificial Logics: Feminist Theory and the Critique of Identity* (New York and London, Routledge, 1996) 127.

[15] I would like to caution that I am using these terms in the specific senses that they have acquired in this debate. At some level, all narratives are performatives, and many performatives involve a narrative dimension. Nonetheless, at the level of identity-constitution these terms suggest distinct theoretical options. Also, the term performativity has been used to refer to a theory of individual identity constitution as well as to a theory of sexual identity formation. In this article I am dealing with individual and collective identities and not with sexual identity alone. I thank Doris Sommer for alerting me to possible misunderstandings in the uses of these terms.

the constitution of identities through "webs of narratives". There is an interesting convergence of literary and philosophical perspectives here: both Woolf and Taylor outline a notion of a "core" self, the constitution of which Woolf leaves mysterious and Taylor tries to account for in several ways. My own views of narrativity develop in interlocution with their writings.

THE NARRATIVE MODEL OF IDENTITY CONSTITUTION I: VIRGINIA WOOLF'S *ORLANDO*

Narrativity and identity, or the manner in which the telling of the story of the self reinforces or undermines a particular understanding of self, is a major preoccupation of high modernist literature from Marcel Proust to James Joyce, from Robert Musil to Virginia Woolf. Due to her incisive disentanglement of the confluence of one's sense of self with fantasies and expectations about one's sex/gender, Woolf's work remains a beacon for navigating the stormy waters of identities.

In October 1928, the month during which Woolf delivered the two lectures that were to form the basis of *A Room of One's Own*[16] (1929) her novel *Orlando* appeared.[17] An exuberant, fantastic, lyrical, satiric novel, *Orlando*, in the words of one critic, "stages the mobility of fantasy and desire; it is a narrative of boundary crossings—of time, space, gender and sex".[18] This biography begins in the late 1500s as the story of a beautiful and talented young man of noble descent, good fortune, and great promise. In fact, so bright is the future held in store for this young man that Queen Elizabeth takes a fancy to him and showers him with amorous advances. After falling madly in love with a mysterious and fickle Russian princess, Sasha, Orlando agrees to be sent to Constantinople as the Crown's ambassador; there he falls into a deep trance that lasts several days and awakens to find himself a woman: "Orlando had become a woman—there is no denying it," writes Woolf.

> "But in every other respect, Orlando remained precisely as he had been. The change of sex, though it altered their future, did nothing whatever to alter their identity. Their faces remained, as their portraits prove, practically the same. His memory—but in future we must, for convention's sake, say 'her' for 'his', and 'she' for 'he'—her memory then, went back through all the events of her past life without encountering any obstacle. Some slight haziness there may have been, as if a few dark drops had fallen into the clear pool of memory; certain things had become a little dimmed; but that was all."[19]

The last phrase, "that was all", conceals the extent to which the entire novel is a meditation on the complex themes of personal identity, sexual difference, the construction of gender, and the quest of the artist to discover the innermost sources

[16] V Woolf, *A Room of One's Own* (London, Hogarth Press, 1929).

[17] V Woolf, *Orlando: A Biography*, ninth reprinting (Glasgow, Triad Grafton, 1977) 106–7. All references in parantheses in the text are to this edition.

[18] K R Lawrence, "Orlando's Voyage Out" (1992) 38 (1) *Modern Fiction Studies* 253.

[19] Woolf, *supra* n. 17, at 107.

from which creativity, art, imagination, and fantasy spring. "Orlando was a man till the age of thirty; when he became a woman and has remained so ever since."[20] Woolf's narrative defies easy categorisation in terms of androgyny, bisexuality, or the polymorphous perversity of all sexual desire. It is "an exuberant and fantastic sexual ideal",[21] a story of multiple and transgressive sexuality. Dedicated to Woolf's lover, Vita Sackville-West, and composed during Sackville-West's travels to the Near East, *Orlando* is both "public and private, directed to an audience of one and many".[22]

Having survived the sarcasm, hypocrisy, and baseness of the savants of the eighteenth century, personified by Pope, Addison, and Dryden, Orlando faces the repressive gender roles of the nineteenth century:

> "One might see the spirit of the age blowing, now hot, now cold, upon her cheeks. And if the spirit of the age blew a little unequally . . . her ambiguous position must excuse her (even her sex was still in dispute) and the irregular life she had lived before."[23]

Fixed sexual identity, as defined by rigid gender roles and categories, is not central to the core identity of the self, Woolf intimates. The sources of the self as a unified being, if there are any at all, suggests Woolf, lie deeper. Looking through her shirt pockets, Orlando discovers a "sea-stained, blood-stained, travel-stained"[24] manuscript of her poem "The Oak Tree". She had started working on this back in 1586, close to "three hundred years" before the point at which the narrator finds her/himself in the second half of the nineteenth century.[25] Meanwhile, as she looks through the pages of the manuscript, she realises "how very little she had changed all these years. She had been a gloomy boy, in love with death, as boys are; and then she had been amorous and florid; and then she had been sprightly and satirical; and sometimes she had tried prose and sometimes she has tried drama. Yet through all these changes she had remained, she reflected, fundamentally the same. She had "the same brooding meditative temper, the same love of animals and nature, the same passion for the country and the seasons".[26]

"Yet through all these changes she had remained, she reflected, fundamentally the same." What is the meaning of this sameness of the self? Through what sets of characteristics or activities, patterns of consciousness or behavior, do we say of someone that she is "the same"? In philosophical language, how is the identity of the self that remains self-same to be thought of?

Woolf gives no unequivocal answer to this question—perhaps it allows none. Sometimes she suggests that the core identity of the self is formed by a set of gender-transcending characteristics that in old-fashioned language would be called

[20] Woolf, *supra* n. 17, at 107.

[21] K E Lokke, "Orlando and Incandescence: Virginia Woolf's Comic Sublime" (1992) 38 (1) *Modern Fiction Studies* 236.

[22] Lawrence, *supra* n. 18, at 257.

[23] Woolf, *supra* n. 17, at 181.

[24] *Ibid.*

[25] *Ibid.*

[26] *Ibid.*

"character": Orlando had "the same brooding meditative temper, the same love of animals and nature, the same passion for the country and the seasons". It is these moral, cognitive, and aesthetic dispositions, Woolf intimates, that constitute her as "fundamentally the same".

THE NARRATIVE MODEL OF IDENTITY CONSTITUTION II: CHARLES TAYLOR'S *SOURCES OF THE SELF*

Charles Taylor's *Sources of the Self* is an attempt to disentangle philosophically the relationships between a sense of core identity and a set of dispositional attitudes, or "strong evaluative commitments", also cherished by the self. Two metaphors dominate Taylor's lucid analysis of identity: "horizons" and "webs of interlocution". Of horizons Taylor writes:

> "My identity is defined by the commitments and identifications which provide the frame or horizon within which I can try to determine from case to case what is good, or valuable, or what ought to be done, or what I endorse or oppose."[27]

"To know who I am," he emphasises, "is a species of knowing where I stand".[28] A horizon of strong evaluations or of strong evaluative commitments is for Taylor "integral" to human personhood.[29] The metaphor of "webs of interlocution" suggests a different approach, one more consonant with a narrative view. It describes, Taylor writes

> "the sense in which one cannot be a self on one's own . . . I am a self only in relation to certain interlocutors: in one way in relation to those conversation partners who were essential to my achieving self-definition; in another in relation to those who are now crucial to my continuing grasp of languages of self understanding—and, of course, these classes may overlap. A self exists only within what I call 'webs of interlocution' ".[30]

The answer to the question of who I am always involves reference to "where" I am speaking from and to whom or with whom.

[27] C Taylor, *Sources of the Self: The Making of the Modern Identity* (Cambridge, Mass., Harvard University Press, 1989) 27.

[28] *Ibid.*

[29] Surely though, this claim is far too specific to a certain ethos of modernity to be generalisable throughout the history of culture. The language of strong evaluations and strong evaluative commitments implies an ethics of autonomy and an ethos of disenchantment. Since our moral and value universes have become disenchanted in characteristically modern ways, we are thrust into the position of making strong evaluations and strong evaluative commitments. In an enchanted universe these evaluations are not "mine," they simply are a "part" of my being by virtue of the constitutive identity that I share with others. They are mine because they are a part of my value universe . The language of strong evaluative commitments, with its Kantian and Weberian overtones, would be curiously out of place here. Joel Anderson analyses the tensions between Taylor's "expressivism" and his "moral realism": "The Personal Lives of Strong Evaluators" (1996) 3 (1) *Constellations: An International Journal of Critical and Democratic Theory* 17.

[30] Taylor, *supra* n. 27, at 36.

The dialogic narrative view, which I share with Taylor and which I shall distinguish from the more essentialist model of "strong evaluative commitments", is the following: to be and to become a self is to insert oneself into webs of interlocution; it is to know how to answer when one is addressed; in turn, it is learning how to address others. Of course, we never really "insert" ourselves but rather are thrown into these webs of interlocution, in the Heideggerian sense of *Geworfenheit*. We are born into webs of interlocution or into webs of narrative—from the familial and gender narratives to the linguistic one to the macronarrative of one's collective identity. We become who we are by learning to be a conversation partner in these narratives. Although we do not choose the webs in whose nets we are initially caught or select those with whom we wish to converse, our agency consists in our capacity to weave out of those narratives and fragments of narratives a life story that makes sense for us, as unique individual selves. Certainly, the codes of established narratives in various cultures define our capacity to tell the story in very different ways; they limit our freedom to "vary the code".[31] But just as it is always possible in a conversation to drop the last remark and let it crash on the floor in silence, or to carry on and keep the dialogue alive and going, or to become whimsical, ironic, and critical and turn the conversation on itself, so too do we always have options in telling a life story that makes sense to us. These options are not ahistorical; they are culturally and historically specific and inflected by the master narrative of the family structure and gender roles into which each individual is thrown. Nonetheless, just as the grammatical rules of language, once acquired, do not exhaust our capacity to build an infinite number of well-formed sentences in an language, so socialisation and accumulation processes do not determine the life story of any unique individual or his or her capacity to initiate new actions and new sentences in a conversation. Donald Spence, a psychoanalyst, formulates the link between the self and narration perspicaciously:

> "It is by means of a continuous dialogue with ourselves—in daydreams, partial thoughts, and full-fledged plans—that we search for ways to interact with our environment and turn happenings into meanings, and we organize these interactions by putting our reactions into words. . . . Language offers a mechanism for putting myself into the world, as Heidegger might phrase it, and for making the world part of me, and language very likely determines the way in which experience will be registered and later recalled."[32]

Are there really significant distinctions between the dialogic and narrative understanding of the self and the view of "strong evaluations" that Taylor also adumbrates? Indeed there are, and spelling them out will give one a firmer grasp of the

[31] It is thanks to Toni Morrison's tremendous contributions in giving voice to Black Americans, and African-American women in particular, that we have learned something about the (invisibility) of "narratives and codes" across groups and cultures and genders. The comparative (body) of narrative voices and codes would contribute to a philosophical understanding of selfhood across racial and gender divides. Morrison's work also demonstrates the indispensability of narrative for the *empowerment* of oppressed and marginal groups.

[32] D Spence, "Turning Happenings into Meanings: The Central Role of the Self" in P Young-Eisendrath and J Hall (eds.), *The Book of the Self: Person, Pretext, and Process* (New York, New York University Press, 1987) 134.

postmodernist objection that any conception of a "core identity" is essentialist, ahistorical, and implausible. Consider some postmodern objections to the concept of "strong evaluations": certainly, the experiences of fragmentation and collage, the senseless being next-to-each-other in space and time of individuals, are authentic. They express and articulate a material and lived reality of our social and cultural world. Particularly postmodern selves seem to suffer from the inability to make strong evaluative commitments. What implications does this have for Taylor's theory? In the face of cultural forms of possible selfhood that contradict his theory, Taylor could give two answers: one response could be that individuals do have strong evaluative and constitutive commitments, although these may not be known to them. It is only the standpoint of the observer or the philosophical analyst or the psychotherapist that could disclose these. A second response could be that individuals whose lives lack strong evaluative commitments also lack the essential conditions of what Taylor refers to as "integral, that is, undamaged human personhood".[33] Taylor entertains both options; it is the second claim that I find particularly problematic and would like to focus on.

How plausible is it to argue that strong evaluative commitments are essential to human personhood—as essential, let us say, as the capacity to be a conversation partner in a web of interlocution? I think that there is a confusion of levels in Taylor's argument at this point: Taylor confuses the *conditions of possible human agency* with a *strong concept of moral integrity*. But it is possible to think of the first without the second. Consider two human types: the seducer and the ironist. The one goes through life accumulating conquests, love affairs, and broken hearts and is unable to make strong commitments or even state where or for what she or he stands. The other, vigilant and self-reflective, self-critical and whimsical, retains a distance from all commitments and thrives on not making strong evaluations or strong evaluative commitments. Of course, Taylor could respond that the strong evaluations out of which the seducer acts are those of narcissistic self-gratification in having others fall for her or him, whereas, for the ironist, a certain sense of sovereign control and not giving oneself too much to any one thing is the secret horizon of strong evaluation. If the philosopher were the psychotherapist for these individuals the task would consist in revealing to them what they implicitly presuppose. One could shift from the language of self-description and self-identification to the language of observational assessment to sustain Taylor's view of strong evaluations.

Undoubtedly, in many instances in human life and interaction, such a shift in perspective from the standpoint of the agent to that of the observer is justifiable and valid. Nonetheless, it cannot be that there is always and necessarily a disjunction between the language of self-evaluation and description and that of the third-person observer's point of view. I think we can entertain the possibility that there are human lives that lack a horizon of strong evaluations and evaluative commitments. Such lives may lack a certain depth, a certain integrity, a certain vibrancy and vitality, but

[33] Taylor, *supra* n. 27, at 27.

we know that they can be and are lived by some. It just seems wrong to say that they are not human life stories at all; should we rather not say that they are not very desirable, deep, or worthwhile ones? What is at stake here?

We have to think of the continuity of the self in time not through a *commitment to a specific set of evaluative goods* but through the *capacity to take and adopt an attitude* toward such goods, even if, and particularly if, this attitude means noncommitment. There can be self-identity without moral integrity; the core identity of a self is better defined through the second order attitudes and beliefs that this self has toward making first-order commitments. In the language of narration, it is not what the story is about that matters but, rather, one's ability to keep telling a story about who one is that makes sense to oneself and to others. Strong evaluative commitments may or may not be part of such narratives or fragments of narratives. Spence writes of the self as a "signature," a "fingerprint":

> "The way a life is conceived or described tells us something important about the teller that he very likely does not know himself . . . The concept of self reminds us that a certain structured constellation of attitudes, principles, and values contributes to our view of everyday happenings and affects the way these happenings are represented in memory and recovered in time."[34]

This "certain structured constellation of attitudes" may or may not entail strong evaluations or evaluative commitments. It is the signature that matters, not the document that is signed. Or, to remain at the level of metaphor, what matters are the marks left by the fingerprint not the ink or what the marks are imprinted on. Taylor's view of the self is not about the signature, however, but about the document, and not about the imprint but the ink and the object on which it is left. This, I am arguing, is a confusion of levels of analysis.

Ironically, objections to views such as Taylor's concept of "strong evaluations" on the grounds that they are essentialist also succumb to the same confusion: they assume that any conception of identity suggests the fiction of a stable, frozen, and fixed subject, preceding in time the multifarious performatives of gender and language, social roles, and individual postures through which we become who we are. The language of strong evaluative commitments suggests a "doer who precedes the deed" (Nietzsche). Yet if we think of the identity of the self in time not in terms of a set of strong evaluative commitments but rather in terms of an ability to make sense, to render coherent, meaningful, and viable for oneself one's shifting commitments as well as changing attachments, then the postmodernist objection loses its target. The issue becomes whether it is possible to be a self at all without some ability to continue to generate meaningful and viable narratives over time. My view is that, hard as we try, we cannot "stop making sense", as the Talking Heads urge us to do. We *will* try to make sense out of nonsense.

Are there constraints, then, on what makes sense? Put differently: What if strong assumptions about narrative with their inevitable overtones of beginning, unfolding,

[34] Spence, *supra* n. 32, at 132–3.

and resolution—the classical model of a tragedy from which we can draw lessons for life—find their way into this model and thus push the illusions of coherence, continuity, and fixity from one level to the next? I would like to suggest that "making sense" does not involve an Aristotelian or Victorian model of narrative, with a coherent beginning, unfolding, and ending. It involves, rather, the psychodynamic capacity to go on, to retell, to remember, to reconfigure. Retelling, remembering, and reconfiguring always entail more than one narrative; they occur in a "web of interlocution", which is also a conversation with the other(s). Others are not just the subject matters of my story; they are also tellers of their own stories, which compete with my own, unsettle my self-understanding, and spoil my attempts to mastermind my own narrative. Narratives cannot have closure precisely because they are always aspects of the narratives of others; the sense that I create for myself is always immersed in a fragile "web of stories" that I as well as others spin.[35] Psychoanalytic feminism both challenges and supplements the narrative model. "The shadow cast by the other subject", in Jessica Benjamin's words, is permanent.

PSYCHOANALYTIC FEMINISM: THE LIMITS OF NARRATIVITY

If we view the human child as a fragile, dependent creature whose body needs to be cared for, sustained, and nurtured and whose various needs have to be satisfied,

[35] Margaret R Somers and Gloria D Gibson write: "Above all, narratives are *constellations of relationships* (connected parts) embedded in *time and space*, constituted by *causal employment*": "Reclaiming the Epistemological 'Other': Narrative and the Social Construction of Identity" in C C Calhoun (ed.), *Social Theory and the Politics of Identity* (Cambridge, Mass., Blackwell, 1994) 59. Emphasising that the narratives within social actions are embedded can only be intelligible against a background, Somers and Gibson attempt to connect views of social structure and social agency through the narrative paradigm: "Narrative identities are constituted by a person's temporally and spatially variable 'place' in culturally constructed stories comprised of (breakable) rules, (variable) practices, binding (and unbinding) institutions, and the multiple plots of family, nation, or economic life" (67). This view of narrative is metatheoretical, or second order, in that it does not prejudge the content of the culturally constructed stories, practices, and institutions that constitute narrative identities, and it should not be confused with theories of relationality and the "relational self" (e.g., the work of Carol Gilligan). Relationality is *one form* of narrative emplotment. Furthermore, in that culturally constructed stories are composed of rules, this view of interlocutive narratives is compatible with universal pragmatics, which seeks to analyse such rules as they would undergird all cultural constructions, insofar as the narratives are reproduced only by the communicative competence of ordinary actors. Equally significantly, although they are experienced by social agents through narrative emplotment, practices and institutions are not narratives themselves; they constrain narratives and limit the agent's abilities to vary the code. As Somers and Gibson write, "Although we argue that social action is intelligible only through the construction, enactment, and appropriation of narratives, this does not mean that actions are free to fabricate narratives at will; rather, they must 'choose' from a repertoire of available representations and stories. Which kinds of narratives will socially predominate is contested politically and will depend in large part on the distribution of power" (73). In this essay, I am developing a metatheoretical, or second-order , perspective for conceptualising narratively constituted identities. Although the details of the social-theoretical implications of this perspective will need to be elaborated in future work, my thesis is that narrativity and critical social theory based on the communicative action paradigm are mutually compatible. The pitfalls of moving too quickly from a metatheoretical perspective on narratively constituted actions and identities to prescribing social science methodologies in incisively analysed by Sayres S Rudy (Rudy, in press).

we must take seriously the psychoanalytic insight that there is a corporal, somatic memory, that is, the unconscious. This is the point at which the insights of psychoanalystically inspired feminism aid in developing the narrative model further. Every story we tell of ourselves will also contain another of which we may not even be aware; and, in ways that are usually very obscure to us, we are determined by these subtexts and memories in our unconscious. The self is not sovereign, or as Freud famously put it, "Das Ich ist nicht Herr im eigenen Haus" (the ego is not master in its own house).[36] Poststructuralist/discourse feminists, alert to the oppressive language of *Herrschaft/Knechtschaft* in Freud's formulation, follow Nietzsche and Foucault in arguing that the Ich—the ego—is something we must get rid of altogether. They translate the psychoanalytic insight that the sovereignty of the "I" is never unlimited but always dependent on contexts, conscious and unconscious, that the I cannot master, into a call to get rid of the I as an instance of coherent mastery in ordering altogether. The I becomes instead an instance of expression, and its sovereignty is viewed as a striving after a form of repressive and illusory unity. Hence identity is viewed as a suspect category. Perhaps, though, we can think of the phrase "Das Ich ist nicht Herr im eigenen Haus" in quite a different way.

The I can never be master in its house because a household is composed of other beings whose needs, desires, and concrete identities always make claims on one and remind one of the inevitable perspectivality and limits of one's own point of view. Only the male subject could consider itself "the master of the household". All others—women, children, domestics, other dependants such as the elderly—have always known that there are limits to mastery and agency. The view that only one perspective dominates could only be the view of the master; the others know how to view themselves as they appear to the master, to each other, and to themselves. A household consists of multiple, complex perspectives and voices often in contest with each other, arguing with each other. Webs of interlocution are often family brawls, and only some family brawls succeed in making good conversations. More often than not they fail. The individual is thus always already situated in a psychosomatic context that we can define as the psychic economy of the household that one is born into and grows up in. Although we can never extricate ourselves from the material and spiritual webs in which these beginnings implicate us, we can nonetheless weave them together into a narrative of the many voices within us and the many perspectives that have constituted our field of vision.

This, however, is an interminable task, for narration is also a project of recollection and retrieval. We can only retrieve more or less, retell more or less those memories ingrained on the body, those somatic impressions of touch, tone and odour that defined our early being-in-the-world. They can only be relived in the present, as meaningful within our present narrative. They are only "for us"; our access to them can never be "in itself", or *an sich*. The attempt to relive these memories

[36] S Freud, "A Difficulty in the Path of Psychoanalysis" in J Strachey (ed. and trans.), vol. 17 *Standard Edition of the Complete Psychological Works* (London, Hogarth, 1974) 143.

outside the temporal horizon of the present would put the self in danger of regression, dissipation, and loss of ego boundaries. For an individual whose childhood was one of abuse and systematic mistreatment, the present may be a constant process of warding against being overwhelmed by memories and by the pull of the past. Yet there may also be ways of recuperating these memories by the pull of the past. Yet there may also be ways of recuperating these memories in the present so as to generate new and future horizons of meaning. Personal identity is the ever fragile achievement of needy and dependent creatures whose capacity to develop a coherent life story out of the multiple, competing, and often irreconcilable voices and perspectives of childhood must be cherished and protected. Furthering one's capacity for autonomous agency is only possible within a solidaristic community that sustains in one's identity through listening to one, and allowing one to listen to others, with respect within the many webs of interlocution that constitute our lives.

COMPLEX SUBJECTIVITIES, THE POLITICS OF DIFFERENCE, AND THE NEW CONSTELLATION

The intuition that certain views of identity and subjectivity are closely linked with collective politics is an old one. At least since the work of the Frankfurt School, which attempted to explain the rise of fascism in Europe through a mix of Marxist and psychoanalytic theory, we have had access to the insight that one's inability at the psychic level to acknowledge the otherness within oneself will, more often that not, manifest itself in the urge to split the "other" off and project it onto an external figuration outside oneself.[37] This projected or "abjected" other is thus excised from oneself, placing it outside, the self feels secure in maintaining the boundaries of its own identity without being threatened by dissolution into otherness. The other is the stranger, the foreigner, the one who is "alien" and "unlike" us. All authoritarian and fascist movements of our century (and not only of ours) manipulate this fear of losing ego boundaries and self-identity by making a group of collective others the bearers and carriers of certain naturalistic traits that are said to be different from and a threat to one's own identity. Already in the sixteenth century, during and after the Spanish Inquisition against the Jews of Spain, the doctrine of *la limpeaza de la sangre* (the cleanliness of blood) was practised.[38] The divider between the Jews and the Catholics was not doctrinal belief or religious practices but a biological category, itself only a phantasmagoric figment of the imagination. How does one prove "cleanliness of the blood"? In the case of the Spanish Inquisition, this meant not only that those who had intermarried with other Jews but also all others who had some Jewish descendants had to be eradicated. It is hard

[37] Julia Kristeva, *Nations without Nationalism*, trans. L S Roudiez (New York, Columbia University Press, 1993) has also explored these links.

[38] B Netanyahu, *The Marranos of Spain, from the Late XIVth to the Early XVIIIth Century, according to Contemporary Hebrew Sources* (Millwood, NY, Kraus Reprint Co., 1973).

to imagine—but historically documented—the mechanisms of state control and persecution that had to be mobilised in a sixteenth-century society in order, first, to establish the fact of Jewish blood in one's lineage and, second, to carry out the extermination or forced conversation of those so identified.

Think now of a more recent example. During the war in Bosnia-Herzegovina it was reported that Bosnian Serb soldiers in several instances not only raped Bosnian Muslim women but detained them in special camps where they were subjected to continuous rapes so that they would become pregnant. To view women as the booty of war is an ancient human practice. However, reflect for a moment on the ethnic genocide behind this act of impregnation. The reasoning of the Bosnian Serbs appears to have been the following: since the Serbs refused to acknowledge a separate Muslim Bosnian identity—since, in their eyes, the Bosnian Muslims were an insignificant and bastard category, a people who should never have been granted official recognition—the Serbs took themselves to be ending this group's identity by impregnating its women. Muslim women would now bear Bosnian Serb offspring. Yet the bizarre blindness in this act is the apparent lack of recognition that these offspring would be half-Serb and half-Muslim; by virtue of being born to a Muslim mother they would continue her ethnic lineage. Paradoxically, then, the attempt to eliminate ethic otherness results in the creation of more "ethnic bastardisation" or "hybridisation", and these children of war become the purest examples of collective impurity and hybridity.

The narrative view of identity regards individual as well as collective identities as woven out of tales and fragments belonging both to oneself and to others. While narrativity stresses otherness and the fluidity of the boundaries between the self and others, authoritarian and repressive movements respond to the search for certainty, for rigid definitions, for boundaries and markers.

"THE SHADOW OF THE OTHER SUBJECT": JESSICA BENJAMIN'S INTERVENTION

In an impressive contribution titled "The Shadow of the Other (Subject): Intersubjectivity and Feminist Theory", Jessica Benjamin deepens understandings of the homologies as well as disanalogies between processes of interpsychic and intrapsychic recognition:

> "The question whether a subject can relate to the other without assimilating the other to the self through identification corresponds to the political question whether a community can admit the Other without her/him having to already be the same, or become the same. What psychoanalysis refers to as omnipotence is thus always linked to the ethical (respect) and the political (non-violence)."[39]

Omnipotence is the name for the fantasy that I can mould the world and others to fit my desires, that I can control them so completely that I will never be rendered

[39] J Benjamin, "The Shadow of the Other Subject: Intersubjectivity and Feminist Theory" (1994) 1 (2) *Constellations: An International Journal of Critical and Democratic Theory* 231 at 240.

vulnerable, dependent, frustrated, and needy. Classical political philosophy named the fantasy of omnipotence the "regime of tyranny".

Yet despite this homology between accepting the other within and respecting the other without, intrasubjectivity in the psyche and intersubjectivity in the political world cannot be mapped onto each other. "The psychological relations that constitute the self" cannot be collapsed "into the epistemological and political positions that constitute the subject of knowledge or history".[40] For each individual, the process of "splitting", as an ongoing active process of idealisation and defence performed with respect to the other, has a unique trajectory and logic. The other is significant in this story only insofar as he or she is introjected by the self in a particular manner and imbued with certain meanings. Whether the political other is conceived as the enemy or the liberator, as the oppressor or the redeemer, as the purifier or the seducer—to play with only some permutations—will depend not only on the cultural codes of the public world but on the individual psychic history of the self as well.

Benjamin makes the important observation that "the opposition recognition/negation is therefore not precisely the same opposition as mutual recognition/breakdown. All negotiation of difference involves negation, partial breakdowns. Breakdown is only catastrophic when the possibility of re-establishing the tension between negation and recognition is foreclosed when the survival of the other self, of self for other, is definitely over".[41] An individual may become incapable of establishing and sustaining this tension because he or she is delusional and violent or completely rigid and fragmented. In either case, the ability to "narrate" proximity and distance, intimacy and alienation is lost or impaired. Using the analogy advisedly, one can say that, politically, a regime of recognition without negation would correspond to despotism. In the eyes of the despot all are one and equal, but there is no democratic sphere of jostling and collaborating, competing and co-operating. That is why depostism is like the death of the political body: it eliminates the possibility of negation.

What is surprising in Benjamin's illuminating contribution is her insistence that "identity is not self. To include without assimilating or reducing requires us to think beyond the binary alternatives of self-enclosed identity and fragmented dispersal to a notion of multiplicity. What kind of self can sustain multiplicity, indeed, the opposition to identity that the relation with the different other brings?".[42] Benjamin understands identity as sameness, indeed as the compulsory re-creation of sameness. However, precisely because, as I have sought to argue, the self cannot be viewed as a substrate that remains self-same over time, other models of identity have been suggested in the Western philosophical tradition. The narrative model of identity is developed precisely to counteract this difficulty by proposing that identity does not mean "sameness in time" but rather the capacity to generate meaning over time so as to hold past, present, and future together. In arguing that inclusion "calls for difference, not synthesis", Benjamin repeats some of the

[40] *Ibid.*, at 234

[41] *Ibid.*, at 241.

[42] *Ibid.*, at 247.

postmodernist prejudices against the narrative search for coherence. Inclusion, I would argue, does not call for symbiosis, but it does call for some kind of synthesis.[43] Retaining the degree of separateness and otherness that the permanent struggle for recognition pushes selves into requires a strong sense of respect for the autonomy of the other and for his or her equal right to retain such difference.[44]

[43] The question of "synthesis"—i.e., whether all attempts at unity and searches for some general rule shared by all particulars are inherently oppressive and repressive—has been at the centre of recent debates in critical theory. Formulated very generally, these debates involve critical theorists who seek to defend the possibility of "synthesis without violence" and poststructuralists, beginning with Jacques Lacan in his work on the ego, who deny this possibility. For a general statement of the epistemological problem see A Wellmer, *The Persistence of Modernity: Essays on Aesthetics, Ethics and Postmodernism*, trans. D Midgeley (Cambridge, Mass., MIT Press, 1991). Joel Whitebook gives an incisive and extensive discussion of different ideals of the ego and of synthesis prevalent: *Perversion and Utopia: A Study in Psychoanalysis and Critical Theory* (Cambridge, Mass., MIT Press, 1995), see esp. 119–65). Philosophically we are dealing with the same issue of how to understand activity that—be it linguistic or epistemological, psychic or social—is rule governed but creative, innovative, and playful in contextually implementing the rules rather than being dogmatically subservient to them.

[44] Benjamin misunderstands my use of the term "autonomy" in the debate with Judith Butler when she writes, "The autonomy and intact reflexivity that Benhabib wants to rescue have been revealed to be an illusion, based on the denial of the subject's social production, on a break that conceals and represses what constitutes it" (*supra* n. 39, at 233). She also claims that there is a contradiction between the conception of autonomy I use in the debate with Butler and my position in my 1992 essay "The Generalized and the Concrete Other" (*supra* n. 39, at 251, n.5). Benjamin confuses autonomy with autarchy—only an autarchical conception of autonomy would deny the "subject's social production". Since *Critique, Norm, and Utopia* (S Benhabib, *Critique, Norm, and Utopia: A Study of the Foundations of Critical Theory* (New York, Columbia University Press, 1986), I have subscribed to the notion that autonomy is not autarchy but rather the ability to distance oneself from one's social roles, traditions, history, and even deepest commitments and to take a universalistic attitude of hypothetical questioning toward them. This is the salvageable and still valid kernel of the Kantian injunction to consider ourselves as beings who, through our actions, could legislate a universally valid moral law. Indeed, the "intersubjective" turn of Kantian ethics, initiated by Karl Otto-Apel and Jürgen Habermas, has been at the centre of my concerns for the last decade. In this discourse ethics model "universalisability" is understood in procedural terms as the ability to take the standpoint of the other in an actual and idealised moral dialogue through a process of reversing perspectives. As Thomas McCarthy has observed, "The emphasis shifts from what each can will without contradiction to be a general law, to what all can will in universal agreement to be a universal norm": T McCarthy, *The Critical Theory of Jürgen Habermas* (Cambridge Mass., MIT Press, 1978) 326. My contribution to this general programme has been the insistence, thoroughly inspired by feminist moral theory and psychoanalysis, that taking the "standpoint of the other" in real and virtual moral discourse be understood as including the "concrete," and not only the "generalised", other. This conception of autonomy requires no denial of the heteronomy of the subject, i.e. of the fundamental dependence of the self on the webs of narrative interlocution that constitute it. Only, to be "constituted" by narrative is not to be "determined" by it; situadedness does not preclude critical distantiation and reflexivity. As I wrote in *Critique, Norm, and Utopia*, "The ideal community of communication corresponds to an ego identity which allows the unfolding of the relation to the concrete other on the basis of *autonomous* action" (342). I see no reason to retract this claim. In these post-utopian times, we have become more sensitive to the breakdown of recognition and communication. We have come to see the recalcitrance of alterity, the violence always lurking in human relationships, the potential for breakdown of communication, and the disappointment and hurt that accompany unrequited recognition and love. But in these hard times as well, the task of critical philosophy is to think beyond the given to the regulative limits of our concepts. "Autonomy" in action, conduct, and thought that is generated through critical reflection and a principled moral stance, is one such limit-concept of modern philosophy. It must not be confused with the fantasy of "autarchy," which also inhabits the early bourgeois male imagination and which I have discussed in "The Generalized and the Concrete Other": S Benhabib, "The Generalized and the Concrete Other: The Kohlberg-Gilligan Controversy and Moral Theory in S Benhabib, *Situating the Self: Gender, Community, and Postmodernism in Contemporary Ethics* (New York, Routledge, 1992) (Cambridge, Polity, 1992).

When some such synthetic narrative is not available, then recognition can indeed break down altogether and result in violence and civil war, armed conflict or silent confrontation. As Benjamin succinctly observes, "Owning the other within diminishes the threat of the other without, so that the stranger outside is no longer identical with the stranger within us".[45] This capacity to own up to the "strange" within and the "stranger" without presupposes the capacity for narrative synthesis: the capacity to generate individual and collective stories of the many voices within us, reflecting the fragility as well as the complexity of the webs of interlocution that constitute us.

THE VOCATION OF THE FEMINIST THEORIST: A CULTURAL BROKER?

During historical periods such as ours, in which economic-technological and political changes effect a restructuring of millions of lives, the search for certainty grows. The more fluid the environment becomes, the more unpredictable and opaque it grows and the more we retreat into the walls of our certainties, into the markers of the familiar. Hence globalisation is accompanied by demands for isolationism, for protectionism, for raising even higher and making even sturdier the walls that divide us and them.

Theories of fragmentary and dispersed subjectivity, which were so fashionable at the height of postmodernism, ignored these demands for stability and understanding. The dispersal of the subject—yes, indeed, the "death" of the subject—was thought to be a good thing. Yet the search for coherence in an increasingly fragmentary material and cultural world and the attempt to generate meaning out of the complexities of life stories are not wrong, or unjust, or meaningless. The challenge in the new constellation is the following. Can there be coherent accounts of individual and collective identity that do not fall into xenophobia, intolerance, paranoia, and aggression toward others? Can the search for coherence be made comparable with the maintenance of fluid ego boundaries? Can the attempt to generate meaning be accompanied by an appreciation of the meaningless, the absurd, and the limits of discursivity? And finally, can we establish justice and solidarity at home without turning in on ourselves, without closing our borders to the needs and cries of others? What will democratic collective identities look like in the century of globalisation?

One consequence of the new constellation for issues of sexual difference and collective identity is a renewed respect for the universal. The feminist movement in the 1980s lived through a "hermeneutics of suspicion". Every claim to generalisation was suspected of hiding a claim to power on the part of a specific group; every attempt to speak in the name of "women" was countered by myriad differences of race, class, culture, and sexual orientation that were said to divide women. The category "woman" itself became suspect; feminist theorising about woman or the

[45] Benjamin, *supra* n. 39, at 250.

female of the species was dubbed the hegemonic discourse of white, middle-class, professional, heterosexual women. We are still reeling from the many divisions and splinterings, the amoeba-like splinterings, of the women's movements.

I sense, however, a new awareness afoot—a recognition of interdependence among women of different classes, cultures, and sexual orientations;[46] more significantly, I detect a renewed respect for the moral and political legacy of universalism out of which the women's movements first grew in the eighteenth and nineteenth centuries. Consider the remarkable "Universalism" issue of the journal *Differences*. In "French Feminism Is a Universalism", Naomi Schor writes:

> "And yet just as some women have resisted the critique of universalism, so, too, universalism has clung to life. This refusal simply to fade away gracefully is indicated by the recent return of the universal among some of the feminists and postmodernist theorists who at other times and in other situations wholeheartedly embraced the critique of universalism. I count myself among them. . . . If Auschwitz dealt the Enlightenment ideal of universalism—a notion rejected by fascism—a death blow, what may pass for the repetition of Auschwitz, the ongoing ethnic cleansing in Bosnia-Herzegovina, has if not revived universalism then called into question the celebration of particularisms, at least in their regressive ethnic form."[47]

A further consequence of the new constellation is a reconceptualisation of the position of the feminist theorist as a critical intellectual. In *Situating the Self* I used the metaphor of the exile to explicate the possibility of social and cultural criticism, which, while being situated and context-bound, nonetheless aspired to transcend its own parish walls. I argued that:

> "the social critic who is in exile does not adopt the 'view from nowhere' but the 'view from outside the walls of the city', wherever those walls and those boundaries might be. It may indeed be no coincidence that from Hypatia to Diotima to Olympe de Gouges and to Rosa Luxemburg, the vocation of the feminist thinker and critic has led her to leave home and the city walls".[48]

The metaphor of exile to describe the vocation of the feminist critic has received a spirited objection from Rosi Braidotti in her provocative *Nomadic Subjects*. Braidotti agrees with me that we must empower women's political agency without falling "back on a substantialist vision of the subject", but she objects to my emphasis on exile.

[46] The work of Mariá Lugones on *mestizaje* "Purity, Impurity, and Separation" (1994) 19 (2) *Signs: Journal of Women in Culture and Society* 458 and Gloria Anzaldúa, *Borderlands/La frontera: The New Mestiza* (San Francisco, Spinsters/Aunt Lute, 1987) (ed.) *Making Face, Making Soul- Haciendo caras: Creative and Critical Perspectives by Women of Color* (San Francisco, Aunt Lute, 1990) and Norma Alarcón, "The Theoretical Subject(s) of This Bridge Called My Back and Anglo-American Feminism" in G Anzaldúa (ed.), *Making Face, Making Soul-Haciendo caras: Creative and Critical Perspectives by Women of Color* on cultural interstitiality deal with parallel themes. I would like to think my student Edwina Barvosa, "Multiple Identity and Citizenship: The Political Skills of Mulitiplex Identities" Ph.D. Dissertation, Harvard University, 1998 for drawing my attention to Chicana women's (viewing) and multiplex identities.

[47] N Schor, "French Feminism Is a Universalism" (1995) 7 (1) *Differences* 15, 28.

[48] Benhabib, *supra* n. 44, at 228.

> "The central figuration for postmodern subjectivity is not that of a marginalized exile but rather that of an active nomadism. The critical intellectual camping at the city gates is not seeking readmission but rather taking a rest before crossing the next stretch of desert. Critical thinking is not a diaspora of the elected few but a massive abandonment of the logocentric 'polis', the alleged 'center' of the empire, on the part of critical and resisting thinking beings. Whereas for Benhabib the normativity of the phallogocentric regime is negotiable and reparable, for me it is beyond repair. Nomadism is therefore also a gesture of nonconfidence in the capacity of the 'polis' to undo the power foundations on which it rests."[49]

This is an eloquent characterisation of some fundamental differences. However, Braidotti has an unrealistic conception of identity. For her, matters of identity seem infinitely deconstructable figuration. She defines nomadic consciousness as:

> "not taking any kind of identity as permanent. The nomad is only passing through; s/he makes those necessarily situated connections that can help her/him to survive, but s/he never takes on fully the limits of one, national fixed identity. The nomad has no passport—or has too many of them."[50]

Yet there is an enormous difference between having no passport and having too many. The refugee, the illegal immigrant, the asylum seeker who has no passport also has no protection from the collective and organised power of her or his fellow human beings. She or he is at the mercy of border patrols, emigration officials, international relief organisations.[51] She has lost, in Hannah Arendt's famous words, "the right to have rights"—that is, the right to be recognised as a moral and political equal in a human community.[52] In a century in which statelessness and the condition of being a refugee have become global phenomena, this is not a matter to be taken lightly. To have too many passports is usually the privilege of the few. Nation-states are still loath to recognise the status of dual citizenship; it is only rare circumstances of family, work, and political history that place one in this situation. I would agree with Braidotti that the complexity of our cultural, ethnic, racial, linguistic identities and heritages are not reflected in our passports, in our identities as nationals of this or that state. However, we must have the right to become members of a polity, and the rules of entry into a polity must be fair and in accordance with human dignity. To achieve this, we must indeed renegotiate the normativity of the "logocentric polis". The feminist theorist at the present is one of the brokers in this complex renegotiation of sexual difference and new collective identities.

Having started with Virginia Woolf, let me end by returning to *Orlando* once more. It is Thursday, 11 October 1928, and Orlando is driving past Old Kent Road

[49] R Braidotti, *Nomadic Subjects: Embodiment and Sexual Difference in Contemporary Feminist Theory* (New York, Columbia University Press, 1994) 32.

[50] *Ibid.*, 33.

[51] S Benhabib, "Democracy and Identity: Dilemmas of Citizenship in Contemporary Europe" in *Democracy—a Culture of the West? Proceedings of the German Political Science Association* (Leverkusen, Leske & Budrich, in press, 1998).

[52] H Arendt, *The Origins of Totalitarianism* (New York, Harcourt Brace, 1951) 290. See also S Benhabib, *The Reluctant Modernism of Hannah Arendt* (Thousand Oaks, Calif., Sage, 1996).

to the family estate of four hundred years. Orlando, now a mother and writer, calls to Orlando at the turn by the barn, but Orlando does not come. However, she has many other selves to choose from: "A biography is considered complete if is merely accounts for six or seven selves, whereas a person may well have as many as a thousand".[53] For some unaccountable reason, complains Woolf, sometimes the conscious self wishes to be one self. "This", she observes,

> "is what some people call the true self, and it is, they say, compact of all the selves we have it in us to be; commanded and locked up by the Captain self, the Key self, which amalgamates and controls them al".[54]

Having winked in the direction of the Nietzschean-Freudian critique of the unitary self as the captain self with the master key, Woolf then bows toward Taylor's theory of strong evaluative commitments:

> "And it was at this moment, when she had ceased to call 'Orlando' and was deep in thoughts of something else, that the Orlando whom she had called came of its own accord. . . . The whole of her darkened and settled, as when some foil whose addition makes the round and solidity of a surface is added to it, and the shallow becomes deep and the near distant; and all is contained as water is contained by the sides of a well. So she was now darkened, stilled, and became, with the addition of this Orlando, what is called, rightly or wrongly, a single self, a real self".[55]

These are not the last lines of the novel, and I do not want to leave the impression that they are. In the last pages of the book, Orlando experiences moments of intense recollection and ultimate reconciliation, uttering, "ecstasy" as she catches a vision of her seafaring captain husband, Shelmerdine, now returned. A quaint, romantic, we might even say regressively traditional female ending to a novel so daring! But I shall resist the temptation to draw a single, coherent philosophical conclusion from Woolf's complex narrative, for I frankly do not know that there is a single conclusion to be drawn. The mark of a great work of art is to hold together in a single intuition those complex conceptual relationships that it is the task of a philosophical reflection to disentangle.

[53] Woolf, *supra* n. 17, at 235.
[54] *Ibid.*, at 236
[55] *Ibid.*, at 249.

7

The Politics of "Presence" and "Difference": Working Through Spinoza and Eliot

MOIRA GATENS*

THE DEGREE TO which the problematic of embodiment[1] has become central to ethical, political and epistemological theory today is indicative of the widespread influence of recent feminist philosophy. The ability to wield such influence is a significant achievement but the problematic of embodiment also presents a series of challenges. This essay is concerned to address some of the challenges arising from the politics of embodiment, identity and difference. It is concerned to acknowledge and explore the import of embodiment for ethical and political theory at the same time as it is concerned to avoid a counterproductive "body-essentialism".

The essay is in five sections. Section one revisits the issue of feminism's troubled relation to philosophy, specifically the charge of feminism's "demonisation" of certain figures in the history of philosophy. This section offers the (double) notion of "working through" the thought of past philosophers in order to create "new"

* This essay is for Barbara Caine who started me thinking about Eliot alongside Spinoza and politics. Thanks are due also to Margaret Harris for her advice and guidance through the secondary literature. Paul Patton and Glenda Sluga offered the right mix of encouragement and criticism. Finally, Susan James's astute comments made this a better essay than it would otherwise have been. Its limitations, sadly, are all mine.

[1] By the "problematic of embodiment" I simply mean the cluster of issues around "the body" found in feminist theory today. They include questions such as: do specific forms of embodiment affect the ideas, values and preferences held by different individuals? More particularly, do historically embodied men and women form their moral judgments from different moral standpoints, as various theorists of an "ethic of care" hold? Do historically embodied men and women adopt different standpoints on epistemological issues? Further complex issues arise in each of the previous cases when one acknowledges that class, "race" and ethnicity may be equally as significant as sexual difference to the formation of ethical, political and epistemological views. Of course, a good deal hangs on how one understands the concepts of "the body" and "embodiment" and how the borders of self-other and individual-community are drawn. Many feminists would insist that the way we experience our embodiment is historically and culturally contingent rather than expressive of a necessary or natural "essence". Therefore, to valorise "experience" as a touchstone of authenticity or "truth" is questionable. Rather, "experience" should be the starting point of critical analysis. Others would add that a relational ontology suggests that embodiment must be understood in much broader terms than the individual. Who and what we are (and/or become) is dependent on our ongoing participation in familial, social and political life. Identities based on sexual preference, gender, ethnicity, "race" and class, all suppose complex relations with others in broader social contexts. (See M Gatens, *Imaginary Bodies: Ethics, Power and Corporeality* (London, Routledge, 1996)).

modes of self-understanding and cultural critique. Section two considers Anne Phillips' analytic distinction between a "politics of ideas" and a "politics of presence" and asks how the unity of the two halves of the distinction may be elucidated. Section three introduces the work of Benedict Spinoza as possible fertile philosophical ground for working through the relation between presence (or embodiment) and ideas. Section four considers depictions of identity and difference in *Daniel Deronda*, by George Eliot, and explores the ways in which these depictions may be read as illustrative of a Spinozistic ethico-political ontology. The final section attempts to draw out how a Spinozistically inspired ethico-political ontology—and the relationship it posits between "ideas" and "presence"—can contribute to a re-thinking of the politics of identity and difference.

I WORKING THROUGH "THE DEMONS"

"Mind-body", "reason-emotion" and "man-woman" may be the most used (and abused) distinctions in twentieth-century feminist philosophy. Western philosophy associates "man" (or masculinity) with the valued terms "mind" and "reason" while "woman" (or femininity) is associated with the denigrated terms "body" and "emotion": if feminist philosophy were to adopt a mantra, it probably would be this. The introduction to a recent anthology of feminist writings on "the body" opens with the claim that the body's status in Western thought "has largely been one of absence or dismissal" and continues with the further claim that:

> "the processes of theorising and theory itself have proceeded as though the body itself is of no account [and] the thinking subject is in effect disembodied, able to operate in terms of pure mind alone."[2]

Such views, though lacking subtlety, have been important in so far as they have enabled feminists to make valuable critical interventions into traditionally male-dominated accounts of epistemology, ethics and politics.

Arguably, the development of feminist ethics, feminist "standpoint epistemology" and feminist politics, relied on an oversimplification of philosophy's past and a degree of demonisation of philosophy's "Great Men". Susan James sums up the limitations of a simplistic critique of the history of philosophy in the following way:

> "feminist research has now reached a point at which the insights yielded by the demonizing approach have been absorbed, and it is safe—and indeed necessary—to muddy the picture by looking more critically at the strategy of vilification. By condemning our forebears as empiricist, rationalist, Christian, or patriarchal, we generate the access of enthusiasm and hope that comes from starting afresh. But at the same time we enact one

[2] J Price and M Shildrick (eds.), *Feminist Theory and the Body: A Reader* (Edinburgh, Edinburgh University Press, 1999) 1. I mean no criticism of the editors or the collection. Rather, I am indicating the pervasiveness of a certain understanding of "the body" (in which I am thoroughly implicated; indeed, the collection includes a reprinted essay of mine).

> of the passionate strategies that philosophers such as Hobbes, Malebranche, or Spinoza identify as a flaw in self-knowledge and an obstacle to understanding."[3]

Such "muddying of the picture", as James shows throughout her study of the emotions, involves acknowledging the continuity of contemporary philosophy with the history of philosophy, acknowledging the intellectual debts and points of convergence, as well as the decisive breaks with the past. On this view, self-knowledge and understanding require attending to the ways in which the present is implicated in, indebted to, and continuous with, the past.

Genevieve Lloyd also has drawn attention to a more "positive" turn in recent feminist approaches to the history of philosophy. While refusing any fixed identity to "feminist" history of philosophy, Lloyd characterises it in terms of a "shifting set of reading strategies" which endeavour to highlight tensions within the text and to open the text to contemporary, culturally enriching meanings. Far from feminist philosophy being limited by a destructive relation to philosophy's past, Lloyd echoes Michéle le Doeuff's view of feminist philosophy as "continuing more constructively the work of past philosophers".[4] Lloyd rightly emphasises the crucial role of imagination in interpreting past philosophies in the light of present concerns. On this view, the "work" of philosophy is to "shift thinking", to move thought onto new, more productive ground through the exercise of philosophical imagination. "The challenge", she writes,

> "is to define and refine the strategies for thinking our way into [the] past—understanding better its processes of exclusion and constitution; appropriating and conciliating its intellectual possibilities, in the hope that by making ourselves more at home in it we can carry philosophical thought on into a more inclusive future."[5]

Feminist philosophy has shown decisively the ways in which women have been excluded and driven away from the practice of philosophy—both materially and symbolically.[6] For female students, the initial encounter with philosophy may be traumatic—Plato, Aristotle, Spinoza, Rousseau, and Kant, all have less than flattering views concerning woman's nature and capacities. These views are part of philosophy's past and continue to exert an influence in the present. Present philosophers—engaged in continuing the cultural practice of philosophy—cannot simply disavow, or excise, those "bits" of philosophy that do not tally with contemporary norms and values, and this is especially true when those philosophers are women. If one is to remain in philosophy, and to feel "at home" in it, one must "work through" philosophy, in a double sense.

[3] S James, *Passion and Action: The Emotions in Seventeenth-Century Philosophy* (Oxford, Oxford University Press, 1977) 19.

[4] G Lloyd, "Feminism in History of Philosophy: Appropriating the Past" in J Hornsby and M Fricker (eds.), *Cambridge Companion to Feminism in Philosophy* (Cambridge, Cambridge University Press, 2000) 256.

[5] G Lloyd, *ibid.*, at 261–2.

[6] Le Doeuff maintains that what ". . .turns women away from philosophical production is intrinsic and structural" to philosophy. See *Hipparchia's Choice An Essay Concerning Women, Philosophy, etc*, trans. T Selous (Oxford, Blackwell, 1991), 141.

The notion of "working through" may be traced to Freudian psychoanalysis where a present trauma, whose cause lies in the past, is able to be overcome through a process of remembering, repeating (differently) and working through.[7] One interpretation of the task of feminist philosophy would be to see it as involving remembering and acknowledging past philosophy, repeating, or re-enacting its assumptions and judgments with an imaginative feminist twist, and conceiving such recollection and repeating differently as a process of working through past philosophical thought in order to move beyond it. This approach, importantly, does not involve disavowing the past but rather carrying it forward in a transformed or restructured way. It involves taking up an active and imaginative stance toward the past in order to affect "the present" differently.[8] Put more dramatically, it is to befriend "the demons" and to get them to work with, rather than against, one's aims.

It is one of the achievements of contemporary feminist philosophy that it has worked through past philosophies in order both to create a transformed conception of embodiment and to establish its conditioning affects on the values and desires of differently situated individuals. However, it remains a challenge to explicate how such insights are to be understood in the context of ethical and political life.

II A POLITICS OF PRESENCE?

Why do feminists, and others, see the democratic extension of equal rights to women, and other marginalised groups, as failing to address adequately the historical and present bases of their exclusion? What is wrong with the metaphor of the "level playing field"? One response is that extending citizenship to previously excluded groups fails to take account of the continuing presence of the past. Our social and political institutions, the norms and "rules of the game", have developed historically in ways which take for granted a range of characteristics, in short, the embodiment of the individuals that those institutions were designed (or have "evolved") to serve.

An obvious example is the structure of labour-market institutions which notoriously assume that individuals are free from the demands of childcare and other domestic duties. In the labour market, women who are mothers do not compete on a level playing field with men (even when those men are fathers). Moreover,

[7] S Freud, "Remembering, Repeating and Working Through", in J Strachey (trans. and ed.), *The Standard Edition of the Complete Psychological Works of Sigmund Freud* (London, Hogarth Press, 1958) Vol. XII, 145–56.

[8] A familiar example may help clarify the point. Susan Moller Okin's use of Rawls' theory of "justice as fairness" may be seen as an instance of "working through" a theory. (See S Moller Okin, *Justice, Gender and the Family* (New York, Basic Books, 1989)). Arguably, Rawls' account inadequately deals with embodiment. Okin both works through, or analyses, the inadequacies of Rawls' account and expresses her revised theory of justice, her "new philosophical work", through the now transformed Rawlsian theory. It is the notion of "working through", in this double sense, that is of interest here.

most women's greater share of domestic duties makes it difficult for them to agitate and organise to have their "difference" represented in political arenas. The difficulty which many women experience in realising their substantive rights (as opposed to "enjoying" their formal entitlements) is then, partly, a problem of being embodied differently to men. The economic, social and political consequences of sexual "difference" are often seen to arise from natural advantage and disadvantage, and as a result the advantages and disadvantages that flow from institutional arrangements are often ignored. The error here is to equate embodiment with individual "biology" and to fail to see that one's embodiment, properly speaking, takes in the context, values and institutions that attach to "biology".

The problem with "equality-as-sameness", as many feminists have argued, is that it is conceived in terms of women's ability to match an already formed masculine standard.[9] Like "race", the differences between men and women are neither able, nor desired to be, erased. As Anne Phillips has observed:

> "[W]omen do not want to change their sex, or black people the colour of their skin, as a condition for equal citizenship; nor do they want their differences discounted in an assimilationist imposition of 'sameness' ".[10]

What previously excluded groups desire is that their difference be recognised and represented in political processes and other institutional settings. They desire to be "present", *in their difference*, to their fellow citizens.

How can "difference" be represented in contemporary democratic societies? Phillips points out that, in liberal democracies, difference is commonly understood to involve diversity in beliefs, values, opinions and preferences, that is, difference is understood in terms of *ideas*. It may be shown that this diversity in beliefs and ideas correlate with different forms of embodiment, and their corresponding ways of life. However, liberal theory tends not to be concerned with such correlations and to take the preferences and desires expressed by individuals at face value. This is to say that liberal theory assumes that the (embodied) sources of difference are able to be separated from the ideas to which they give rise. A liberal "politics of ideas" is thus unable to adequately address the problem of the embodied nature of political exclusion and,

> "[i]ssues of political presence are largely discounted, for when difference is considered in terms of intellectual diversity, it does not much matter who represents the range of ideas."[11]

Feminist political theory has resisted the separation between ways of being and ways of knowing, insisting rather on the complexity of the relation between ideas,

[9] In her criticism of "benchmark man", Margaret Thornton argues that a conception of an embodied polity would recognise that embodiedness generates a range of activities (childcare, housework, nurturing) to which responsible citizens should contribute. See M Thornton (ed.), *Public and Private: Feminist Legal Debates* (Oxford, Oxford University Press, 1995).

[10] A Phillips, *The Politics of Presence: The Political Representation of Gender, Ethnicity and Race* (Oxford, Oxford University Press, 1995) 8.

[11] A Phillips, *ibid.*, at 6.

experience and desires, on the one hand, and specific forms of embodiment, on the other. But the insistence on the singularity of each embodied speaking position may serve to erode any viable notion of the political representation of difference at the same time as it forecloses the possibility of communication across differences. The unappealing result is a situation in which only someone who has had exactly my experiences is entitled to represent me—that is, only I have the authority to represent myself.[12] But "experience" cannot stand as a reliable guarantor of truth or authenticity and part of what it means to participate in collective political discussion, debate and deliberation is surely to be willing, at least in principle, to examine and re-interpret one's habituated views and values along with the "experiences" that underpin them.

At least part of the problem appears to derive from the assumption that embodied identities are static, or fixed, whereas ideas are fluid and may change. A more plausible view is that the identities we express are inextricably tied to the ideas we hold, and vice versa—a change in one is a change in the other. Part of the point of some political struggles is to shift present identities, not to entrench them. The political recognition of difference then does not necessarily involve a commitment to a rigid "identity politics". Rather, it may be linked to a transformative politics which views present identities as a starting point for negotiation with different others. We do not have to choose between a politics of ideas or a politics of presence. Anne Phillips rightly claims that:

> "[t]aken in isolation, the weaknesses of the one are as dramatic as the failings of the other. Most of the problems, indeed, arise when these two ['presence' and 'ideas'] are set up as exclusionary opposites: when ideas are treated as totally separate from the people who carry them; or when the people dominate attention, with no thought given to their policies and ideas. *It is in the relationship between ideas and presence that we can best hope to find a fairer system of representation, not in false opposition between one or the other.*"[13]

The challenge, it would seem, is to find a way of recognising and representing difference without "essentialising" it; to build into processes of political representation and deliberation a tolerance for the mobility of identities as well as the mobility of ideas and preferences.

This thought may be pursued further by considering the conundrum generated by the theory that men and women exercise different—sometimes conflicting—styles of reasoning in the market-place and in the home. The claim here is that men typically pursue a style of reasoning and pattern of action grounded in the pursuit of their self-interest against a background of rights and entitlements. Their actions are deemed reasonable and explicable just to the degree that such action leads to maximising preference satisfaction. Women, on the other hand, typically pursue a style of reason and pattern of action grounded in concern and care for others, especially (but not only), family members. Even in the market-place, women's modes

[12] Kathleen Jones has exposed the hopelessness of this position in *Compassionate Authority: Democracy and the Representation of Women* (New York, Routledge, 1993).

[13] A Phillips, *supra* n. 10, at 24–5, emphasis added.

of action tend to be cooperative and sensitive to the interests of others and their reasoning has a moral rather than instrumental bias. This moral bias in their reasoning often works against women's interests and, in economic terms, their actions may even be deemed "irrational".[14]

Male and female "embodied identities" and corresponding different ways of life, unsurprisingly, are matched by their different ideas and preferences. Many feminist theorists have pointed out that women's "difference", and their preferences, are not adequately represented in political arenas and public policy. Some argue further that an "ethic of care" style of reasoning is much needed in the market-place and in politics and that increased representation of women in political and policy arenas would enhance the quality of life for all.[15]

Other feminists argue that to identify women too closely with the "care" style of reasoning would be to essentialise the identity of "woman" and to uncritically value a style of thinking and acting that may have its roots in women's subordinated position.[16] But one could equally viably contend that "masculine" styles of reasoning and acting—the identity of "man"—has its roots in men's superordinate position. If one attends to the contexts of preference-formation (rather than focus solely on the preferences expressed) the grounding for the elusive unity of "presence" and "ideas" begins to emerge (as I will indicate in the following section). What appears to be crucial if one is to avoid essentialising difference is to conceive identities, desires and preferences as unstable, interdependent and conditioned by the social contexts in which they are formed.

Would an increase in the level of representation of previously excluded groups necessarily lead to entrenching a "politics of identity"? This is a question that calls for an ethico-political ontology, that is, an account of how political identities are formed and transformed, as well as an account of why we should value such transformations. An ethico-political ontology would need to be able to explain which historical exclusions of types of person, or groups, are politically significant, and why they are significant. Phillips has argued that the "slippery slope" of demands for the representation of *every* difference (for example, those of blue-eyed bee-keepers) may be avoided by specifying the historical conditions of the political exclusion of certain groups that today make claims to be represented.[17] However, this argument will go through only if one can demonstrate that those past exclusions continue to affect present individuals. In order to demonstrate that, an historically sensitive ethico-political ontology is required. In the following section I suggest that aspects of the philosophy of Spinoza may be helpful in working towards this requirement.

[14] I have offered a fuller discussion of these themes in "Institutions, Embodiment and Sexual Difference" in M Gatens and A Mackinnon (eds.), *Gender and Institutions: Work, Welfare and Citizenship* (Cambridge, Cambridge University Press, 1998).

[15] See M F Katzenstein and D D Laitin (1987), "Politics, Feminism, and the Ethics of Caring" in E Kittay and D Meyers (eds.), *Women and Moral Theory* (Totowa, NJ, Rowman and Littlefield, 1987) 261–81.

[16] See M Dietz , "Context is All: Feminism and Theories of Citizenship" in (1987) 116 (4) *Daedalus*, 1–24.

[17] See A Phillips, *supra* n. 10, at 46–7.

III SPINOZISTIC INSIGHTS

> "But, perhaps, someone will ask, whether women are under men's authority by nature or institution? For if it has been by mere institution, then we had no reason compelling us to exclude women from government. But if we consult experience itself, we shall find that the origin of it is in their weakness. For there never has been a case of men and women reigning together, but wherever on the earth men are found, there we see that men rule, and women are ruled, and that on this plan, both sexes live in harmony."[18]

Spinoza's views on women and politics make him an easy target for demonisation. However, he is also a fascinating philosopher to "work through" and proves to be fertile ground for elucidating the source of the necessary unity of "presence" and "ideas".[19] What follows is an attempt to work through some of the more important respects in which Spinoza's ethical and political philosophy represents a fundamental challenge to liberal assumptions about identity. Three themes—extracted and adapted from his philosophy—are central to the concerns of this chapter: Spinoza's mind-body identity thesis; his views on imagination; and his ethical ontology.

Spinoza's naturalistic monism understands human being as a part of nature. The human mind, he says, is the idea of an actually existing human body.[20] All that exists does so immanently and the mind does not and cannot transcend, or exist independently, of the body. His mind-body identity thesis yields a relational ontology. Individual identities are understood to emerge from our relations with others and require an effort, or striving (*conatus*), as well as a relatively hospitable context, if those identities are to endure and flourish. Individuality is an attainment, or an achievement, in a world where "self" and "other" are understood in mutually conditioning and co-constitutive terms. Human being on the Spinozistic view is thus conceived as part of a unitary, dynamic and interconnected whole.

Spinoza's ontology allows one to re-think embodiment, difference and identity in a non-dualistic and non-essentialist way. Desire, knowledge and ethics are embedded in particular ways of life and express, in the first instance, the kind and complexity of an individual's encounters with others. From this perspective it does not make sense to affirm the existence of a sex-less, or "race"-less atemporal "mind" which is joined only contingently to a sexed or raced "body"—"ideas", in other words, are not separable from the "presence" of those who hold them. If the mind is the idea of the body then each mind must, in some respects, reflect the

[18] B Spinoza, *A Theologico-Political Treatise and A Political Treatise*, trans. R H M Elwes (New York, Dover Publications, 1951) 386–7.

[19] Genevieve Lloyd and I have explored some of the possibilities of Spinoza's philosophy for the present in *Collective Imaginings: Spinoza Past and Present* (London, Routledge, 1999). Much of section 3 of this essay is a highly compressed version of the interpretation and "working through" of Spinoza's philosophy offered in *Collective Imaginings*.

[20] B Spinoza, *Ethics*, Part II, Proposition 13 in *Collected Works of Spinoza* vol. I, trans. E Curley (Princeton NJ, Princeton University Press, 1985). Hereafter references to the *Ethics* will be given in the body of the text (e.g. E, II, Prop 13).

specificity of the body of which it is the idea, including the traces of culturally entrenched conceptions of that body's value and meaning. That which a specific mind "experiences" are the pleasures, pains and powers of a specific body, at a specific time and in a specific place. In some instances, differently embodied individuals may experience the same pleasures and pains, in other cases, these may differ. The pleasures of cryptic crosswords, for example, are unlikely to differ by gender but the pleasures of sexual intercourse probably are gender-specific. The multifaceted character of human bodies leaves permanently open the question of the formation and transformation of identity.[21]

For Spinoza, then, the capabilities, desires, and powers of any individual are conditioned by that individual's encounters with the rest of nature (E, III, Prop 2, Scholium), which includes the "second nature" constructions of collective human life, such as institutions, norms and values. More abstractly, he contends that the capacities of any particular body will be dependent on the total context of that body (E, IV, Appendix, VII). Human bodies always exist in human communities and the powers of any given body will reflect the social and symbolic worth of that type of body within that type of community. Organisations, institutions and other forms of political order will differentially condition the desires, preferences and experiences of the individuals whose identities have been formed within and through such structures.

It is especially in human collective life that the role of the imagination takes centre stage. Imagination is the lowest and first kind of knowledge we come to have. Significantly, however, Spinoza does count it as a *kind of knowledge*, that is, a way of coming to know one's body, one's context, and one's powers to affect and be affected (E, II, Props 40–1). Imagination is the source of error, superstition, religion, fictions and illusions, fear and hope (E, I, Appendix), but it is also what makes us distinctively human and what facilitates the formation of human collectives, shared meanings and values. Imagination is initially a confused awareness of one's own body along with the body (or bodies) by which it is affected or affects. The sheer complexity of the human body ensures not only the consciousness of such affections but further the retention of their "traces", or memory (E, II, Props 17–18). In this way imagination, passion and time are always intimately connected.

The development of language and culture allow human beings to convey to others imaginings of which those others have had no direct experience. Thus, a shared imaginary may be created, which defeats the mortality of the individual, by constructing a collective memory which takes on an objective existence through its "materialisation" in ritual, religion, habits and norms. Spinoza also notes the tendency of human beings to imitate the emotions of others (E, III, Prop 27). His account of the contagious and mimetic character of passions, or affects, shows the degree to which the imagination is at work in the construction of human sociability and signals the important role that the imagination plays in ethico-political life.

[21] See G Lloyd, "Woman as Other: Sex, Gender and Subjectivity" (1989) 10 *Australian Feminist Studies* 13–22.

It is this sociable aspect of the imagination which feeds mass affects. It is these "collective imaginings" that link past to present to future and so provide individuals with a sense of identity and belonging. That such identities are fabricated, or "fictitious" does not cancel the force of their "objective", or "objectified", material reality. The various institutions and rituals through which human communities express their collective beliefs across time challenges the utility of a "true" or "false" judgment about those beliefs. The truth or falsity of the beliefs which underlie a person's religious identity, for example, has little, or no, impact on the ability of such beliefs to confer meaning and value on that person's life and actions. Nor does the truth value of belief, or set of beliefs, correlate with the efficacy of such beliefs to bind together a number of people and give them a group identity. Thus, the imagination—especially in its social dimension—is crucial to Spinoza's ethical and political philosophy. Understanding who and what we are necessarily involves understanding the ways in which our present individual identities are embedded in ongoing, collective ways of life.

On Spinoza's ethico-political ontology, understanding identity necessarily means considering difference. No individual can exist independently of, or in isolation from, others. Individuals are not "atoms" or "monads" but are themselves made up of "parts" that are in constant interchange with each other. The continuing existence of an individual depends on its ability to maintain a metastability between its parts across time, as well as on the achievement of a more or less harmonious relation with its context. An "inside" and an "outside" one may think—but this is misleading because for an individual to endure requires exchange, struggle and cooperation with other individuals, who are also made up of parts. This effort to persevere requires a constant communication between body and context, a constant regeneration and recreation of self through time.[22] What one "is", is never exactly identical with what one was—what one is, is always in process. Consciousness of the processes through which ones strives to persevere in existence will be experienced as passions and pleasures, hates and loves, fears and hopes. Identity is structured by this "consciousness of appetite", or what Spinoza terms desire (E, III, Prop 9).

Spinoza's insights allow a way of theorising the impact of social and political arrangements on human embodiment that posits neither an essential sameness nor an essential difference among individuals. Rather, difference will be understood as the unfolding—in particular times and places—of the ways in which encounters with each other and with social and political institutions condition specific forms of individuality, along with the specific ways of knowing which attach to those forms. This notion of the interdependent and dynamic individual defies traditional divisions between the way of being of an individual (ontology), what and how that individual can know (epistemology), and the values which underlie how that individual is disposed to act (ethics). The reason, politics and ethics of human

[22] Spinoza writes to Oldenburg, "men are not created, but only generated, . . . their bodies already existed before, though formed differently". Letter 4 in *Collected Works of Spinoza* vol. I, trans. E Curley (Princeton NJ, Princeton University Press, 1985) 172.

communities are always developed from actually existing, embodied forms of life and as such will bear the traces of their own peculiar histories. Spinoza's theory of identity is deeply anchored in his ontology, epistemology and ethics. All three are related by the necessity of human endeavour to take the form of *collective* endeavour, or more simply by politics.

Spinoza's ethico-political ontology facilitates understanding difference as enabling identity and relations of interdependence as enabling autonomy. Just as an isolated individual does not make sense on the Spinozistic view, neither does an isolated reason or solitary moral sensibility. Reason and ethics both assume the existence of a community of (more or less) rational, ethical individuals (see E, IV, Prop 73 and Appendix). Spinoza's claim is not that (more or less) rational communities, based in friendship, would cease to imagine or cease to experience passions but they would imagine and experience passions differently—a theme which will be revisited in the final section of this essay.

IV A POLITICS OF PRESENCE—REVISITED

> "Can a fresh-made garment of citizenship weave itself straightaway into the flesh and change the slow deposit of eighteen centuries?"[23]

Daniel Deronda is a meditation on identity and difference, history, inheritance, religion, culture and nationhood. Among other things, it is concerned with questions of self-knowledge and relations of power and subordination (between husbands and wives; between different classes; and between dominant ethnic groups and those they would exclude or "assimilate"). The hero, Deronda, acts as a hinge between Eliot's presentation of Victorian English social life (comfortably familiar to her nineteenth-century reading public) and her depiction of Jewish culture and aspirations (which "scandalised" her contemporaries, as well as later critics for the frank way it confronted English bigotry and anti-Semitism). Some critics have claimed that *Daniel Deronda* is, in fact, two novels: one about Victorian life and values (the "world" of Gwendolen Harleth), and the other about "the Jewish question" and the aspiration to Jewish nationhood through the "reclamation" of Palestine as the "promised land".[24] F R Leavis, for example, thought *Daniel Deronda* would be greatly improved by excising the "Jewish episodes" and renaming the novel *Gwendolen Harleth*.[25] Such interpretations fail to grasp Eliot's extraordinary philosophical and literary ambition,

[23] G Eliot, *Daniel Deronda* (Harmondsworth, Penguin, 1995) 528.

[24] Eliot's apparent endorsement of Jewish aspirations to nationhood—the nascent Zionism in *Daniel Deronda*—should, I think, be given a charitable reading. She was not, and arguably could not, have been aware of the extreme difficulties that a Jewish "nation" would present to Palestine. Her belief in "the nation" as the primary stay of identity, and as indispensable to the preservation of a culture, is obvious from her essay "The Modern Hep! Hep! Hep!" in D J Enright (ed.), *The Impressions of Theophrastus Such*, (London, Everyman, 1995) 135–55. In spite of Eliot's "nationalism", which I do not endorse, many of her observations on Jewish culture and on anti-Semitism remain pertinent and valuable.

[25] See T Cave's introduction to G Eliot, *Daniel Deronda*, *supra* n. 23, at xv. For further background to the reception of *Daniel Deronda*, see Cave's introduction, xiii–xviii.

namely, to show the internal multiplicity within modern individuality and to convey the desire to understand how we become who and what we are, both as individuals and as members of broader cultural unities.

The narrative structure of *Daniel Deronda* emerges alongside the pattern woven from Deronda's double attachment to English and Jewish values; to Gwendolen Harleth and the Jewish girl, Mirah; to (his adoptive father) Sir Hugo and (the Jewish visionary) Mordecai. The strength of Eliot's character portrayals in *Daniel Deronda* derives from the complexity of the relations and connections she weaves between friends, families, villages, cities, and nations. History is not understood as a grand stage, peopled with equally grand actors, but as constructed out of the intricate (positive and negative) affective connections between individuals and their social milieus, which taken together constitute the rich tapestry of their political and ethical lives. Eliot shows how the past is thoroughly entwined with the present and how the dead may reach out to the living, reminding them from where they came and the responsibilities they bear. When Mordecai provokes his fellow enquirers at the informal "Philosopher's Club" (a group of "poor men given to thought" who meet in the local hotel, the *Hand and Banner*) with the question cited at the beginning of this section, he reminds them of the weighty and fleshy materiality of the past, of the history of a people, compared with the light cover of the present.

Eliot's narrative lavishly illustrates, in imaginative literary detail, the comparatively dry "physics of bodies" sketched by Spinoza in Part II of the *Ethics*, as well as his views on the passions in Parts III and IV.[26] From its unforgettable opening scene in the casino at Leubronn, where Daniel Deronda first sees Gwendolen Harleth at the roulette table, George Eliot weaves her account of the apparently improbable encounters which constitute the web of interlocking stories of *Daniel Deronda*.[27] Deronda's gaze "arrests" Gwendolen's haughty survey of the casino, and feels like "a pressure which begins to be torturing". The effect of these collisions, connections and linkages between individuals—the affects they "communicate" to

[26] This is, perhaps, not quite as far-fetched as it may sound. George Eliot was a keen student of Spinoza's philosophy and even undertook a translation of the *Ethics* (from Latin to English). In his study of George Eliot, David Carroll has commented on the parallels between Spinoza's three-tiered theory of knowledge, which leads to a grasp of the unity of all things, and Eliot's fiction. See D Carroll, *George Eliot and the Conflict of Interpretations: A Reading of the Novels* (Cambridge, Cambridge University Press, 1992) 16. In addition to the influence of Spinoza's philosophy, Eliot also was influenced by the philosophy of Feuerbach (whose *Essence of Christianity* she had translated). Both philosophers share a concern with the significance of religious belief and tradition in early modern and modern societies. Both may be seen as re-interpreting scripture as cultural history—or, to use Nietzsche's phrase—to be interpreting religion as a kind of "sign language of the affects". In keeping with the spirit of these philosophers, Eliot does not attempt to explain *away* religion as mere fiction, falsity, error—but to explain how such imaginative human creations have been woven into history and culture, and into the very being of the individuals who both inherit and continue that history and culture. It is not possible to simply refuse or discard such an inheritance—rather, it must be "worked through".

[27] Eliot is not unaware of the apparent improbabilities that link her characters and she offers a quotation from Aristotle's *Poetics* for the reader to ponder: "This, too, is probable, according to that saying of Agathon: 'It is a part of probability that many improbable things will happen.'" *Daniel Deronda*, *supra* n. 23, at 509.

each other—is to engender hopes and fears, sadness and joy, love and hate. And all this takes place against the background of already formed cultures, habits, beliefs and prejudices. As Eliot's epigram to Chapter One of *Daniel Deronda* states, everything human "really sets off *in media res*", human beginnings always start in the middle. We are born into a (hi)story that is already under way and gaining self-knowledge means coming to understand the past, those bits of the story which have made us what we are.

The story of Deronda's quest for self-knowledge inevitably unfolds a series of questions about identity and the inherited values of specific cultures, religions, and ethnic groups. Daniel Deronda is raised as an English gentleman (adopted by Sir Hugo Mallinger) and the knowledge of his birth and Jewish heritage is revealed to him, relatively late in the novel, by his dying mother. Born into the world of Gentile Victorian values, Deronda is gradually introduced into the world of Jewish culture and religion. His desire—to become,

> "an organic part of social life, instead of roaming in it like a yearning disembodied spirit, stirred with a vague social passion, but without fixed local habitation to render fellowship real"[28]

—is realised only with and through his encounters with others. The strange romantic attachment between Deronda and Gwendolen serves to bind him affectively, as well as in other ways, to English values and expectations. However, his encounter with the suicidal Mirah, and the awkward romance that develops between them, bind him no less to Jewish values and communities. It is Mirah who, indirectly, connects Deronda to Mordecai who, in turn, uncannily intuits Deronda's Jewish background. These connections are significant examples of the multiple encounters in the novel that bring the characters to knowledge of who and what they are, or will become.

Book II, entitled "Meeting Streams", opens with the words: "The beginning of an acquaintance whether with persons or things is to get a definite outline for our ignorance." The movement of the characters who drive the plot of *Daniel Deronda* is a movement away from ignorance and passionate imaginings towards self-knowledge and a developing reflective moral sensibility.[29] Deronda's growing anxiety about his own heritage reaches its climax when he is summoned to Genoa to meet his dying mother, Leonora. Deronda's problematic embodiment of both the Gentile and the Jewish "worlds" emerges sharply in discussion with his mother who, bitterly resenting the "feminine" duties of daughter-wife-mother attached to her Jewish identity, desired complete "assimilation" to European Christian culture, both for herself and for her son. Surprised that Deronda appears to resent her efforts to deliver him "from the pelting contempt that pursues Jewish separateness",[30]

[28] G Eliot, *supra* n. 23, at 365.

[29] It is significant that Grandcourt—one of Eliot's more unpleasant characters—is distinguished by his passivity, boredom and immobility. When Gwendolen first meets her future husband, the description of him includes: "it was perhaps not possible for a breathing man wide awake to look less animated". *Daniel Deronda*, *supra* n. 23, at 111.

[30] *Ibid.*, at 635.

Leonora asks Deronda if he intends to "turn himself into a Jew", like his (deeply orthodox, maternal) grandfather. Deronda answers:

> "That is impossible. The effect of my education can never be done away with. The Christian sympathies in which my mind was reared can never die out of me . . . But I consider it my duty—it is the impulse of my feeling—to identify myself, as far as possible, with my hereditary people, and if I can see any work to be done for them that I can give my soul and hand to I shall choose to do it."[31]

It is not only ethnicity and religion that bite deeply into identity. Sexual difference, with its institutionalised relations of power and domination, plays a large role in *Daniel Deronda*. Leonora's bitter struggle with her father, Gwendolen's subjection to her sadistic husband Grandcourt, and Mirah's abject subjection to her feckless father, unite these women across Gentile/Jew and class divisions. It is the woman Deronda chooses to marry, Mirah, who seems content to take up the duties of a good Jewish sister–wife–mother. When Leonora asks "who and what" Mirah is, Deronda's response heightens the contrast Leonora has already drawn between Mirah and herself. "Not ambitious? . . . Not one who must have a path of her own?" asks Leonora. Deronda responds: "No, I think not. . . . I think her nature is not given to make great claims."[32] Ethnic differences are further complicated by sexual difference and Deronda's assumption of an inter-culturally denigrated identity does not alter his culturally superior position in relation to the female characters in the novel.

Significantly, the patterns that mark out Deronda's life—the threads which run from Deronda to Mirah to Mordecai, and which ultimately lead to Deronda's projected journey to Palestine—trace over the patterns of the broader ethical and political whole of which he is a small part. Deronda's identity—his embodied "difference"—cannot be understood independently of the "others" he encounters and the ethico-political context they all share. Mordecai's provocative question about what the "fresh-made garment of citizenship" has to offer to Jews cannot be reduced to "ideas" about "equality". Rather, the question signals his scepticism about an increasingly influential liberal ideology which assumes that the beliefs and ideas held by individuals can be separated from their embodied, historical forms of life. His own response to that question makes it clear that, for him, desires and ideas are woven into history and culture, indeed, into the very flesh of all individuals.

V "PRESENCE", "IDENTITY" AND ETHICO-POLITICAL ONTOLOGY

The highly complex problems which Eliot set herself to explore through literature have many parallels with those Spinoza set himself to explore through ethical and political analysis. Both thinkers were concerned to study the ethical and political significance of theological, political, and ethnic difference in an immanent world.

[31] *Daniel Deronda*, *supra* n. 23, at 661.

[32] *Ibid.*, at 664.

Spinoza writes, at the beginning of his *Tractatus Theologico-Politicus*, that our notions of religion are based in misconception, superstition and ignorance and are like "scars of our former bondage".[33] His view resonates with Eliot's own words on our religion as placing us,

> "in bondage to terms and conceptions which, having had their root in conditions of thought no longer existing, have ceased to possess any vitality, and are for us as spells which have lost their virtue."[34]

These errors and misconceptions, as Eliot stressed elsewhere, are not "a mere incrustation [but] have grown into the living body and we cannot in the majority of cases, wrench them away without destroying vitality".[35]

The problem, for both theorists, is how to acknowledge the material presence of the past and the embodied nature of our beliefs—the ethico-political structure of human ontology—without being entirely determined by them. Like a "demon" that cannot be ignored, the past acts on and through the present. This chapter has contended that, when confronted with the effects of the past on the present, both Spinoza and Eliot adopted a similar strategy—a strategy already alluded to in section one of this essay—that is, to "work through" the way the past dwells in the present, and through such work, to effect a restructuring or transformation of the present: a transformation that opens the future to new possibilities.

In spite of Leonora's efforts to erase Deronda's Jewish heritage, *Daniel Deronda* illustrates the impossibility of "forgetting", repressing, or disavowing, the past. The historical, cultural and political situations of Deronda, Gwendolen, Mirah and Leonora, condition their identities and the contours of their (religious, class, sexual and ethnic) differences from one another. The movement towards self-understanding of Eliot's protagonists always involves a growth in their understanding of the vast causal web in which they are situated and which determines, forms and limits their powers of action. On this deeply Spinozistic view, each of Eliot's characters are "free", and so able to act ethically, precisely to the degree that they have a reflective grasp of their part *in relation to* the whole. The degree of moral maturity they achieve involves an understanding of their own identities in relation to others, and the power they have to change their individual situations, is shown to be a power coextensive with this understanding. The attainment of a degree of understanding and moral maturity do not prevent Eliot's characters from imagining their lives differently, nor does it protect them from passions or suffering. The point is rather that what they imagine, and how they experience their passions,

[33] B Spinoza, *supra* n. 18, at 6.

[34] George Eliot, "The Progress of the Intellect" in R Ashton (ed.), *George Eliot: Selected Critical Writings* (Oxford, Oxford University Press, 1992) 18–19, quoted in D Carroll, "George Eliot Martyrologist: The Case of Savonarola" in C Levine and M W Turner (eds.), *From Author to Text: Re-reading George Eliot's "Romola"* (Aldershot, Ashgate, 1998) 105.

[35] G S Haight (ed.), *The George Eliot Letters*, 9 vols. (New Haven, Yale University Press, 1954–78, vol. 1, 162, quoted in D Carroll, *George Eliot and the Conflict of Interpretations: A Reading of the Novels*, *supra* n. 26, at 17.

have been altered through the reflective transformations they have wrought on their past identities.

The traditional liberal assumption that "ideas" can be separated from "presence" fails to acknowledge the relationship between who we are and what we think. One of the challenges facing feminist political theory is to conceive a politics in which "difference" may be acknowledged and represented while retaining a conception of identity as dynamic and open to transformation through encounters with others. In this essay I have suggested that such a theory would need to be capable of explaining the necessary unity between the preferences, desires and "ideas" of individuals, and their specific, embodied ways of being in the world. I have argued that an explanation of how the past continues to dwell in the present—and thereby to affect our present identities—requires an historically sensitive ethico-political ontology. I have attempted to show that a Spinozistic approach, illustrated here through *Daniel Deronda*, reveals that individual difference matters not as a brute *fact* of "race", ethnicity or sex, but rather matters because such difference is always historically embodied and embedded in larger networks of institutionalised values and meanings. I hope also to have suggested that these institutional values and meanings are themselves able to be worked through and transformed.

8

Freedom and the Imaginary

SUSAN JAMES*

THE THEORETICAL TOOLS with which arguments are fashioned are the product of an elaborate pattern of exchange, and just as feminists have lent their concepts and approaches to theorists working in other fields, so they have borrowed categories and metaphors from elsewhere. One of the terms that has circulated most rapidly in recent years, moving between psychology, psychoanalysis, social theory, philosophy and literary criticism, is the *imaginary*. Seductive in its power and adaptability, the imaginary has provided a means to explore a wide field of questions, many of them concerned with the self, and it is mainly in addressing this theme that feminist theorists have found the term helpful. It has featured in discussions about our theoretical representations of masculine and feminine selves, about the fluidity and changeability of the self, about the embodied self and the kinds of damage that the self can sustain, and other problems besides.

An exhilarating but also perplexing feature of this development is the sheer variety of ways in which the notion of the imaginary has been interpreted. Even less than usual has there been a consensus as to how the term is to be understood, with the result that, as well as being a tool, the imaginary is a subject of philosophical debate. What is it? How does it work? How does it change? What can it explain? As one might expect, many answers have been offered, and although they diverge, they are bound together by overlapping assumptions and aspirations which give the debate a loose kind of unity. At the same time, recurring tensions and disagreements hold the answers apart, and make for the diversity of appeals to the imaginary that is so striking in recent feminist work.

One tension—the most obvious and perhaps the most significant—separates theorists for whom the imaginary is a social phenomenon which plays a role in the construction of individual subjectivity from theorists for whom it is an individual, psychic phenomenon which can be enhanced or damaged by the social environment. While neither of these positions is found in a pure form, and the differences between them are a matter of emphasis, they can nevertheless be distinguished in current writing. For instance, I think it is fair to say that the first view is held by Michéle le Doeuff and Moira Gatens, while the second is defended by Drucilla

* I am grateful to Quentin Skinner and to members of the graduate seminar of the Philosophy Department of Birkbeck College, London for their helpful comments on an earlier draft of this paper.

Cornell.[1] For le Doeuff and Gatens, the imaginary contains collective metaphors, narratives and other resources which play a part in constructing us as embodied and socially-situated individuals; for Cornell, the imaginary is,

> "the space of the 'as if' in which we imagine who we might be if we made ourselves our own end and claimed ourselves as our own person."[2]

All three authors suggest that, by taking account of the imaginary, we can deepen our understanding of sexual difference and undermine social institutions that are oppressive to women, but because they interpret the imaginary in different ways, they also (more or less explicitly) advocate different routes to this goal.

My first aim is to ask how it has come about that such different understandings are at work in contemporary feminist discussion. The answer I offer will be familiar to many readers: it is that that feminism borrows from an earlier generation of theorists (of whom Lacan, Althusser and Castoriadis are among the most influential) and reiterates a fissure to be found in their writings. I nevertheless hope to illuminate some of the overlaps and divergences within this body of work which help to explain how the imaginary has been used by a succeeding generation of feminist authors. As I shall show, le Doeuff, Gatens and Cornell each take up aspects of earlier positions in creating their conceptions of the imaginary. Moreover, the tensions between these earlier stances are part of what enable them to arrive at their own divergent accounts, some leaning towards a broadly social interpretation of the imaginary, others to a more individualist one.

For some readers, this conceptual and historical mapping of views about the imaginary may prove philosophically interesting. It also bears, however, on more practical questions about the sorts of measures that are likely to be effective in overcoming hierarchical interpretations of sexual difference. The problem can be put by asking how one has to conceive the imaginary in order to conclude, as Cornell does, that it can be protected by individual rights, and what view of the imaginary will yield Gatens's conviction that it often has to be "worked through", and is slow to alter. Although neither of these stances completely excludes the other, their different emphases are significant, and bear on recent discussions of the role of the law in overcoming gender hierarchy. In the last section of the essay I shall take up this theme, and identify what seems to me to be a limitation of Cornell's interpretation of the imaginary as the object of individual rights.

I

For the feminist authors I have mentioned, the imaginary is closely linked to a sequence of themes—embodiment, sexual difference, subjectivity, social identity—

[1] M le Doeuff, *The Philosophical Imaginary*, trans. Colin Gordon (London, Athlone Press, 1989); M Gatens, *Imaginary Bodies. Ethics, Power and Corporeality* (London, Routledge, 1996); D Cornell, *The Imaginary Domain. Abortion, Pornography and Sexual Harassment* (New York, Routledge, 1995) and *At the Heart of Freedom. Feminism, Sex and Equality* (Princeton, Princeton University Press, 1998).

[2] Cornell, *At the Heart of Freedom*, *ibid.*, at 8.

which are not on the face of it closely tied to imagination or imagining as we ordinarily understand the term. To appreciate their place and relevance, we need to go back a bit. The English word "imaginary" is a translation of the French "*l'imaginaire*", a term which gained philosophical currency during the 1930s and 40s in the work of Jean-Paul Sartre, Gaston Bachelard, Maurice Merleau-Ponty and Jacques Lacan.[3] The most important of these for our purposes is Lacan, who drew both on Freud and on the work of early theorists of the body image such as Schilder to articulate an account of what he called the Imaginary Order.[4]

Prompted initially by an interest in pathological phenomena such as phantom limbs, Schilder and others had argued that the body image is a necessary condition of our abilities to understand ourselves as agents and perform everyday actions.[5] To walk through a door, or brush one's hair, one needs to have a sense of the boundary around one's body. Our grasp of this boundary is spatial in that it is a three-dimensional diagram of the actual and potential positions of the surfaces of the body. At the same time, it is affective; the boundary between oneself and the rest of the world is partly constituted by the fact that we identify with and care about our bodies in a way that we don't identify with, or care about, door frames. If we are to act successfully in the world, our image of the spatial dimensions of the body needs to be reasonably accurate; for example, unless you know where your fingers are you will not be able to pick up your hairbrush. But picking up your hairbrush is not just a matter of perceiving a spatial boundary as you might notice that a hairbrush lying on a tabletop is touching a book. And our inward sense of the boundary between ourselves and the world—of the difference between inside and outside—is constituted by our affective investment in the beings we are.

In a number of senses, the body image is a work of imagination. If we turn first to its spatial aspects, its imaginary character emerges in the fact that it does not consist in a literal map of the body, and may diverge from it as to proportion and detail. Some parts may be more intricately mapped than others (for example, the map of my fingers may be fuller than that of the space between my shoulders) and some parts may be out of proportion to the rest (for example, I may imagine my feet as larger than they are). Turning to the body image as a chart of our emotional investments, the effects of imagination may be manifested in the fact that some features are more prominent than others (emotional investment in the front of the body may be stronger than investment in the back) and in the fact that we are more protective of some parts of the body boundary than others. To some extent, these spatial and affective aspects of the imagination cooperate (for instance, if I have no

[3] On the history of the term see R Kearney, *The Wake of Imagination* (London, Hutchinson, 1988); M Whitford, *Luce Irigaray. Philosophy in the Feminine* (London, Routledge, 1991) 54–7.

[4] J Lacan, *Ecrits. A Selection*, trans. Alan Sheridan (London, Hogarth Press, 1977) 77–90. See also B Benvenuto and R Kennedy, *The Works of Jacques Lacan. An Introduction* (London, Free Association Books, 1986) 80–90.

[5] P Schilder, *The Image and Appearance of the Human Body: Studies in the Constructive Energy of the Psyche*, trans. D Rappaport (New York, International Universities Press, 1978). See also E Grosz, *Volatile Bodies. Towards a Corporeal Feminism* (Bloomington and Indianapolis, Indiana University Press, 1994) 62–85.

affective investment at all in my hand, I won't know where my fingers are). But they can also diverge. I may have an adequate spatial map of the entire front of my body, and yet my differential affective investments may prompt me to respond in different ways to a stranger's attempt to touch my shoulder, and her attempt to touch my face.

While theorists of the body image draw attention to the fact that, in order to understand ourselves as agents, we must first experience ourselves as located in a unified body and as separate from other people, Lacan aims to give a psychoanalytic explanation of what it takes for us to experience ourselves in this way, and his account of the imaginary order (one of three sets of processes which structure the mind) is partly addressed to this question. For Lacan, who takes up Freud's view that the bodily ego is a mental projection of bodily sensations, chiefly of those springing from the surface of the body, this is also a question about the formation of the ego; and because the ego emerges at a particular stage of life, Lacan associates the imaginary with a developmental stage, the so-called mirror phase.[6] However, the capacities and structures that are first manifested in the mirror phase, and found the ego, are by no means confined to it, and continue to operate throughout our lives.

Around the age of eighteen months, small children derive intense pleasure from their own mirror image, and from games in which another person becomes a substitute mirror image by imitating the child's expressions, sounds or gestures. According to Lacan, the child identifies with the image, thereby acquiring an integrated sense of its body as a whole, which goes beyond its actual capacity to control its body. This is the source of its delight. It takes a fundamental pleasure in its own bodily integrity, which is soon matched by an equally fundamental anxiety about losing it.[7] In calling this process imaginary, Lacan evokes several familiar connotations. First, the kind of thinking he describes is pre-linguistic and consists in images, traditionally the stuff of the imagination. Secondly, the mirror phase depends on the child's ability to let one thing stand for another, to make the integrated mirror image represent its own fragmented body. Here we find a further trait traditionally ascribed to imagination: unreality. The child's representation of its body is imagined in the everyday sense of departing from reality; it goes beyond the child's actual body and invests it with an integrity it does not in fact possess. Finally, just as imagining is widely understood as an emotional kind of thinking, so the projection of the mirror phase is accompanied by intense pleasure and anxiety. The imaginary image captivates, and the young child experiences powerful emotions about its own embodied wholeness.

This characterisation of the imaginary extends to the whole structure of thought of which the mirror phase is the inception. The child's non-linguistic, imagistic thinking continues in the adult unconscious, where fantasy works by letting one thing stand for another, and in particular by letting parts of the body stand for things

[6] Lacan, *Ecrits. A Selection, supra* n. 4, at 1–7; E Grosz, *Jacques Lacan. A Feminist Introduction* (London and New York, Routledge, 1990) 24–31; Whitford, *Luce Irigaray, supra* n. 3, at 63–4.

[7] See Lacan, *ibid.*; Benvenuto and Kennedy, *The Works of Jacques Lacan, supra* n. 4, at 47–62.

in the world. Equally, the adult ego continues to project an image of the self which, by effacing disintegration and lack, and by creating a unified body image, goes beyond reality. In addition, the emotions of the mirror phase remain with us, so that the ego continues to experience pleasure in its ability to project a unified image of itself, and to suffer disquiet when this is threatened. The fear of disintegration that hangs over the child as it struggles to achieve a rudimentary unity continues to afflict the adult ego, and explains its vulnerability to the myriad ways in which recognition can be given or denied. In short, the profound feelings that accompany our efforts to maintain and modify our projected sense of self hark back to the primordial affects of the mirror phase, and the task of sustaining an understanding of ourselves as embodied and whole continues to require psychic effort.

Lacan distinguishes the Imaginary from the Symbolic Order, from structures of thinking that depend on language and social rules.[8] While he has weighty theoretical reasons for keeping the two separate, there are, as he acknowledges, obvious ways in which they must be interdependent. On the one hand, the ability to understand oneself as embodied, located in space, and distinct from others is a precondition of the more complex forms of self-understanding which become available to us once we enter the social world, so that without the imaginary there could be no symbolic. On the other hand, the imaginary presupposes the existence of the symbolic—the existence, for example, of adults capable of imitating the behaviour of small children, or the existence of the psychoanalytic discourse in which Lacan theorises it. It remains to ask, however, whether there are interrelations which undermine the distinctness of the two orders, an issue taken up during the 1960s by social theorists who had been struck by the continuity between Lacan's account of the imaginary, and the processes by which individuals become social subjects—bearers of names, members of families, adherents of religions or devotees of political parties. These authors had no wish to challenge Lacan's account of the process by which individuals begin, and for the most part continue, to understand themselves as located in a unified body. Rather, they questioned an aspect of Lacan's division between the imaginary and the symbolic. In an essay written in 1964 and revised in 1969, Louis Althusser endorsed the Lacanian view that to enter the symbolic is to enter a world governed by law, a law to which each individual must submit in order to become a social subject. As Althusser puts it, the Law,

> "has been lying in wait for each infant since before his birth, and seizes him before his first cry, assigning to him his fixed place and role, and hence his fixed destination."[9]

Six years later, in a discussion of ideology, Althusser pursued and elaborated this line of thought. We are constructed as subjects, he argued, not simply by the law, but by ideology, working through social practices to which Althusser gave the name Ideological State Apparatuses.[10] However, the process by which ideology

[8] Lacan, *ibid.*, at 30–9.

[9] L Althusser, "Freud and Lacan" *in Lenin and Philosophy and Other Essays*, trans. B Brewster (London, New Left Books, 1971) 195.

[10] L Althusser, "Ideology and Ideological State Apparatuses" *in Lenin and Philosophy and Other Essays*, *ibid.*, at 123–73.

turns us into subjects, although clearly social, can fruitfully be conceived as analogous to that by which we come to understand ourselves as embodied individuals.

In explicating this claim, Althusser adapts Lacan's account of the relationship between the child and its mirror image. Rather as the child's perception of the image prompts and enables it to identify with the image, so intervention by the Ideological State Apparatuses prompts and enables individuals to come to understand themselves as subjects. Ideological State Apparatuses "interpellate" or hail individuals, much as one person may hail another on the street.[11] In the case of Christianity, for example, its religious practices transform individuals into subjects who recognise themselves as free to obey or disobey God's commandments.[12] While interpellation involves social exchange, and is thus located in the symbolic, Althusser also represents it as an encounter between the personification of an Ideological State Apparatus such as the Christian God, and an individual. Like Lacan's imaginary, the identification that the encounter sparks off seems to work in part through images, by making one thing stand for another, and is in this may continuous with the imaginary. At the same time, this process gives us an understanding of ourselves that is unreal, and thus imaginary in a further sense. To understand oneself as a subject is, Althusser claims, to understand oneself as by nature a free, responsible agent. Somewhat as the child imagines itself to possess a degree of bodily integrity which goes beyond its actual powers, and is unable to acknowledge the act of projection by which it arrives at this self-image, so subjects imagine themselves as the natural possessors of free will, while failing to take account of the role of Ideological State Apparatuses in giving them this self-understanding. Their grasp of their relation to their real conditions of existence is thus distorted insofar as its lacks a full account of the means by which subjectivity is constructed, and is to be contrasted with the true understanding of this relation that an adequate theory of ideology will yield.[13]

Althusser's argument suggests that our identity as subjects is imaginary, not only because the fantasies of the ego are never still, but also because the symbolic order, like the imaginary one, contains processes that enable us to function by providing us with self-representations that are inaccurate and in this sense unreal. Since they are imaginary on both these counts, the distinction between the imaginary and the symbolic begins to look more fragile, and also more intricate, than Lacan allows. This conclusion is one of a series of proposals designed to expand the scope of the imaginary that emerged during the 1960s and reached their limit in the work of Cornelius Castoriadis. For Castoriadis, our ability to see in a thing what it is not is the basis both of the founding fantasy around which the self is organised, and of the symbols that construct and individuate societies. This radical imaginary, as Castoriadis calls it, is a condition of all conceptualisation and language, and thus

[11] L Althusser, "Ideology and Ideological State Apparatuses" *in Lenin and Philosophy and Other Essays*, at 160–5.

[12] *Ibid.*, at 165–7.

[13] *Ibid.*, at.153–5 and 168–9.

grounds the actual imaginary (the symbols that are actually imagined) whether in the individual psyche or in society.[14]

Unlike Lacan, whose primary concern is with the structures of the mind, Castoriadis is mainly interested in societies, and appeals to the imaginary to construct an ontology with which to answer such questions as "Why are social institutions organised around symbols?" and "How do particular sets of symbols emerge?", "What holds societies together?" and "How do societies change?" To get a grip on these issues, he argues, we need to take account of the extent to which social life is a manifestation of what he calls the social imaginary—the networks of interconnecting symbols that give meaning to our existence, together with our capacity to generate and modify such networks—and need at the same time to take the social imaginary itself as our most basic ontological category.[15] Efforts to reduce it will not succeed. For example, any attempt to explain it in functional terms, Marxist or otherwise, will be unable to do justice to the fact that many symbols exceed the functional requirements placed on them. The punishments meted out by the God of the Old Testament, for instance, are excessive if their point is simply to exact obedience; you don't have to stone people to death to get them to respect the Sabbath.[16] Equally, theorists who try to explain symbols in terms of the reality they represent are unable to acknowledge a central aspect of their imaginary character, the very fact that they go beyond reality. Nor do theorists who try to reduce social imaginary significations to individual representations fare any better.[17] To explain the social imaginary as an effect of the thoughts of subjects is to put effect before cause, since the existence of social imaginary significations is a condition of the existence of subjects. We are all, as Castoriadis puts it, walking and complementary fragments of the imaginary institution of society, produced in conformity with its significations.[18]

How, though, are we to gain a more positive understanding of the social imaginary? We can think of it, first of all, as constituting institutions, each organised around certain key symbols that may then be embedded in narratives. For instance, the claim that God created the world in seven days is part of what Castoriadis calls the central imaginary of the institution of Mosaic religion. At the same time, however, symbols exceed the institutions to which they belong. For example, while the significance of the number seven is rooted in Mosaic religion, it can transfer to other institutions where it acquires peripheral meanings, as when the seventh day becomes the day of rest.[19] Castoriadis's point here is that the social imaginary is a stock of inherited significations which not only constitutes existing institutions and

[14] C Castoriadis, "Radical Imagination and the Social Instituting Imaginary" in D A Curtis (ed. and trans.), *The Castoriadis Reader* (Oxford, Blackwell, 1997) 321–2.

[15] C Castoriadis, *The Imaginary Institution of Society*, trans. K Blamey (Cambridge, Polity Press, 1975) 344–66.

[16] *Ibid.*, at 128.

[17] *Ibid.*, at 366.

[18] C Castoriadis, "The Imaginary. Creation in the Socio-Historical Domain" in *World in Fragments. Writings on Politics, Society, Psychoanalysis and the Imagination* (Stanford, Stanford University Press, 1997), 7.

[19] Castoriadis, *supra* n. 15, at 129.

gives meaning to events and actions, but also provides society with a means to express and solve its problems. As he emphasises, it is a creative force, continually adapting existing meanings and producing new ones, and is thus the source of social change.[20]

Looked at in this way, the social imaginary is a pervasive resource, at work in all our social dealings, of which any systematic attempt at social explanation must take account. However, Castoriadis also argues that societies are bound to face certain crucial questions to which the social imaginary is particularly relevant. One of these concerns identity. Answers to the question "Who are we?" ("We are macaws, the sons of heaven, the children of Abraham, the Hellenes, we call ourselves German, Frank, Teutsch, Slav . . .")[21] always involve imaginary significations which extend beyond "us" and place us in a landscape, an historical narrative, a cosmology, a moral order, and so on. The same goes for questions of the general form "What natural world do we inhabit?" and "What do we need?"[22] The self-conceptions that societies construct are shaped by myth, history, residues of abandoned theories and the scientific innovations of the moment, and each of these is constituted by symbols belonging to the social imaginary.

What understandings of the imagination is Castoriadis drawing on in this account? Central to his conception of imagination is the ability to see in a thing what it is not.[23] The view that imagining involves letting one thing stand for another, and the view that imaginings are unreal or fictional, each of which we have already come across in the works of Lacan and Althusser, are thus integral to Castoriadis's definition. One of the points he stresses is the extent to which institutions are organised around imaginary significations, such as God, money, justice or the economy, which, he claims, do not represent anything real, but through which things or events become meaningful.[24] However, whereas Lacan takes imaginary thinking to be archetypically non-linguistic, Castoriadis observes no such restriction. In his view, we can use words or images to think what is not, so that the imaginary does not lose its purchase at the borders of language, as Lacan seems to propose. Instead, it extends not only across the psychological realm, where it offers a means to articulate something about the individual psyche, but also across the social one, where it provides a means to capture the character of social phenomena, linguistic and otherwise.[25]

This radical reconceptualisation of the imaginary contains other divergences from the Lacanian position, and breaks in particular with its account of the mirror phase. For Lacan, as Castoriadis presents him, the metaphor of the mirror captures a structure of the mind. Castoriadis objects, however, that the mirror metaphor is "a byproduct of Platonic ontology", profoundly indebted to the social imaginary

[20] Castoriadis, *supra* n. 15, at 345.
[21] *Ibid.*, at 148.
[22] *Ibid.*, at 147–50.
[23] *Ibid.*, at 127.
[24] *Ibid.*, at 362–5.
[25] *Ibid.*, at 345f and "The Imaginary" in *World in Fragments*, *supra* n. 18 at 11.

of the West, and is itself an example of the way that a symbol originating in one context can move to another. Lacan does not succeed in providing an account of an imaginary prior to and distinct from the social imaginary, but rather offers a narrative which is *part* of the social imaginary, and thus part of a creative force much vaster than any individual fantasy.[26] This re-evaluation of the Lacanian analysis shifts attention away from its content, and encourages us to reflect instead on the position of its authorial voice. Because we can only speak from within the social imaginary, Castoriadis contends, we can only conceptualise what lies outside it in the barest terms. We cannot directly grasp the content of the fantasy that founds the self, and can only do our best to reconstruct it from its manifestations, using the tools that the social imaginary provides.

If Lacan's interpretation of the imaginary is a product of the social imaginary, the same may presumably be true of his description of the central task that the imaginary performs—that of making the fragmented human body whole. The story of the mirror phase may perhaps be understood as providing an answer to the question "Who am I?", and this, as we have seen, is part of the social imaginary's role. The significations of the social imaginary construct us as individual and collective subjects, thereby putting us in a position to think about, or imagine, the emergence of the most basic conditions of selfhood. This approach enfolds the Lacanian account of the imaginary, together with its emphasis on bodily integrity, within a more extensive interplay of parts and wholes. The social imaginary makes the world (including ourselves) whole by imbuing it with meaning; it provides the resources with which we create social wholes ("we are the sons of heaven") and with which we come to understand ourselves as subjects. The means by which we acquire and maintain integrity, Castoriadis seems to be saying, are more diverse than the Lacanian account of the imaginary conveys.

Underlying the conceptions of the imaginary defended by Lacan and Castoriadis is an overlapping understanding of imaginariness; for both writers, the imaginary involves unreality, and is therefore manifested in symbols, images and metaphors. Yet these authors exemplify, perhaps more clearly than any others, the tension between the imaginary as a social and as a psychic phenomenon. For Lacan, the imaginary is primarily psychic, an individual capacity to achieve an integrated sense of oneself on which social identity depends. For Castoriadis, it is first and foremost social, a name for shared forms of self-understanding which are the source of meaning. By mapping the areas of overlap and divergence between these two positions we are able to identify fault lines within the notion of the imaginary that are both fruitful and contentious. Fruitfully, they pose the problem of finding a way to hold together the elements that the imaginary contains; contentiously, they draw attention to the strains and stresses within it. This is the unstable landscape inherited by feminist theorists of the imaginary, who have followed its contours to novel destinations.

[26] Castoriadis, *supra* n. 15, at 3.

II

If, as Castoriadis argues, the imaginary permeates all aspects of our existence, what role does it play in philosophy? This question has been taken up by Luce Irigaray who, in several influential discussions, has examined philosophical writings in order to reveal the complex means by which they exclude the feminine, and reaffirm the masculinity of the symbolic.[27] However, alongside the idea that philosophical discourse propagates symbols and meanings that are at work in many areas of the symbolic, there is also the idea that philosophy has its own imaginary, its own stock of inherited images which it uses to construct and reconstruct itself. This conception of the philosophical imaginary, elegantly articulated by Michèle le Doeuff,[28] reiterates Castoriadis' claim that the social imaginary is always changing and is therefore historical, but departs from his all-encompassing approach. There is not, le Doeuff insists, just one imaginary, or indeed one dominant imaginary. Instead, images which gain currency within a discourse such as philosophy acquire their own relatively local meanings, and constitute the imaginary of a particular community. This is not to say that the range of circulation of philosophical images is fixed; but within a sequence of philosophical texts we find images "through which subjectivity can be structured and given a marking which is that of the corporate body".[29]

By learning these images and the contexts in which they occur, philosophers put themselves in a position to use them in novel ways. But because philosophy has traditionally distinguished reason from imagination and regarded itself as the bastion of rational argument, the moments when images are employed are, le Doeuff suggests, moments of tension. "Such imagery is inseparable from the difficulties and sensitive points of an intellectual venture" because imagery deals with problems posed by the theoretical enterprise itself, and engages with the possibilities and limits of an explicit line of argument.[30] Ideas or feelings that hover around the edges of an argument, or cannot be directly expressed without threatening to disrupt it, are often expressed in images, in a register which is not reducible to discursive argument and does not impinge directly on the overt claims of a philosophical position. When le Doeuff identifies images as the stuff of the philosophical imaginary—"islands, clocks, horses, donkeys and even a lion . . . scenes of sea and storm, forests and trees" she is relying on the by now familiar view that images are manifestations of more or less unconscious thought.[31] Within a philosophical text, they often stand for something they are not, namely something about the argument. We as readers can learn to decode both their meanings and the affective charges they

[27] See in particular L Irigaray, *Speculum of the Other Woman*, trans. G C Gill (Ithaca, Cornell University Press, 1985).

[28] Le Doeuff, *supra* n. 1.

[29] *Ibid.*, at 19.

[30] *Ibid.*, at 3.

[31] *Ibid.*, at 1.

carry. To do so, we may use the concepts and techniques of psychoanalysis; but we also need to use our own philosophical learning to see how, when a particular philosopher uses an image, he or she departs from, reiterates or reimposes meanings already established within philosophy.

Le Doeuff's conception of the philosophical imaginary is helpful, not only to philosophers interested in the interpretation of texts, but also to a wider range of theorists. Extending her argument, one might propose that the sets of images contained in a discourse carry meanings (some central, some peripheral) which can serve shifting purposes. In discourses not directly concerned with images (philosophy or politics, for example), images, metaphors or narratives often make a contribution to arguments of which authors and readers are not fully conscious, but which we can nevertheless recover by using ordinary, if sophisticated, interpretative techniques. There is, moreover, a *longue durée* of the imaginary; certain images have a complex history and a correspondingly rich set of significations, and become constitutive of particular debates. Theorists use them unselfconsciously and would find it virtually impossible to avoid doing so. (Think, for example, of the role of integrity in this essay.) They contribute to our most basic formulations of a subject-matter or its problems and, while not immovable, are hard to shift.

Like Castoriadis' account of the social imaginary, le Doeuff's discussion of the philosophical imaginary is not immediately concerned with the embodied self so central to Lacan, nor with sexual difference. It does, however, offer a framework for addressing these problems, and le Doeuff herself has written illuminatingly about images of woman within philosophy. At the same time, her approach has been taken up by other philosophers, including Moira Gatens, who has brought it to bear on our understanding of embodiment, thus drawing together the concerns of broadly psychological conceptions of the imaginary with those of theorists of the social imaginary. For Gatens, as for Castoriadis, the imaginary "refers to those images, symbols, metaphors and representations which help construct various forms of subjectivity",[32] and enables us to answer the questions "Who are we?" and "Who am I?" It is therefore primarily social. Furthermore, Gatens holds, like le Doeuff, that the imaginary is not unique, so that the relations between social imaginaries may be inconsistent or paradoxical.[33] Within this framework, and with the help of Spinoza, she develops a conception of the self as an active source of imagining, and as created by its encounters with its environment.[34] Its self-understanding is therefore an understanding of its interrelations with other physical bodies, and its perceptions and passions are shaped by its own body, the bodies it encounters, and its own history. Part of Gatens' aim here is to accommodate within the imaginary both the cultural difference emphasised by Castoriadis and sexual difference. The way the imaginary shapes subjectivity depends on the physical traits

[32] Gatens, *supra* n. 1, at viii.

[33] *Ibid.*, at ix.

[34] See M Gatens, "Spinoza, Law and Responsibility" in *Imaginary Bodies*, *ibid.*, at 108–24; M Gatens and G Lloyd, *Collective Imaginings* (London and New York, Routledge, 1999) and M Gatens, "The Politics of 'Presence' and 'Difference': Working Through Spinoza and Eliot", *supra* chap. 7.

of our bodies and also on our histories as embodied individuals. Our individual bodily differences play a part in the creation of sexual differences; and at the same time, people who share a culture, and have been exposed to a particular range of metaphors and images, will have attitudes and affects in common. The social imaginary thus plays a part in making us who we are, and it is as embodied selves that we internalise and live by it.

Gatens engages with the imaginary at several levels and forges an intricate set of connections between the themes so far discussed. Somewhat like le Doeuff, she aims to explore and question images embedded in imaginaries in order to uncover the genderings implicit in them and find ways to move beyond them. At the same time, she offers a view of the imaginary which takes account of the discontinuity between those conceptions which focus on its role in creating and maintaining bodily integrity, and those which are more broadly concerned with its contribution to subjectivity. As we have seen, the second of these conceptions has tended to lose sight of the body, and fails to ask how it figures in social identities, whether those of Australians, Latinos or sons of heaven. By contrast, Gatens argues that the imaginary always works on the body as much as on the mind; the changes that the child undergoes in the mirror phase are as much physical as psychological, and the same is true of an adult Australian's exposure to nationalist propaganda or to the heart-searchings of a post-colonial state. All our encounters with the world leave traces on both body and mind, and these may strengthen or weaken the integrity of the self, sometimes saliently, sometimes insignificantly. While Gatens can, and no doubt would, allow that certain types of experience may play a special role in founding and maintaining the embodied self, she stresses not so much the preconditions of subjectivity as its continued openness to, and dependence on, the world. The self she portrays is not a bounded entity set down in the environment of the social imaginary; rather, its boundaries continue to be created by its interactions with other people and things.

If we listen for the senses of imagination that are most prominent in this work, we hear the reverberating assumptions we have come to expect. First, according to Gatens, imaginary thinking is pervaded by affect; our encounters with the social imaginary evoke affects which shape the way we respond. Secondly, images, metaphors, symbols and representations constitute, and are therefore central to, the kind of thinking we call imaginary. Thirdly, imaginary thinking is always the thought of embodied individuals. What, though, about the further assumption that the imaginary in some way departs from, or goes beyond, reality? For Lacan, the child's image of itself does not accurately reflect the disorder of its body; for Althusser, the imaginary is the realm of ideological representations that are to be distinguished from the reality mapped by science; for Castoriadis, the social imaginary contains terms which do not represent anything and are in this sense unreal. Gatens is wary of claims like these and emphatically rejects the identification of the imaginary with the ideological, partly on the grounds that this allies it to a misleading distinction between true and false consciousness.[35] The images and symbols

[35] Gatens, *Imaginary Bodies*, *supra* n. 1, at 176.

of the social imaginary are not, in her view, fruitfully viewed as unreal but are better seen as incomplete, as providing us with a partial grasp of reality which we can supplement and modify.

Le Doeuff and Gatens are agreed that the images and symbols of the social imaginary demand to be explored and analysed precisely because they play an important role in shaping subjectivity. It is through our encounters with social imaginaries that we create our conceptions of ourselves as men and women, and as men and women of particular kinds. Becoming aware of how this process works at least opens up the possibility of altering our understandings of sexual difference. Change is not easily brought about, however, when symbols, metaphors or images are what Genevieve Lloyd has called "deep".[36] A powerful imaginary symbol will sustain a range of normative judgments, social relationships and individual habits, either within a delimited social imaginary (the philosophical one, for instance) or across several. The process of "working it through", in Gatens' phrase, is bound to be both intellectually and socially demanding, and to meet with resistance at various levels. While coming to understand the workings of social imaginaries is a vital condition of change, there is no recipe for success, no procedure for undermining or replacing particular images or their effects. In many cases, the task of modifying the way we understand ourselves and others, together with the way we feel, will be long and unpredictable, and will be achieved by imaginative techniques over which we have at best imperfect control.

In the light of these cautious conclusions it is instructive to look at the work of Drucilla Cornell, who has argued in two recent books that the imaginary can be protected and nurtured by individual rights.[37] The substantive inequalities between women and men that have so obstinately resisted attempts at reform can be eroded, Cornell proposes, by ensuring that women and men possess equal rights over what she calls the imaginary domain.[38] There is thus a juridical means of modifying the imaginary which can produce greater equality, and can help to free individuals from coercive social imaginaries which limit their liberty. To some degree, Cornell's position turns away from the concern with social imaginaries that inspires le Doeuff and Gatens, and moves back to the preoccupations shared by Lacan and the theorists of the body image. Relying on the basic elements of the Lacanian view,[39] she argues that the imaginary creates and maintains our sense of bodily wholeness, and that the pleasure and aggression aroused by the body image during the mirror phase endure in the unconscious, fuelling our adult satisfaction in our integrity, our resistance to disintegration, and our ability to recover from violation. However, although Cornell's position is indebted to a psychoanalytic account of the initial creation of the individual psyche, it is mainly concerned with socially-situated, and above all sexually-differentiated selves, and with the ways in which their integrity can be

[36] G. Lloyd, 'Maleness, Metaphor and the "Crisis" of Reason', in L Antony and C Witt eds. *A Mind of One's Own* (Boulder, Colorado; Cornell University Press, 1993), 69–83.

[37] Cornell, *The Imaginary Domain* and *At the Heart of Freedom supra* n. 1.

[38] Cornell, *At the Heart of Freedom, supra* n. 1, at 23.

[39] Cornell, *At the Heart of Freedom, ibid.*, at 34–7; *The Imaginary Domain, supra* n. 1, at 38–43.

threatened. Our fundamental self-understandings are embodied and sexuate, and the task of maintaining our integrity as sexuate beings depends on our continuing ability to imagine ourselves both as whole and as worthy.

Cornell draws on a rich vein of feminist writing which has examined the relation between the descriptive and affective dimensions of bodily integrity, and the congruent connection between the way we imagine ourselves and what we can do. For example, a woman who imagines her feet as disproportionately large may avoid looking at them in the mirror or wearing sandals but, more interestingly, may also be bad at dancing and prone to trip over things. To take a far more serious case, a woman who has been raped may be unable to drive by herself at night or stay alone in the house. Discussions of such links between imagination and action, Cornell's included, tend to work with several conceptions of bodily integrity. First, a person's imaginary body image may be characterised as integrated in contrast to that of a person who imagines themselves as an assemblage of parts and has a comparatively weak emotional investment in the wholeness of their body. Emily Martin has argued, for example, that some forms of gynaecological examination induce the latter self-conception.[40] Secondly, it is sometimes claimed that the integrity of the imaginary body image may be damaged by the quality of our emotional investments in it. The integrity of the image is held to be constituted and strengthened by broadly positive emotional investments so that the woman who is discontented with her feet has a less integrated body image than one who likes herself the way she is. This assumption underlies the view that, because we live in societies filled with such numerous and demanding female bodily norms, women are liable to invest their body images with negative emotions, thereby damaging both the quality of their feelings for themselves and their ability to function.[41]

While these interpretations focus on the contrast between integrity and fragmentation, a third approach directs attention to the boundary around the body. We first need to take account of the way we imagine the body image as a whole, and with the pleasure or distress that we take, for example, in our overall size or shape. As Iris Young has pointed out, the admiration with which some people gaze on heavily pregnant women can strengthen their investment in their imaginary body image.[42] By contrast, an anorexic's image of herself as fat can fill her with hatred for the imagined shape of her body. In addition, the integrity of the body boundary is sometimes held to lie not so much in its overall properties as in its firmness. We need to remember at this stage that the boundary round the imaginary body image is at best only relatively firm; it changes as we age and with the way we wear our hair, and may incorporate tools or instruments which function almost as parts of the body. When theorists write about firmness they usually seem to be claiming

[40] E Martin, *The Woman in the Body. A Cultural Analysis of Reproduction* (Boston, Beacon Press, 1983) 71–91.

[41] S Bartky, *Femininity and Domination* (London and New York, Routledge, 1990); S Grogan, *Body Image. Understanding Body Dissatisfaction in Men, Women and Children* (London, Routledge, 1999).

[42] I M Young, "Pregnant Embodiment. Subjectivity and Alienation" in *Throwing Like a Girl and Other Essays in Feminist Philosophy and Social Theory* (Bloomington and Indianapolis, Indiana University Press, 1990) 167.

that a person with a firm boundary invests enough in it to maintain a relatively clear sense of the difference between inside and outside and to create a degree of resistance to change, whereas people with weak boundaries are liable to respond to external pressures by altering their imaginary body images. For instance, they may come to imagine themselves as too thin, or as badly proportioned.[43]

Cornell appeals to all these senses of imaginary integrity. Women are threatened by fragmentation, she argues, when they are unwillingly pregnant and experience the foetus as an alien being in their midst, or when pornographic images represent female body parts as objects of male desire. At the same time, their imaginary images of the boundaries around their bodies are challenged by a plethora of representations of "perfect" female forms. Their bodily integrity (their capacity to imagine, and keep imagining, their bodies as whole) is thus reinforced or undermined, for example by prohibitions on abortion, by exposure to pornography, by laws about adoption, and so on. There is, however, a further aspect of integrity which plays an absolutely central role in Cornell's argument, namely a sense of sexual integrity, or an ability to represent oneself as a sexuate being.[44] This interpretation of wholeness focuses not so much on bodily parts or boundaries as on their pleasures, and thus on the body image as an affective mapping. It also returns us to the relation between the imaginary body image and action. To achieve integrity of the kind Cornell is advocating, sexual pleasure must be integral to the way one imagines oneself; one must be able to acknowledge and enjoy one's sexuality without experiencing what Cornell calls unworthiness,[45] and one must be free to express it in relationships with other people. Practices which constrain this aspect of imagination—homophobic ones, for instance—therefore threaten the projection and confirmation of bodily integrity that is fundamental to the most basic sense of self.[46]

In this account, the imaginary integrity we achieve is a matter of degree, and also strongly normative. An unhappily pregnant woman denied the possibility of an abortion, for example, does not altogether lack integrity; she continues to invest in her body and to function accordingly. But insofar as she experiences the foetus in her womb as dividing her from herself, she has less integrity than before she became pregnant. Furthermore, because this reduction of integrity damages her fundamental sense of self, it is a morally significant loss. The woman's reduced integrity prevents her from imagining herself as whole and worthy and cuts her off from a moral ideal of proper individual functioning. The normative status of integrity therefore underpins Cornell's further claim that it ought not to be damaged by social practices, and thus that individuals have a right not to be exposed to such damage. These conclusions rest on two contentions: that individuals have rights over the self, and also have a right to be protected from significant forms of harm.

[43] Perhaps the most famous example of this vein of argument is Simone de Beauvoir, *The Second Sex*, trans. H M Parshley (Harmondsworth, Penguin Books, 1972).

[44] Cornell, *At The Heart of Freedom*, *supra* n. 1, at 24.

[45] Cornell, *The Imaginary Domain*, *supra* n. 1, at 148.

[46] Cornell, *At The Heart of Freedom*, *supra* n. 1, at 42.

Cornell extends the widely-held view that, since the body is constitutive of the self, individuals have rights over it, and argues that, since the ability to imagine ourselves as integrated is also constitutive of the self, we have a right to this ability as well. Furthermore, just as my right to my body correlates with a duty on the part of others not to injure me and a duty on the part of the state to create conditions in which injury is not a threat, so my right to imaginary integrity correlates with a duty on the part of others not to damage my capacity to imagine myself as whole and to represent my sexuate being, and a duty on the part of the state to make it possible for me to achieve and maintain this representation . The case for rights over the body would of course be weakened were it not that physical injury (damage to our physical integrity) is a significant kind of harm and we therefore have an interest in being protected against it. Analogously, Cornell argues, violations of our imaginary integrity do serious damage, and therefore warrant protection.[47]

There is some overlap between the rights that individuals are commonly held to possess over their (physical) bodies, and the rights envisaged by Cornell. For example, women can be granted a right of protection against rape on the grounds that rape is a form of physical coercion, as well as on the grounds that Cornell favours, that rape damages women's imaginary integrity. However—and this is Cornell's point—there is also divergence. Casual exposure to pornographic images of women, for instance, does not involve physical coercion, but according to Cornell does involve violation of women's rights over the imaginary domain. "In my own case", she writes, "these images continuously assault my own self-conception and my own imaginary domain as I must continuously rework and live through the process of claiming my bodily integrity. They portray my 'sex' as something shameful, as something to be despised. They challenge my self-respect as a woman, since I am portrayed in these images as unworthy of personhood."[48] Women therefore need protection against this infringement of their freedom.

This picture focuses on the existence of social practices which damage the liberty of women more than of men, and which need to be modified if women and men are to be equally free. For instance, Cornell suggests, a right of protection against injury to the imaginary domain could be used to demand pornography-free zones in which women would not suffer the kind of assault she describes.[49] Liberated from the pressure to conform to established and demeaning images of femininity, and from the need to use up psychic energy in resisting such images, women would be as free as men to let their imaginations run free, and engage in what John Stuart Mill called experiments in living. A free imaginary domain thus requires a social setting in which no social practices prevent one from imagining oneself as whole and worthy, and in which one is able to express one's imaginary self in one's actions and lifestyle.

[47] Compare Catherine Breillat's remark, "The imaginary has never hurt anyone". Made during a dramatised "trial of the Marquis de Sade" on French television. Quoted by S Feay in "Marquis Mania", *The Independent*, London, 22 October 2000.

[48] Cornell, *The Imaginary Domain*, *supra* n. 1, at 147–8.

[49] *Ibid.*, at 150.

In the line of thought that runs through the work of Castoriadis, le Doeuff and Gatens, the social imaginary figures as a creative, though not always a benign, force. The fact that it can contribute to the construction of subjectivity in ways that are oppressive is balanced by the fact that it can contribute to our freedom, for example by providing tools for critical reflection. We often, for example, deploy one image or narrative to challenge another. In Cornell's argument, by contrast, a patriarchal social imaginary figures as an obstacle to self-realisation, and the creative ability to overcome it lies in the individual imaginary. Once freed from the constraints and inequalities imposed by society or groups within it, our individual powers of imagination will enable us to reimagine ourselves.

> "[The] spaces in which we reimagine the meanings of 'kin', 'love', 'sex' and 'intergenerational friendship' are not necessarily places we have been or know and so they demand imaginative creation. We are dreaming them up . . . And the imaginary domain is crucial for these dreams."[50]

The emphasis shifts, then, from the interrelation between society and individual, to the individual who makes claims on society in the name of her or his own freedom.

Cornell is emphatic that people must be as free as possible to live the lives they imagine in all their variety, and must in particular be as free as possible from any attempt on the part of the state to restrict them. Any practice which infringes their equal rights to imagine and express themselves as whole and worthy is therefore open to challenge. While she concedes in passing that the state may intervene when a person's way of life harms others or is bad for her,[51] Cornell is overwhelmingly concerned to argue for the protection of all imaginary representations that bear on integrity and sexuality. However, it is not immediately obvious how this is to be done. An initial problem stems from her assumption that, left to themselves, individuals will imagine lives they will find fulfilling. But how freely, we might wonder, is the imagination to be left to roam? Am I to be able to live out the life I yearn for, in which I am eight feet tall or a descendant of the Romanoffs, and do I have a right to be supported in these projects? Less fancifully, if individuals have the capacity to imagine themselves in a great variety of ways, almost any social practice will be an obstacle to someone's personhood. Given that each individual cannot be awarded rights to protect her against every practice that grates on her integrity and sexuality, how is society to decide which practices to change?

Versions of this problem are confronted by all forms of liberalism, and raising it may seem small-minded. It is, however, one of the points at which Cornell's conception of the individual imaginary interconnects with the social imaginary, to which, as we have seen, she gives an unusually marginal role. When Cornell argues, for example, that displays of pornography damage the imaginary domains of women, she appeals for support to our knowledge of shared patterns of subjectivity. In doing so, she appeals to nothing other than the social imaginary, to the

[50] Cornell, *At The Heart of Freedom*, *supra* n. 1, at 43.
[51] *Ibid.*, at 59.

embedded narratives, pervasive images and potent symbols that run through our practices, and turn out on reflection to bear on our sense of bodily wholeness and worthiness. Her repertoire of practices that harm the imaginary domains of women derives from various more or less local studies of female subjectivity, which have uncovered deep metaphors at work in social imaginaries, particularly in those which operate across practices and are encountered in many areas of life. For example, studies of pornography have revealed that its images are experienced by many women as demeaning, as undermining of the worthiness of their sexuality, and on this basis Cornell argues that women should be able to avoid encountering them. The social imaginary therefore plays a crucial, though tacit, role in her account of what is involved in realising the rights of individuals over the imaginary domain, and it is only by studying it that we are able to identify practices that do more and less significant damage. The liberation of the imaginary domain cannot consist in the demand that the state should protect and support any way of life that represents the sexuate being of an individual. Hard choices will have to be made, and the state will have to reach a view about where to exert itself, where to refrain from intervention and how to modify existing practices. These decisions need to be grounded, at least in part, on an examination of the social imaginary and its effects on subjectivity. If, as Cornell claims, any assessment by the state of the relative gravity of harms to the imaginary domain is a violation of the individual, it is difficult to see how the state can take on the obligations that amount to protecting the imaginary domain.[52]

Although Cornell does not ignore the social imaginary—she acknowledges, for instance, that we are shaped by the world into which we are thrown and cannot be the original source of our own values [53]—she refrains from much explicit discussion of its relation to the individual imaginary domain. Implicitly, however, her interpretation argues for a division between the individual imaginary and its social counterpart. As her discussion proceeds, it becomes increasingly clear that an individual's imaginary domain is constituted by those of their more and less conscious thoughts and feelings which are directly or indirectly about bodily or sexual integrity. Some of them are about what is; for example, the satisfaction a particular woman takes in her mirror image is part of her imaginary domain. Some (and these are the ones Cornell emphasises) are about what might be, as for example when Toni Morrison's heroine, Sula, imagines a time when "there'll be a little love left over for me".[54] Everyone has such thoughts and feelings and therefore possesses an imaginary domain; but some imaginary domains conform better than others to the normative ideal of wholeness and worthiness we have already encountered. For example, a woman's ability to continue to imagine herself as integrated and able to represent her sexuate being may be abruptly damaged by an unwanted pregnancy and the unavailability of an abortion.

[52] Cornell, *At The Heart of Freedom*, *supra* n. 1, at 23.
[53] *Ibid.*, at 38.
[54] Quoted in Cornell, *ibid.*, at 25.

In this account, the dependence of the imaginary on images and symbols which is so prominent in work on the social imaginary is displaced. Consider, for example, a woman's ability to recognise and use an image of a pair of scales in a conversation about justice. This symbol belongs to the social imaginary, but would not, on Cornell's analysis, form part of the woman's imaginary domain unless it somehow bore on her understanding of her integrity. What distinguishes the imaginary domain is not so much its reliance on images or symbols as the fact that it encompasses thoughts and feelings that are fundamental (whether or not she acknowledges this) to an individual's sense of herself as more or less whole and worthy. These thoughts and feelings will be imaginary, sometimes in the everyday sense of knowingly representing what is not, sometimes in the more technical sense of unconsciously covering over fragmentation and lack. In either case, however, what qualifies them for entry into the imaginary domain is their subject matter. The question of how they arose and how they will be received (their relation to the social imaginary) thus becomes marginal to the project of specifying the character and content of the imaginary domain.

This interpretation is well suited to Cornell's ends. The idea that thoughts, feelings and their expression can, and sometimes should, be protected, has long been central to liberal political philosophy, and by presenting the imaginary domain in these terms Cornell fits it to enter the arena of rights theory. Inhabitants of liberal democracies are already comfortable with the view that individuals possess a right (albeit not an unlimited one) to express their thoughts and feelings. If these are what constitute an individual's imaginary domain, the latter is already defined as the sort of thing over which rights extend. Cornell thus incorporates the imaginary domain into a liberal framework and challenges liberal political philosophers to explain why it should not be protected, both by negative rights which prevent interference, and by positive rights to the conditions that make it possible for people to express their imaginary domains in their lifestyles. One striking feature of this assimilationist strategy is the extent to which it draws on a conception of rights already embedded in philosophical and legal social imaginaries. As many theorists have pointed out, rights to self-defence, to freedom of the person, or to freedom of speech, are intimately connected with the idea of ownership, which operates as a guiding metaphor in our many explications of what such rights involve. Whether we are owned by God, as some founding theorists of natural right believed, or own ourselves, as some philosophers think nowadays, the notion of ownership often provides a justifying interpretation of our freedom to control our bodies and actions. When Cornell argues that these rights over our person extend to the imaginary domain, she implicitly appeals to the idea that our thoughts and feelings, together with the actions that express them, belong to us and should therefore be under our own control. An attempt to limit another person's imaginary domain (unless it can be justified by some version of the harm principle) should be seen as analogous to assaulting them, as an unwarranted attack on their person, which they own. Here, the metaphor of ownership plays the part that Castoriadis identifies as characteristic of the social imaginary in that it makes sense of certain rights claims and the social practices to which they belong. As an aspect of philosophical and legal social imaginaries, it not only shapes our understanding of the negative rights that are central to classical liberalism, but also functions as a resource that can be used to defend a range of positions, including Cornell's. What is ownership and what can we be said to own? As long as answers to these questions are contestable, this aspect of the social imaginary can play a role in debates about the character and extent of individual rights.

Cornell's account of the imaginary domain fits it to enter into liberal discussion about the scope of rights over the person. Rather than challenging the basis of liberal conceptions of rights, as a number of feminist writers have done, she employs it for her own purposes, opting to argue on liberal terms.[55] As we have seen, she draws on a conception of rights embedded in the social imaginary to sustain her argument, and to this extent connects the individual imaginary domain with the social imaginary. At the same time, however, she opens up a gap between the two, a gap between an imaginary domain firmly embedded in a particular moral and political theory, and a social imaginary which stands outside it. While the imaginary domain becomes an entity to be fought for on the page and in the courts, the social imaginary remains a theoretical, diagnostic tool, a means of critically examining what goes on in particular debates or historical changes. It would, of course, be misleading to present the social imaginary as altogether above the fray when its position is equivocal. At one level, it is part of a theory of social explanation that is itself contested and the object of debate. At another level it belongs to a metatheory which aims to provide us with a means of reflecting on our everyday theories and practices. At the first level it may need to be defended, and in defending it we may appeal to the very social imaginary being theorised. At the second level it aims to keep a certain distance, to examine the workings of key images and metaphors in terms other than their own.

Viewed in this second way, interpretations of the social imaginary are distinguished by the emphasis they lay on images, metaphors, symbols, and the narratives to which these contribute. Running through them is the idea that collective images are often an extremely potent yet elusive element in our ways of understanding ourselves; a distinct register, one might say, of the social inheritance that shapes individual subjectivity. To understand how our social practices are constructed, how they change, and how they can both limit and empower us, we need to pay careful attention to the images that constitute social imaginaries, and to the mechanisms (if that is not too blunt a word) by which they work on our embodied selves and our embodied selves work on them. Images and metaphors will sometimes only give way to images and metaphors; and the processes by which they are dislodged or gain ascendancy are, in contrast to the comparatively clearcut procedures of the law, often slow, roundabout and unpredictable.

[55] For discussion and criticism of feminist objections to rights theory see S Palmer, "Feminism and the Promise of Human Rights: Possibilities and Paradoxes", *supra* chap. 4.

Advocates of this conception of the social imaginary can be seen as outlining a research programme which has begun to prove its worth but has not yet developed (and perhaps should not develop) a unified theoretical basis. Many questions therefore remain open. What exactly do people have in mind when they say that the social imaginary is constituted by images? How profound is the link between the imaginary and embodiment, or between the imaginary and integrity? To what extent are we capable of deliberately modifying the imaginary? The fact that these issues, and others like them need to be further explored is part of what makes work on the social imaginary significant for feminist research. It holds out the possibility of modes of investigation that take account of the depth and pervasiveness of gendered images and their effects, and of the intricate measures required to change them. While appeals to rights are undoubtedly an important means of enhancing the status of women, Cornell's strategy of turning the imaginary domain into an individual possession over which its owner holds rights runs the danger of directing attention away from the broader issues that the social imaginary raises. First, it exposes her position to the strengths and weaknesses of liberal conceptions of persons, rights, freedom, and the power of legal categories to facilitate change, and thereby to the assumptions that have made liberalism inhospitable to many forms of feminism. Secondly, it emphasises the creative power of individuals to represent themselves as whole and sexuate beings at the expense of a consideration of the conditions in which they try to do so. Here, surely, attention to the social imaginary is crucial. If women are to do more than reiterate oppressive or deferent forms of life, we need to reflect on the inherited images through which we understand ourselves, and on the processes through which we may internalise or change them.

Index

Printed in the United States
20754LVS00003BC/139-156